Warring Friends

A volume in the series

CORNELL STUDIES IN SECURITY AFFAIRS

edited by Robert J. Art, Robert Jervis, and Stephen M. Walt

A list of titles in this series is available at www.cornellpress.cornell.edu.

WARRING FRIENDS

Alliance Restraint in International Politics

Jeremy Pressman

CORNELL UNIVERSITY PRESS

Ithaca and London

First published 2008 by Cornell University Press
First printing, Cornell Paperbacks, 2008

Printed in the United States of America

Library of Congress Cataloging-in-Publication Data

Pressman, Jeremy, 1969–
    Warring friends : alliance restraint in international politics /
Jeremy Pressman.
        p. cm. — (Cornell studies in security affairs)
    Includes bibliographical references and index.
    ISBN 978-0-8014-4671-9 (cloth : alk. paper) — ISBN 978-0-8014-
7443-9 (pbk. : alk. paper)
    1. Alliances.   2. Deterrence (Strategy)   3. Conflict management—
International cooperation.   4. War—Prevention—International
cooperation.   5. International relations.   6. United States—
Foreign relations—20th century—Case studies.   7. United States—
Foreign relations—2001—Case studies.   I. Title.   II. Series.

    JZ1314.P74 2008
        327.1'16—dc22   2007048432

Cornell University Press strives to use environmentally responsible suppliers
and materials to the fullest extent possible in the publishing of its books.
Such materials include vegetable-based, low-VOC inks and acid-free papers
that are recycled, totally chlorine-free, or partly composed of nonwood fibers.
For further information, visit our website at www.cornellpress.cornell.edu.

Cloth printing   10 9 8 7 6 5 4 3 2 1

Paperback printing   10 9 8 7 6 5 4 3 2 1

In memory of
Goldie Pressman,
my grandmother

Contents

Acknowledgments

Many people helped me develop this project. In my graduate studies, I was guided by Malik Mufti, Barry Posen, and Stephen Van Evera. Each offered incisive comments on my work. Steve Van Evera in particular challenged me intellectually while offering unending encouragement and food for thought. My thinking was further stimulated by a postdoctoral fellowship at the Belfer Center for Science and International Affairs at Harvard University. I have enjoyed working with my colleagues at the University of Connecticut and especially express my appreciation to my four colleagues in international relations, Mark Boyer, Garry Clifford, Betty Hanson, and Jennifer Sterling-Folker. I appreciated the research and intellectual support of Shai Feldman and Kristina Cherniahivsky at the Crown Center for Middle East Studies at Brandeis University.

At Cornell University Press, I thank Roger Haydon for shepherding me through the publication process. Series editor Stephen M. Walt offered excellent feedback on the manuscript. I also valued the suggestions of an anonymous reviewer. I thank Susan Barnett, Kay Banning, Ange Romeo-Hall, and Kim Vivier for helping to publish this book.

Many other people offered comments and suggestions. I thank David Art, Boaz Atzili, Thomas Christensen, Michal Ben-Josef Hirsch, Robert Blecher, Jonathan Cutler, Kelly Greenhill, Mark L. Haas, Waleed Hazbun, Alan Kuperman, Scott Lasensky, Sarah Kenyon Lischer, Sara Jane McCaffrey, Monika L. McDermott, Daniel Metz, Benny Miller, Jessica Piombo,

Benjamin L. Read, Howard Reiter, Jonathan Rynhold, Chris Twomey, Cory Welt, and Amos Zehavi.

On the administrative side, I thank Anne Carbone, Helen F. Ray, Scott Schnyer, and Tobie Weiner at the Massachusetts Institute of Technology. At the University of Connecticut, I am deeply indebted to Jennifer Fontanella, Justine Hill, and Christine Luberto. I am also grateful to librarians at MIT, UConn, Harvard, the National Archives and Records Administration, the British National Archives, and a number of other presidential and university libraries.

My parents nurtured my interests in the political world, and I am grateful for their continuing friendship and that of my siblings and the Sobel family. Audrey Sobel, my wife, has been incredibly supportive throughout this project, and I would not have reached this point without her. I deeply appreciate her love, wisdom, and kindness.

My four grandparents were an example of educational achievement and lifelong learning. They set the tone for their children and grandchildren. In late 2006, my last living grandparent, Goldie Pressman, passed away at the age of 97. She was reading and discussing the *New York Times* until she died. It seems fitting to dedicate this Cornell University Press book to her, a member of the Cornell University class of 1930.

Warring Friends

1

Alliance Restraint

In the months leading up to the U.S. invasion of Iraq in March 2003, several close U.S. allies frenetically worked to stop the war. In different ways, France, Germany, Saudi Arabia, and Turkey all took actions or issued statements that sought to restrain the United States by blocking American military intervention to topple Saddam Hussein. They failed to stop the world's lone superpower.

Nearly fifty years earlier, the situation was reversed as the United States worked to restrain its British and French allies. In 1956, after Egypt nationalized the Suez Canal, Britain and France considered military action against Egypt to retake control of the canal. The United States opposed Anglo-French military intervention. But the opposition of the American superpower was to no avail, and British and French military forces, along with Israeli troops, invaded Egypt.

Lest one think that allies always fail to restrain each other, the history of international politics also demonstrates the opposite tendency. In the 1991 Persian Gulf War, the United States led a coalition to expel Iraq from Kuwait. The United States feared that Israeli military retaliation against Iraqi attacks would fracture the U.S. war-fighting coalition. Even before the start of the American military operation, U.S. officials worked to rein in their Israeli ally. Using both inducements and the threat of punitive policies, the United States successfully restrained Israel.

In a much earlier example, the United States had to abandon military intervention because of British opposition. In 1954, with French forces under siege at Dien Bien Phu in Indochina, France pleaded with the United States for direct military support. The United States was willing to do so only along with Britain, but Britain opposed intervention and adamantly refused to join its American ally. The United States declined the French request, and the French forces at Dien Bien Phu fell.

More generally, as the case studies in this book demonstrate, efforts by one ally to restrain its partner are common in international affairs, but these attempts at alliance restraint have not received sustained scholarly attention.[1] This book asks two central questions. First, does alliance restraint cause the formation of some alliances? Second, what explains the success or failure of alliance restraint attempts? Both questions address alliance restraint, but they deal with distinct categories of the alliance literature. The first question concerns the origins of alliances whereas the second one is about alliance management, or how decisions are taken inside an existing alliance. The case studies in chapter 2 address the first question. Chapter 3, on Anglo-American relations, and chapter 4, on American-Israeli relations, explore the second.

The second question, on the success or failure of alliance restraint, is particularly puzzling because neither of the dominant answers about alliance decision making fits the empirical evidence. Some scholars have argued that powerful allies get their way, just as powerful states more generally dominate international affairs. As Thucydides wrote long ago, "The strong do what they have the power to do and the weak accept what they have to accept."[2] Within alliances, the most powerful ally gets the outcome it wants.[3] Other scholars have emphasized ways that weak allies prevail over their stronger partners through shared normative commitments or institutional constraints. The stronger ally is often at the mercy of its partners—or at the very least the allies have equal standing despite the power disparity.[4] Yet neither of these explanations can explain the variation we see in the success *and* failure of alliance restraint attempts. Neither stronger nor weaker allies always get their way in restraint debates.

This book proposes a different way of explaining alliance restraint success that accepts and rejects part of each existing answer. The more powerful ally must *mobilize* its power resources and not, as it often does, rely solely on rhetoric and persuasion to restrain its allies. The 800-pound gorilla has to throw its weight around; merely being heavy is not enough to force allies in line. At the same time, the institutional factors matter as tools or pathways for the mobilization and use of power rather than as limits on the policies of the powerful allies.

This answer—that alliance management in terms of the success or failure of alliance restraint turns on power mobilization—leads to two obvious questions. First, when will a powerful ally mobilize its resources either to restrain an ally or to ignore a restraint attempt by one of its weaker partners? Case studies of Anglo-American and American-Israeli relations show that the powerful ally mobilizes its resources when it is not deceived and thus has sufficient information about its weaker ally's policy; its leadership is unified on the alliance restraint question; and the mobilization furthers its highest national security objectives. When the more powerful ally is the restrainer, there is one additional factor: power mobilization may also be necessary to create an alternative to the military policy it sought to block.

The focus here on power mobilization in the domestic realm is consistent with the work of several neoclassical realists whose recent writings address the relationship between national and international elements, resource mobilization, and the factors influencing strategic policy choice. Structure alone does not determine the strategic choices of states. Instead, domestic variables act as intervening variables. To Randall Schweller, for instance, some states fail to balance against threats because of domestic political factors; they fail to mobilize their resources. When states have a weak extractive capacity, meaning they lack the political power and governmental tools to draw on the material resources of their country, they end up with policies that vary with those predicted by structural realism. In his study of underbalancing, Schweller focuses on elite and social consensus and fragmentation. When elites and societies are divided, resource mobilization is limited, and that, in turn, constrains state policy.[5] In sum, his work shares three characteristics with this study of alliance restraint: domestic factors shape the selection and pursuit of strategic policies; domestic resource mobilization or the lack thereof is a central determinant; and leadership (elite) unity is an important variable.

A second question might also be raised: if alliance restraint is about power mobilization, how is that different from restraint attempts among *non-allies?* States try to stop military policies they do not like all the time. But there are important differences. When non-allied states try to stop a military policy, it is called deterrence or compellence. They may threaten or use force to do so. With alliance restraint, however, the restrainer never threatens to use force against its own ally to stop the disputed military policy. An ally may try to coerce its partner, but it will almost never threaten direct military action. In alliance restraint, allies neither resolve disputes harmoniously nor attack each other to get their way.

Furthermore, the alliance itself creates institutional links that facilitate the use of power to shape the restraint attempt. Alliances facilitate the exchange of information, allow for closer monitoring, and create channels for issue linkage and side payments.[6] Rather than constrain the powerful ally, as one might assume based on previous claims, these institutional aspects of the alliance provide mechanisms for the powerful ally to flex its muscles if it so chooses. Alliances serve as institutional "arenas for acting out power relations." In other words, if a powerful ally mobilizes its resources for alliance restraint, the fact that it takes place within an alliance gives that ally additional or enhanced policy tools.[7]

Lastly, the act of joining the alliance itself may send signals that are absent in the regular ebb and flow of international affairs. The act of forming an alliance sends a costly signal to both the new ally and the adversary. Other scholars have focused on the impact on the adversary.[8] Yet the fact that the restrainer in the alliance was willing to absorb some costs and risks associated with the alliance indicates to its new partner, the restrainee, just how much the former values the policy of alliance restraint.

Figuring out how alliance restraint works has profound implications for policymakers. Is a rival alliance being formed for protection because both states view a third state as a potential menace or is the alliance an effort by one state to rein in a second and reduce the risk of a conflict with the third state? The same holds for prospective partners: is a potential ally seeking to deter a third party, increase control of its soon-to-be ally's defense policy, or both? Much as the spiral and deterrence models offer states two contradictory lenses through which to view diplomatic and military action, alliances can be seen in a protective, outward-directed manner or a controlling, inward-directed manner.[9] Similar confusion may occur as states seek to differentiate between "offensive" and "defensive" alliances.[10] The policy response that follows could be different depending how one views and interprets an alliance.

Alliance restraint is one of a range of possible policy answers to a dilemma a state faces, namely, how to prevent war among two other states. How, for instance, can the United States stop Indo-Pakistani or Greco-Turkish conflict? Timothy Crawford describes an alternate answer to this question. Whereas alliance restraint involves aligning with one state to prevent a battle between that ally and a third party, Crawford's pivotal deterrence involves deterring both sides from attacking the other while avoiding "firm alignment with either side." In alliance restraint, the restrainer uses a mixed policy approach of alliance (with the restrainee) and deterrence (with the third state). In pivotal deterrence, the same state seeks to deter states two *and* three: "the pivot tries to obscure its ultimate allegiances in order to restrain both sides." Yet in considering three types of pivotal deterrence, Crawford describes one approach—the "straddle strategy"—that looks very similar to alliance restraint, a fact that Crawford acknowledges in linking the strategy to Glenn Snyder's *Alliance Politics*. Crawford, citing the work of Georg Simmel and Theodore Caplow, further notes that triads tend to become "segregated," or in Caplow's words, "two-against-one," exactly the kind of triangle described in this book.[11]

Deepening our understanding of how alliance restraint works also offers guidance to strong and weak states about how to maximize their influence within alliances. This has important implications for the contemporary policies of both the United States and its many allies. The United States has many bilateral military ties, such as those with Australia, Israel, Japan, and South Korea. The North Atlantic Treaty Organization (NATO) has 26 members, and the Organization of American States has 34 members.[12] How the members of these pacts try to affect U.S. policy and how the agreements might be used by the United States to affect its allies is a crucial question. At a time when some analysts recommend ending NATO because it does little for American national security but others advocate deepening U.S. involvement because such self-binding restrains America's destabilizing, unilateral impulses, a focused study of alliance restraint could provide crucial insights.[13]

In terms of definitions, alliances have often been described as either formal or informal. They have also been contrasted with alignments, which are less committed relationships between two states. Since restraint may play a role in all these categories, the definition in this book breaks down alliances into five components.[14] An alliance is a relationship between two or more states based on shared interest, an exchange of benefits, security cooperation, specific written agreements, and/or an expectation of continuing ties. Every alliance need not have all five components, and the five are not mutually exclusive; they can and do overlap. Though this definition does not a priori include an exact minimum combination that determines the threshold beyond which a given international relationship is an alliance, shared interest alone is not sufficient for an alliance, though it probably is for an alignment. At the same time, specific written agreements are not necessary.[15] Two states could be allies without formally signing an agreement. The definition includes security cooperation in order to stress that the focus is military alliances.

Alliance restraint is an actual or anticipated diplomatic effort by one ally to influence a second ally not to proceed with a proposed military policy or not to continue an existing military policy. The focus is military policies, not the entire range of an ally's policies. Military policies include military intervention, war, arms sales, nuclear proliferation, and the formation of alliances. This focus is also restricted to restraint attempts within an alliance, a subset of efforts to shape policy among all states, be they allies, neutrals, or adversaries. Alliance restraint is an attempt; it may be a success or a failure. It is a failure when the restrainee goes ahead with the policy despite allied objections. It is a success when the restrainee modifies, drops, or accepts a substitute for the military policy contested by the restrainer.[16]

The Alliance Literature and Beyond

In studying alliance restraint and its impact on both the origins and management of alliances, this book draws on three scholarly streams within the study of alliances and, in some cases, international relations more broadly. First, a handful of scholars have written directly about alliance restraint. But they have not framed the same research questions and have addressed varied slices of the alliance restraint issue. This book is the first to compare restraint with another explanation for the formation of alliances. It is also the first to compare explanations for the success or failure of attempts at alliance restraint.

Second, many scholars have studied the origins of alliances, but these studies tend to be associated with Stephen Walt's balance-of-threat model. This perspective has kept the spotlight off motivations such as alliance restraint, which are about influencing or controlling one's ally more than using the alliance to counter an external threat. Since Walt's book, which primarily addresses the question of whether to ally, much of the work of the last decade on alliance formation and regime type has emphasized a slightly different question—with whom to ally.[17]

Third, when is alliance restraint successful in existing alliances? Scholarly works on how decisions are made by strong and weak allies (alliance management) or strong and weak states more generally provide possible answers. Many of the existing answers, whether originally intended for alliance frameworks or not, have trouble explaining the variation we see in alliance restraint success and failure.

Alliance Restraint

Paul Schroeder put the issue of alliance restraint on the map in 1975, but he takes a very broad view of restraint in his review of "pacta de contrahendo."[18] He notes that alliances can be both "weapons of security and instruments of management." His description of World War I and World War II suggests that the former function will be most important just before and during times of war.[19] Schroeder describes a lot of restraint, and he demonstrates how prevalent it is in international affairs. His biggest contribution is in proving that the desire to control one's ally is a frequent occurrence. But he includes a much wider range of contested policies, not just military ones, ranging from the management of the international system to the status of particular rulers.[20] Schroeder does not systematically address questions about when and why alliance restraint works, and consequently, his many cases are not organized to answer that particular research question. He concludes by noting briefly that there "is no magic formula for using alliances as tools of management for the purpose of promoting international peace and stability."[21]

In contrast with Schroeder, Snyder is concerned with the causality of alliance restraint. His book, *Alliance Politics,* addresses both alliance formation and management. In general, Snyder develops the linkage between one's adversaries and allies. For Snyder, policies toward both are part of the same game, the composite security dilemma. Alliance restraint may hinder deterrence of one's adversary and vice versa. Restraint may prevent entrapment, being drawn into war, but facilitate abandonment, the defection of one's ally.[22]

Snyder lists three ways in which the formation of an alliance might lead to restraint: reassuring an ally so it feels more secure, creating dependence so it does not want to jeopardize the alliance, and developing norms that "facilitate controlling the ally." These in turn suggest methods for restraining: threatening defection, withholding diplomatic support in a crisis, insisting on consultation, and offering inducements. Snyder develops a rational approach, a "calculus of restraint," that emphasizes the entrapment/abandonment dichotomy and the balance of interests between the restrainer and the restrainee.[23] According to Snyder, the success of alliance restraint turns on credibility, interests, dependence, and commitment to the alliance. This framework is a useful starting point for thinking about alliance restraint but is at a general enough level of abstraction that it would need further specification to help guide a researcher working inside actual cases. Snyder does not frame and test competing explanations for success. Alliance restraint is a secondary issue in his book in two senses: it occupies a limited amount of space in the work on alliance politics more generally, and he writes that it is only a secondary purpose of most alliances.[24]

The most recent treatment of alliance restraint is Patricia Weitsman's work on tethering and alliance formation and cohesion, which is most useful for thinking about states of relatively equal power and how they manage their strategic rivalry.[25] Weitsman rightly notes that these states have other options besides direct confrontation. They may form a tethering alliance, in which they ally together in order to contain each other and dampen the rivalry. This approach is an important contrast with work focused on the external threat orientation of alliance origins. At the same time, her focus is on tethering—one kind of alliance restraint—rather than alliance restraint as a whole category. Tethering assumes a direct threat and a conflict of interest. In contrast, with alliance restraint the threat might be direct or indirect; states may have a clash of interests but may also share common interests, though they may disagree about the best policy instrument to pursue those interests. Furthermore, Weitsman is not concerned with the success or failure of alliance restraint attempts. None of these three restraint pioneers considers allied battles over military policies and the role of material power advantages or normative and institutional factors.

Alliance Formation

Turning to the thread of the literature on whether states should form alliances, we find that the major explanation has been Walt's balance-of-threat theory. This approach, however, leaves out an equally important category of motivations: alliances as mechanisms of control. According to Walt, "states tend to ally with or against the foreign power that poses the greatest threat." Walt tests other explanations for alliance formation, such as domestic lobbying and the provision of foreign aid, but not alliance restraint.[26] By forming alliances, states protect themselves from a threat that exists outside the confines of the alliance. As one observer notes, international "relations scholarship is nearly unanimous in the view...that [alliances'] primary motivation is to enhance state security in the face of some immediate or future external threat."[27]

This focus on motivations related to outsiders underplays the extent to which alliances are also formed to control and influence those parties within the alliance, the members themselves.[28] In other words, states may also come together, as Weitsman notes, because they fear each other as much or more as a country outside the alliance. Schroeder explains that "allies often clash with each other more than they unite in a common cause."[29] In the context of this book, restraint, a type of control, can also cause alliances to be formed.

These two ideas, protection from threat and control, are not, however, mutually exclusive. They often jointly explain the origin of an alliance. One of the reasons state A may want to control or restrain state B is the fear that state B may start a conflict or confrontation with state C.[30] So A forms an alliance with B to mitigate the threat to A from C. Control may be necessary to avoid or minimize threats to one's survival or welfare. This way of thinking about threat and restraint parallels the claim of George Downs et al. that arms-racing states may shift to cooperative relations due to "the activity of a third power." For example, the Anglo-French arms race of 1852–1853 ended when both parties became concerned with Russia (and thus brought about the Crimean War).[31] As Robert Keohane notes, "without the specter of conflict, there is no need to cooperate."[32]

The point is not to challenge the idea that protection from threats is a viable motivation for alliance formation but rather to suggest that the emphasis on protection neglects a second important category. Moreover, the interplay between the two categories is an important dynamic as well.

Alliance Management

The third relevant literature covers explanations for how decisions are made within an alliance and which ally tends to prevail. This approach includes both works that explicitly address alliances and those that offer explanations applicable to an alliance context. What have scholars said that might explain how allies make a decision and which ally gets its way? As alluded to earlier in this chapter, the works break into two categories, one that privileges the powerful ally and one that favors the weaker ally. I build on this literature to develop my explanations for why alliance restraint is successful or unsuccessful.

One group has given great deference to the most powerful ally. In Kenneth Waltz's discussion of bipolar systems, he emphasizes the importance of capabilities as the central determinant of alliance decisions. Although he accepts that some "concessions" to lesser allies will occur, his general position is that the great power (e.g., the United States or Soviet Union during the Cold War) will set the tone: "Both superpowers can make long-range plans and carry out their policies as best they see fit, for they need not accede to the demands of third parties."[33] The reason is that each superpower controls so much of its respective alliance's capabilities that it can act unilaterally without fearing a shortfall of resources: "Because of the vast differences in the capabilities of member states, the roughly equal sharing of burdens found in earlier alliance systems is no longer feasible."[34] Capabilities determine alliance policies. One observer stated in 1944 that "the American people would not fully join an organization which they could not dominate."[35] In NATO, "a thin patina of equality barely disguises the hegemonic power of the strongest partner."[36]

Drawing from the empirical experience of post-1945 U.S. foreign policy, a second group has highlighted normative and institutional ways in which the weak constrain the strong. Karl Deutsch hypothesizes that the "tighter an alliance becomes, or the more a political community is knit, the more constraints it imposes on each of its members in their right to decide upon peace or war in the light of their own national consideration."[37] Although the United States has talked as if it had the right to dominate NATO decision making, Inis Claude writes, it "has also promoted and participated in a process of organizational involvement and entanglement which suggests—and is intended to suggest—that it has in fact forfeited that right."[38] Thomas Risse-Kappen emphasizes the role of normative factors in alliance outcomes. Looking at examples from NATO and comparing realist and liberal explanations for the alliance decisions, he finds that the liberal notions were more persuasive. In particular, he points to the importance of consultation and a normative culture of policy codetermination.[39] Some scholars of patron-client relations emphasize the client's bargaining advantages, at least in a bipolar setting.[40]

G. John Ikenberry argues that "institutional binding" restrains powerful actors. More specifically, alliances themselves constrain powerful allies: "Security alliances are the most important and potentially far-reaching form of binding."[41] The United States was in charge of NATO, "but the mutual understandings and institutional mechanisms of the alliance would reduce the implications of these asymmetries of power in its actual operation."[42] In a similar vein, Lisa Martin argues that the United States did not "occupy the privileged position of the hegemon." Instead, "this immensely powerful state championed principles and norms that served to bind itself; it created institutions premised on the notion that even the United States would play by the rules it asked others to accept." Martin mentions non-alliance organizations such as the Bretton Woods economic institutions and the United Nations, but she also highlights the role of NATO. In her view, the United States believed constraining itself inside the NATO alliance and other postwar organizations was in its long-term interest.[43]

In the Anglo-American and American-Israeli cases in this book, however, the normative argument is unsupported while the institutional claims prove half correct for cases of alliance restraint. An institution, the alliance, is a factor, but it does not tend to serve as a constraint on the most powerful allies. Instead, the institutions serve as conduits for the mobilization of these allies' power resources. At the same time, power alone—meaning the possession of superior capabilities—is insufficient; powerful allies must mobilize their power resources in order to prevail in alliance restraint disputes.

Competing Explanations

Do allies form alliances in order to restrain? To answer this first core question on the origins of alliances, this book contrasts explanations for forming alliances based on threats and based on restraint. Then it turns to the second core question: what explains the success or failure of alliance restraint attempts in existing alliances? This question relates to alliance management, the decisions that are taken inside existing alliances. Explanations based on power, norms, and institutions are plausible, but the key factor turns out to be power *mobilization*.

In terms of alliance formation, the contrast is between the dominant explanation, balance-of-threat theory, and the restraint explanation. The former suggest that states form alliances in response to threats from actors outside the alliance. It is embedded within a larger belief that states form alliances to seek military protection. In contrast, the restraint alternative argues that states form alliances to rein in their soon-to-be partners. Rather than protection, the restraint explanation highlights the role of control. Restraint demonstrates that one ally may use the alliance to control the behavior of other allies.

The point is not to determine whether one of these two approaches is dominant but rather to see if there are cases in which the restraint explanation is relevant. This is an exploratory exercise to see if the explanation is merely a theoretical construct or actually explains some cases. Does the restraint explanation deserve a seat at the table when scholars or practitioners are assessing why alliances are formed? By looking at threats and restraint, one may also see the interplay between the two. It may be the mixture of the explanations rather than either one singly that is most compelling.

Alliance management looks inside the alliance to see how decisions are made and which ally gets its way. Alliance restraint involves a dispute among allies over a military policy. Why does the restrainer or the restrainee get its way? Is the restraint effort a success, meaning that the ally is restrained?

One explanation is that the decision turns on the power relationship, with power understood as capabilities. The more powerful ally prevails. If true, restraint failure would be consistent with this explanation if the restrainer was the less powerful partner. The logic might be that since military policies often involve the projection of military and economic power, the ally that controls more of those capabilities has the final say on alliance policy. If the restrainee is more powerful, it can ignore its allies' restraint effort and go it alone, if necessary. If the restrainer is more powerful, it can deny the restrainee the support it needs to carry off the proposed military policy. In short, power means that one (less powerful) ally is more dependent on the other (more powerful) ally. However, the power approach sometimes results in uncertain predictions, as in the case of allies of equal capabilities—for example, same gross domestic product, population, and military expenditures—or, as is more likely in the real world, situations in which each ally is stronger in certain areas: for example, one ally has more people and a larger military while the other ally has a stronger economy and nuclear weapons. In these two scenarios, a simple power-based explanation does not differentiate between the two parties.

A second explanation is that weaker allies may shape the alliance restraint outcome. Rather than treat all the possible normative and institutional constraints, this book focuses on a particular normative explanation: alliances are governed by norms of policy coordination. Allies tend to align their policy preferences. When they have disagreements, they work them out. Allies consult, share information, maintain contact, and respect each other's views: "procedural norms insure that superior material power does not necessarily carry the day and that the lesser states have a fair chance of being heard and of influencing decisions."[44] In a similar light, other scholars emphasize that the powerful and the peripheral influence each other, and the superpower at the center does not dominate decision making. For instance, the Western order built during the Cold War is "reciprocal," and "subordinate states achieve effective representation."[45] Weak states, as restrainer or restrainee, are on a level playing field. The norm turns the power disparity into a secondary concern.

Given such a norm, one would not expect allies to deceive or defy each other when arguing over a contested military policy. Consultation is an important part of coordination, but it is only one element; it is not the same as coordination. If a norm of coordination dominates in a given alliance, one would expect the allies to agree to go forward with the policy or to drop it; by the end of the debate they should be in accord on the preferred pathway. Cases that would pose problems for this explanation include those that lack consultation altogether, are infused with deceptive actions, or are not resolved by agreement, even informally, between the allies.

Method and Case Selection

This book is built on case studies. Understanding restraint in terms of both alliance formation and alliance management depends on assessing the motives of the allies. Case studies allow for careful attention to the decision-making process. Process tracing follows the discussions and seeks clues about the policymakers' motivations for particular actions, giving the researcher the ability to test unique predictions and draw meaningful distinctions between alternative explanations for outcomes. Case studies are also well suited for uncovering and understanding causal mechanisms and intervening variables.[46] Given the limited amount of previous research on restraint, it would be difficult to delineate a universe of cases for large-N research. But case studies can be used to build toward large-N work, as large-N coding would require in-depth research; for the study of restraint, large-N work and case studies are not mutually exclusive.

In the alliance formation cases, the case studies allow for clear tests of two alternatives, threat-based and restraint-based explanations. Because restraint-based explanations are not applicable to every case, some cases were, by definition, not relevant. In contrast, balance-of-threat is purportedly a universally applicable explanation. Part of the aim of this book is simply to demonstrate that a phenomenon exists in the empirical world—alliance restraint—and that objective informs the case selection as well. Cases where restraint was not a factor do not tell us anything about whether it exists or not, unless all cases fit into that category. Evidence comes from both the direct statements of policymakers and the analysis of later scholars. In some of the cases, only one of the allies was motivated by restraint.

Chapter 2 includes six cases in which both threat and restraint explanations are plausible motivations for alliance formation: Germany-Austria (1879), Britain-Japan (1902), the North Atlantic Treaty Organization–West Germany (1949), United States–South Korea (1953), United States–Taiwan (1954), and Egypt-Syria (1964). Each of these cases is useful because the parties faced a threat from a party external to the alliance yet one member of the new alliance also feared the provocative behavior of its new ally. In contrast to the later case studies examining alliance management, cases of alliance restraint and the formation of alliances tend to rely on a more expansive definition of restraint. Rather than focus on stopping a *specific* policy, the restrainer is often concerned about more *general* provocative behavior, resurgent militarism, and the possibility of a plan to attack in the future instead of a concrete policy that has been proposed.[47]

When the book shifts to alliance management and the success or failure of restraint, the focus is on multiple cases within two bilateral relationships: Britain–United States and United States–Israel. The United States is the stronger party in both relationships. The Anglo-American cases include two variants: Britain restraining the United States, and the United States restraining Britain. In 1951, the United States blocked British military intervention in Iran. In 1954, Britain stopped American intervention in support of France in Indochina. In 1954–1955, Britain failed to prevent what it saw as an overly broad U.S. treaty commitment to defend Taiwan. In 1956, the United States failed to stop Anglo-French military intervention in Egypt but then used economic pressure to force British soldiers out.

For Israel and the United States, the former is always the restrainee and the latter is always the restrainer. But the cases vary in terms of the success or failure of the restraint effort.[48] The United States failed to stop Israeli nuclear proliferation in the early 1960s, to prevent an Israeli preemptive attack in 1967, and to block an Israeli invasion of Lebanon all the way to Beirut in 1982. The United States successfully restrained Israel in four situations. It prevented an Israeli preemptive attack in 1973, forced Israel to remove Israeli military equipment from Lebanon in 1977, avoided Israeli retaliatory attacks on Iraq in 1991, and rolled back Israeli arms sales to China in the early 2000s.

In all the Anglo-American and American-Israeli cases, both policy coordination and power variants are plausible explanations on the surface.

Both relationships have been described as "special," making them conducive to a norm of policy coordination. But both also embody large disparities in capabilities, so weak-strong relations could make sense as well. This book helps evaluate these alternative explanations.

Moreover, both relationships are well documented, a key ingredient for learning more about motives. That said, assessing motives becomes harder with the cases closer to the contemporary period. Most documents are still classified for U.S.-Israeli relations from the 1970s forward, for instance. One final benefit of the case selection in this book is that looking at several cases within the same bilateral framework allows for holding constant many factors, including any differences in relative capabilities or culture. Of course, such factors could change over time even within the same bilateral linkage. This is not an issue with the Anglo-American cases, which all took place in the 1950s, but might be relevant for the American-Israeli ones, which ran across several decades.

Findings

The case studies in this book suggest four central findings about alliance restraint. First, some states form alliances with the intent of restraining their new ally. The desire to restrain causes the alliance to be formed. But that does not mean restraint is the only motivation for forming the alliance; these alliances often highlight the interrelationship between restraint and threats. In a larger sense, the restraining alliances point to the role of control and influence in alliance formation, a role that has been overshadowed by the emphasis on threat and protection.[49]

Second, the success or failure of alliance restraint attempts depends on the willingness of the most powerful ally to mobilize its power resources. If the powerful ally mobilizes, it can compel weaker allies to be restrained. If the powerful state is the restrainee, it can mobilize its power resources to go it alone and ignore the restraint attempt. Merely being the more capable ally is not sufficient to prevail in an alliance restraint dispute. An explanation based on a normative commitment to policy coordination is not persuasive.

Third, there are several conditions that make power mobilization more or less likely in the case of alliance restraint: deception, leadership unity, national security priorities, and policy alternatives. *Deception* may block restraint by preventing an attempt from even being made or by preventing the mobilization of resources, though withholding information from one's allies is especially tricky in alliances that embody a thick institutional web of interaction. An ally must be aware of the military policy. This seems self-evident, but allies sometimes go to great lengths to conceal from an ally a military policy that they imagine might be objectionable to that ally.

Unified leadership promotes successful mobilization; divided leaders make it less likely. Mobilizing one's power resources is costly, so disagreement about whether to do so may stymie the effort. It is one thing simply to ask an ally not to do something. It is quite another to threaten to penalize, sanction, or bribe that ally if it does not accept one's position. Disunity matters on both sides of the equation, for the restrainee and the restrainer. Unity is not necessarily a cause of power mobilization but is at least correlated with it.

Most important, restraint attempts are part of a larger national security framework that indicates the importance of each issue: the allies' *hierarchy of national security objectives* directly shapes their stance on the restraint attempt.[50] When a state has an overarching objective, as was the case with the United States during the Cold War, other international issues are evaluated in light of that objective. At the same time, that overarching objective includes a variety of smaller goals, each of which competes for priority. If, for example, the restrainer feels its ally's contested military policy will undermine the larger security objective, the restrainer will mobilize its resources to stop it. If, in contrast, the contested military policy is inconvenient and even dangerous but will not adversely affect the restrainer's highest national security priorities, it will be more likely to rely on rhetoric rather than material sanctions or inducements. Another way to frame this issue would be in terms of the balance of interests, not only across allies but also within each state.[51]

Restrainers may see a way to focus their resources on creating an *alternate pathway* to the same outcome desired by the restrainee. Substitution can help restrainers restrain their allies. Sometimes this means substituting one military policy for another. Other times it means jump-starting the diplomatic track between one's ally, the restrainee, and its adversary. In short, it might be worth mobilizing one's resources if one can see an alternate policy pathway by which to restrain. One other possible element is domestic pressure, but I saw only limited evidence for the proposition that domestic interest groups determine whether a state will mobilize its resources.

Fourth, alliance restraint is different from efforts to influence policies among non-allies, the "regular" influence attempts in international relations. Unlike non-allied states, allies do not directly attack each other or threaten to do so. Allies gather information and monitor each other, tasks made easier by the alliance's organizational structure. The alliance creates mechanisms and institutional pathways by which the two sides can try to influence each other, such as military training exercises, officer training, joint planning, high levels of elite interaction, and shared intelligence.

2

Allying to Restrain

Some states form alliances in order to restrain other states. This chapter reviews six alliances in which alliance restraint and balance-of-threat theory each purport to explain the formation of a military alliance. In three cases, the alliance restraint explanation is more persuasive: United States–South Korea, United States–Taiwan, and Egypt-Syria. With the Anglo-Japanese alliance, threat and restraint played about equal roles. In the fifth and sixth cases, the German-Austrian alliance and the North Atlantic Treaty Organization, the restraint element played a secondary, albeit important, role.

However, this does not mean that balance-of-threat theory is irrelevant in the three cases in which restraint was the primary motivation for the origin of the alliance. In fact, threats usually work in tandem with alliance restraint. The existence of a threat sets the stage for one ally to pursue provocative policies that scare its soon-to-be ally into forming a restraining alliance. If no threat existed, the need for a restraining alliance often would not exist. There is an interplay between the two explanations for the formation of alliances; they are not mutually exclusive.

The importance of these cases goes beyond alliance restraint and its role in alliance formation. Alliance restraint should be considered along with other possible explanations when scholars study the origin of an alliance or list the theoretically plausible explanations. But these cases also suggest a broader point: the predominant emphasis on the external orientation of understanding alliance formation needs to be modified.

There is little doubt that many alliances are primarily about affecting the decision making and behavior of those countries external to the alliance. An alliance formed in response to an external threat is an obvious case in point. Some alliances, however, are formed to modify the behavior of someone within the alliance itself more so than any external party. If deterring a party external to the alliance is the cause of some alliances, controlling an ally through restraint or other mechanisms is the cause of many others.

In sections 2 through 7, I analyze historical cases in which restraint was a major factor in the decision to form the alliance. The six cases of alliance formation that at least in part were motivated by restraint are Germany-Austria in 1879; Britain-Japan in 1902; the formation of the North Atlantic Treaty Organization (NATO) in 1949; United States–South Korea in 1953; United States–Taiwan in 1954; and Egypt-Syria in 1964 and 1966. The final section of this chapter summarizes the results.

The cases in this chapter are varied along a number of dimensions. Most of them involve bilateral alliances, but NATO is a multilateral alliance and Egyptian-Syrian ties occurred in the context of multilateral summits. The treaty language varies as well; some spell out very specific scenarios, such as the Anglo-Japanese treaty, whereas others are more general, such as NATO.[1] In most of the cases the restrainer fears the restrainee will provoke an attack by a third party, but in the NATO case France was concerned about an attack by Germany, the same state being brought into the alliance. The former fear is that the restrainee will provoke an attack by someone else whereas the latter concern is that the restrainee itself will be the attacker. Although many articles have been written about these and other differences in alliances, this chapter does not attempt to ascertain what if any impact they have on alliance restraint.[2]

However varied, all the cases in this chapter were selected in order to test whether restraint as a motivation for alliances is even a plausible argument. They are not hard cases for an alliance restraint explanation. In terms of balance-of-threat theory, my contention is that balance-of-threat is a universal explanation and could be applied to any case. The point is not that a previous theorist has actually done so in all six cases in this chapter.

The cases share the idea that one side intends to restrain the other by forming the alliance. Evidence of intent in terms of statements by policymakers or the judgments of later observers is important. Alliance restraint can occur in alliances formed for other reasons, but that is not the focus of this chapter. The motivation for forming the alliance is not always a two-way street. Often only one party is trying to restrain the other. That means the other ally (or soon-to-be ally) may have an entirely different motivation for forming the alliance.

To some readers, the argument of this chapter may seem counterintuitive. Why would a state that feared being dragged into war form an alliance and thereby become more formally committed to defending its new ally? Why not keep its distance? The assumption in this chapter is that in many situations states already feel bound to come to the aid of a second state whether or not they are allies. They already feel they could not stand aside. They may have this feeling because they fear the accumulation of power resources by another state. If state A does nothing as state C gobbles up state B, the combined state of B-C may be too powerful for state A to defend itself. So whether A is allied with B or not, it feels it must help B if a B-C war erupts. Alternatively, a state may feel aligned with another state even if they are not allies. Alignment might be another way of restating fears about power accumulation or it might be the result of political or ideological affinities or other shared interests.

Given that a state (A) will have to come to the aid of another country (B) anyway, it becomes more willing to form an alliance in the hopes of gaining more leverage over its new ally, leverage it can use to restrain. In forming the alliance, the restrainer (A) accepts a slightly elevated chance of having to fight to defend its new ally (B) if war occurs in exchange for the belief that the probability of the outbreak of war will decrease because it (A) is restraining its new ally (B). Of course, this calculation may be mistaken, especially if the restrainee actually feels emboldened by the alliance. The U.S.-Taiwan treaty may have been intended to restrain Taiwan, but nothing stopped Taiwan from seeing the treaty as insurance against the risk of attacking or provoking communist China. As a result, restrainers must balance the restraining aspect of a treaty with concerns that the agreement could spark adventurist policies.[3] But just because it might be mistaken to assume that states can better control their new partner inside an alliance does not mean that states have stopped making that assumption.

In studying alliance formation, scholars have really been considering two questions about alliances: whether to ally and, if so, with whom? Balance-of-threat theory answers the first question. The state identifies a threat and then has to mitigate that threat. Because, the theory concludes, states tend to balance, they react against the threat and find other partners. The theory says little about which partners will be most appealing, though one would expect there to be a limited pool given basic screens such as geographic location and possession of the proper quality and quantity of capabilities. The more, contra balance-of-threat, states tend to ally with the source of the threat (bandwagoning), the more a theory based on threat would answer both questions. When I argue that balance-of-threat theory has overshadowed other explanations, my emphasis is on the question of whether to ally. Other explanations for alliance formation, such as regime type, ideology, and reputation, have tended to be most helpful in answering the second question.[4] In other words, given a need to ally, why did policymakers pick state A over state B? This means that a hybrid explanation may be most helpful. For example, a state may want to balance against a threat but chooses to do so with other democracies like itself or with states that have a reputation for reliability in alliances.

Alliance restraint provides an answer to both questions. Restraint is a motivation to form an alliance, but it also is focused on the need to ally with a specific state.

Germany-Austria (1879)

Although Germany's primary motive for allying with Austria in 1879 was to preclude it from allying with another state, an additional important motive was to prevent war between Austria and Russia by influencing Austrian policy decisions. After Russo-German relations worsened in the latter half of the 1870s, Germany became more interested in an alliance with Austria. Austria had been interested in such a pairing for much of the decade.[5] The actual Russian threat to Germany probably played a lesser role in the formation of the alliance because Germany both felt that Russia was unlikely to attack and believed that Germany would have to come to Austria's aid even without the treaty. In an indirect sense, however, the adversarial nature of the Austro-Russian relationship meant that Germany feared *Austria* might provoke the Russians and drag Germany into a war against Moscow; the hostile state of Austro-Russian relations set the stage for restraint as an explanation for the German interest in an alliance with Austria.

Given the long-term importance of this alliance, understanding what led to it is significant. According to one scholar, the treaty "is perhaps the most important of all the treaties negotiated by [German Chancellor Otto von] Bismarck and it remained the corner-stone of German foreign policy till 1918."[6] William Langer calls the alliance the "kernel of the whole Bismarckian system....All other arrangements centred about it."[7] A. J. P. Taylor guesses that "probably even Bismarck did not fully realize the decisive nature of the step that he had taken."[8] By calling for a long-term rather than ad hoc alliance, the treaty marked a significant shift in German (and European) foreign policy. With the 1879 pact, Bismarck ended Germany's role as an honest broker untied to any one state until the last moment. Furthermore, the agreement helped set in place the European alignments over the next three-plus decades leading to World War I. By joining together Austria and Germany and antagonizing Russia (as St. Petersburg saw it), the alliance was an important step along the way to defining the two sides for future European political competition and war.

Austria and Germany signed the treaty on October 7, 1879. It had two key clauses. First, each party pledged to come to the other's aid in the event of a Russian attack. Second, both parties agreed to benevolent neutrality if attacked by any party other than Russia. In other words, Germany would not join a third state in attacking Austria, and Austria would not join a third state in attacking Germany.

The primary German motive for the alliance was preclusive: prevent Austria from allying elsewhere. According to Snyder, Bismarck thought the alliance would preclude a Russo-French-Austrian alliance against Germany and would draw in England as a "silent partner," given shared Anglo-Austrian interests in the Near East.[9] "I wanted to dig a ditch between her [Austria] and the western powers," Bismarck noted.[10] Bismarck moved to cement the alliance with Count Andrassy, the Austro-Hungarian foreign minister, before Andrassy was replaced by Austrian officials who Bismarck expected to be less sympathetic to an alliance with Germany. Bismarck also sought to act before leadership preferences moved Austria toward a rival state; he did not want Austria "drifting into the arms of France."[11]

In addition, Germany may not have needed the alliance to mitigate the Russian threat directly. Germany would have been expected to defend Austria with or without the formal alliance, according to Bismarck.[12] According to Snyder, Germany did not need an alliance with Austria to meet the Russian threat; there was "little objective likelihood of an attack by Russia [on Germany], and Germany could plausibly defend itself against such an attack without Austrian assistance."[13] Germany would have needed Austrian help only for opposing a joint Russo-French attack on Germany, but good German-French relations in 1879 meant that such a combination was unlikely. Moreover, the German military felt it was superior to the Russian armed forces. Busy at home with nihilists and terrorists, Russia "was quite clearly unprepared to embark upon another war."[14] One historian claims that Bismarck highlighted the Russian threat to Germany only to convince the reluctant German emperor, William I, to support the Austro-German alliance.[15]

Even if Germany did fear Russia, Russia offered Germany an alliance that would have dealt with Russian-German hostility. In late September 1879, Bismarck rebuffed Russian feelers for an alliance that included Russian respect for Austria-Hungary and a Russian pledge to stay neutral in a Franco-German war. From this episode, Taylor deduces Germany's true motives: "If Bismarck had really feared Russia, this offer gave him everything he wanted. But Bismarck's real anxiety was the Austro-Hungarian desire to follow a 'western' policy, and Russian aggressiveness was his excuse, not his motive."[16]

If the threat from Russia was not a major factor in German decision making, why else besides preclusion did Germany seek an alliance with Austria? A second reason was that the alliance would allow Germany to restrain Austria and prevent a needless (Austrian) drive to war with Russia. Germany wanted "to exert some control over Austrian policy and hence to forward one of Bismarck's primary aims: to prevent the outbreak of war between Russia and Austria."[17] In every alliance, "there was a horse and a rider, and he [Bismarck] did not wish Germany to be the horse."[18] By allying with Austria, Germany could rein in Austria and stop policies that might provoke Russia and lead to war. Bismarck's "real fear," writes Taylor, "was of Austro-Hungarian restlessness, not of Russia aggression."[19]

The idea of an Austro-German alliance contrasted favorably in Bismarck's eyes with the possibility of a Russo-German alliance. In the latter case, Bismarck feared, Russia would have the upper hand. In an alliance, Russia would be able to dictate the direction of the alliance's policies, and this might lead to German entanglement in peripheral issues such as Russia's Balkan policies.[20] If Germany allied with Russia and then opposed an alliance policy, "the Tsar could enforce submission by threatening to join forces with France." Austria had no similar alternative ally. Also, "Russian policy was restless and aggressive. . . . A Russo-German alliance would embroil Germany in every Russian quarrel." Austria, in contrast, was a "satiated state . . . her friendship need not involve dangerous obligations."[21] Although Austria could recklessly provoke Russia, Austria was not actively seeking expansion elsewhere, which made it a safer bet than Russia.

In signing a treaty with Austria, Germany faced a common challenge: how to form a restraining alliance without empowering its new partner so the partner feels free to be even more aggressive. The agreement needed by one state (e.g., Germany) to gain some restraining influence, a treaty, may also give the other ally (e.g., Austria) more of a security cushion and thus more of an incentive for aggressive behavior.[22] In this case, for instance, increasing Austrian security through the alliance could have made Austria "less accommodating in confrontations with Russia."[23] "Once he [Bismarck] had given Austria-Hungary a guarantee of existence, he was always in danger of being drawn into her quarrels," Taylor notes.[24] Austrian leaders, who had favored an alliance with Germany to get support against Russia in the disputed Balkans, could have decided to propose or pursue more militant policies now that they had a treaty guarantee of German support in an Austro-Russian war (or at least such a war that Austria could paint as a defensive one against overbearing Russia). As noted below, Britain faced a similar balancing act in its 1902 alliance with Japan, as did the United States with South Korea in 1953.

Although Germany and Austria were both considered great powers, their alliance was not a tethering alliance because they were not equally strong and Germany's fear was not a direct attack by Austria on Germany. Germany was the stronger party by a wide margin. In 1870, for example, Germany possessed 16 percent of European wealth, more than three times Austria's 5 percent; by 1880, it was 20 percent to 4 percent. In 1875, Germany's standing army was 51 percent larger; by 1880, Austria's standing army was even smaller than it had been in 1875 and so the German advantage was 75 percent.[25] Tethering alliances are also designed to prevent the new allies from attacking each other. They manage a strategic rivalry by bringing the rivals into the same alliance. In this case, Germany was concerned Austria would provoke Russia, not attack Germany.

In sum, the German motivation for allying with Austria was twofold. First, Germany wanted to prevent Austria from allying with France and/or Russia. Second, Germany wanted to prevent Austria from starting a war with Russia, which would inevitably mean Germany would have to fight as well. This second motive is an example of desiring an alliance to restrain one's soon-to-be ally.

Britain-Japan (1902)

Britain formed an alliance with Japan in 1902 both to counter the Russian threat and to restrain Japan. In terms of the Russian threat, Britain was concerned by Russia in general, Russo-French naval gains, the Russian penetration of China, and the possibility of a Russo-Japanese agreement that might further strengthen the Russian position in East Asia. British leaders believed the Russian threat to Britain was real. At the same time, London did not want Japan to confront Russia and drag England into a war Britain opposed and could not afford. Britain wanted to control Japanese policy such that Japan neither appeased nor provoked Russia. Within two years, however, a convergence of Anglo-French thinking made British restraint of Japan less crucial; Britain and France would both stay out of a Russo-Japanese war. Russia and Japan could (and did) fight without the need for Britain to join the battle.

The Anglo-Japanese alliance was signed on January 30, 1902. Britain agreed to stay neutral in a Japanese-Russian war.[26] Britain also agreed to support Japan if France joined on the Russian side of the war. The treaty was signed at a time when Britain was looking to decrease its foreign commitments, end conflict where possible, and rely more on alliances and burden sharing. The British empire was costly, and the British public was unwilling to consider further taxation or reduced social welfare spending at home in order to prop it up. The Anglo-Japanese alliance provoked a Russo-French counteragreement on March 17, 1902.[27]

Russia threatened Britain in several ways, as British leaders saw it. First, for both military and economic reasons, Britain wanted to limit Russia's involvement in China. China was the big prize for all the imperial powers, and they repeatedly sought to slow or block one another's access. Second, Britain saw that its long naval superiority was under threat in the Far East from Russo-French naval increases. Lastly, Britain wanted to avoid a Japanese rapprochement with Russia that might further bolster Russian power in the region.[28] Britain believed Japan had the option of settling with Russia rather than allying with Britain, even though this was not a viable option for Japan because Russia made "exorbitant" demands.[29]

Although Britain considered three policies to deal with these problems, only one was successful. Each policy was meant to avoid war and protect British interests. Britain's attempts to negotiate an understanding with Russia (1898) or a treaty with Germany (1898, 1901) all ended without an agreement.[30] Only the third option, an alliance with Japan, was successful.

At least one British leader figured that since England would have to defend Japan anyway, London may as well form an alliance and get some concessions from the Japanese. Lord Lansdowne, the British foreign secretary, described his logic: "The question, he added, was whether

Britain should allow Japan to be wiped out by France and Russia in certain given circumstances: 'If the answer is "no," may we not as well tell her so beforehand and get what we can out of the bargain?'"[31]

Restraint was also a major British motivation for the treaty. By allying with Japan, Britain hoped, Japan would feel more secure and less likely to drag Britain into a war with Russia or with Russia and France. In a dispatch to Claude MacDonald, British minister at Tokyo, on January 30, 1902, Lansdowne explained the signing of the treaty. British officials "had been largely influenced in their decision to enter into this important contract by the conviction that it contains no provisions which can be regarded as an indication of aggressive or self-seeking tendencies in the regions to which it applies. It has been concluded purely as a measure of precaution." He further hoped the treaty would "make for the preservation of peace."[32] On May 9, 1902, a British permanent undersecretary, situating restraint within the larger British effort to control Japanese policy, said the agreement was signed to avoid a Japanese effort either to "go for the Russians" or to "lose heart and give way."[33] Whereas prior to the treaty Britain had been concerned that a Russo-Japanese agreement would strengthen the Russians at Britain's expense, London welcomed the Russo-Japanese understanding on Manchuria in April 1902, just a few months after the signing of the Anglo-Japanese treaty. The understanding called for a reduction of Russian forces in Manchuria (in China) and meant that Russo-Japanese conflict over the Manchuria issue, a conflict that might drag Britain into the battle, was less likely.

The handling of Korea in the Anglo-Japanese treaty provides mixed support for the idea of restraint. Japan's interest in Korea was one issue that could have dragged Britain into an unwanted conflict, and thus both parties were concerned with how the treaty dealt with Korea. On the one hand, the treaty recognized Korea's independence, and both parties "declared themselves to be entirely uninfluenced by any aggressive tendencies in either country [China or Korea]." This fit with Britain's desire not to be drawn into a war over Korea. On the other hand, the treaty recognized that Japan was "interested in a peculiar degree" in Korea and could safeguard those interests if they were threatened by the aggressive action of another state. This meant that Britain would have been expected to come to Japan's aid in a war over Korea if one or more states joined Korea in the fight against Japan.[34]

Just two years after the Anglo-Japanese alliance, Japan went to war with Russia. Did the outbreak of war demonstrate that British restraint of Japan had failed? Possibly, but another interpretation is that London may no longer have felt the need to restrain Japan in order to achieve its goal of not being drawn into an Asian war. In 1904—unlike 1902—Britain and France had both come to the realization that not only did they each not want to be drawn into a war in the Far East but also that the other had no interest in such a war either. This shared Anglo-French interest in the avoidance of war meant that neither would have to go to the aid of Russia or Japan; the Anglo-Japanese and Franco-Russian treaties were worded such that London and Paris had to join the war only if a second state intervened on Russia's or Japan's behalf. In 1902, restraint of Japan was the British mechanism for avoiding being drawn into a Russo-Japanese war.[35] In 1904, an implicit (made explicit in late 1904) agreement with France was the mechanism for avoiding being drawn into war based on the phrasing of the Anglo-Japanese treaty.

In tandem, Britain's fear of the Russian threat and Japanese provocation led to the Anglo-Japanese alliance. Britain did not want Russia to undermine British interests in Asia, but neither did it want Japan starting a war over those same interests. Alliance restraint was part of Britain's motivation for forming an alliance with Japan.

The North Atlantic Treaty Organization–West Germany (1949)

The formation of the North Atlantic Treaty Organization, a multilateral defensive alliance, was part of the U.S. policy response to French pressure on the possibility of a renewed German threat. The United States was eager both to rebuild Germany and to accommodate French security concerns, which centered on renewed German aggression. NATO came to be seen as providing an opportunity to reassure France on security matters without totally excluding Germany from the calculus. Absent French pressure, the United States could have chosen from a range of possible responses to the Soviet Union. But NATO provided a framework that met three oft-mentioned objectives: keeping the Soviet Union out (of Western Europe), the United States in, and Germany down. Meeting the Soviet threat was probably the most important factor, but restraint was of at least secondary importance.

France, a member of NATO, felt that a rebuilt Germany still could pose a threat to France. In other words, just after World War II, France saw Germany as a strategic rival. But ultimately, France accepted the U.S. argument that the best way to deal with this threat was to bring

Germany into the alliance rather than direct the alliance against West Germany.

On March 17, 1948, the same day France, Britain, and others signed the Brussels Treaty, which formed a West European security alliance without Germany, President Harry Truman told the U.S. Congress, "I am sure that the determination of the free countries of Europe to protect themselves will be matched by an equal determination on our part to help them protect themselves."[36] Soon thereafter U.S. and European officials began to meet to consider ways to implement Truman's pledge. His pledge could have meant a number of things: doctrinal changes and rhetorical support, a multilateral treaty, bilateral treaties, and/or military assistance.

Although the NATO treaty was signed on April 4, 1949, without German membership, the three major NATO players all foresaw German involvement or came to accept it over the next year. On June 28, 1948, a U.S. National Security Council staff report advocated eventual German membership in the Brussels pact.[37] On becoming secretary of state in 1949, Dean Acheson argued that Germany must be included in an Atlantic alignment, but he was aware that France wanted to keep Germany out permanently.[38] As for Britain, in January 1948, in a draft of a treaty of "Western union," Foreign Secretary Ernest Bevin envisaged German participation. But the treaty was also aimed at preventing renewed German aggression.[39] The United States saw these two points as contradictory and pushed for a treaty that envisioned German inclusion and did not specifically target Germany (or any one state).[40]

The French were the last to support German inclusion; French opposition to a rejuvenated Germany had been a persistent postwar theme. At the end of July 1948, Paris "expressed grave doubts about the idea of the eventual inclusion of West Germany."[41] When the French Assembly approved the treaty on July 27, 1949, it attached several reservations, including one calling for assembly approval of any new NATO members.[42] This reservation could have been used to try to block German inclusion. However, in September 1950, Robert Schuman, French foreign minister, proposed eventual German participation in NATO instead of rearmament.[43]

Moreover, certain aspects of NATO were developed with the idea of keeping Germany down. Wallander explains:

> Many of NATO's distinctive features had nothing to do with coping with the Soviet threat at all and were a result of NATO's more subtle purpose of preventing a cycle of mistrust, competition, and instability in security relations among its members. NATO therefore developed specific assets

for coping with risks among its members—primarily but not exclusively with Germany in mind. These features include mechanisms for political-military integration, multinationality of alliance structures, supranational defense policy, and the principles and procedures of civilian democratic control of defense affairs.

Wallander also claims that "NATO's existence constrained Germany from acquiring nuclear weapons or creating a general staff."[44]

The French role differs from that of Britain and the United States. Since France did not envision that Germany would come into the treaty (or at least did not do so until after the treaty was signed), in the French case it was not an alliance that was based on restraint of an *ally*—Germany would never be an ally. But Britain and the United States saw a place for Germany in NATO, and thus the acceptance that NATO would help contain Germany was acceptance of the idea of restraining an ally.

Many years later, in 1990, U.S. Secretary of State James Baker used the argument that NATO restrained Germany but this time as a tool in his discussion with the Soviet Union. Baker told the Soviets that a reunited Germany should be part of NATO to prevent a resurgent Germany from threatening either Russia or Western Europe.[45]

Although the threat posed by the Soviet Union was the primary motivation for NATO, the desire to restrain Germany was a secondary factor. The Soviet problem was more apparent. The Soviet Union was a victor in World War II and emerged somewhat intact. Germany was defeated, devastated, and under military occupation by four countries. The Soviets were taking steps to solidify their control over East European states, but the Germans had no foreign state under their control. Though alliance restraint was a factor, it was probably secondary because it dealt with a future fear (about Germany), not a growing threat in the present (the USSR).

The case of Germany and NATO provides some support for alliance restraint as a motive for alliance formation. Given Soviet strength, restraint was not the only factor, but it was an important element for some policymakers.

United States–South Korea (1953)

After nearly three years of fighting, the Korean armistice talks had reached a crucial stage by mid-1953. U.S. officials correctly believed a final agreement with the communist forces was within reach, but they worried about threats by the Republic of Korea (the ROK, or South

Korea) to take military and political steps to undermine and block an agreement. In the end, the United States formed a bilateral alliance with the Republic of Korea in order to restrain Seoul from pursuing military policies that would undermine the armistice talks.[46] The defense pact was not the only U.S. concession to restrain the ROK from unilateral military action, but it was one of the most important and had significant long-term ramifications. Inducements, alliance restraint, and successful negotiations may go together.

The nature of restraint in this case is slightly different from that in many other cases of restraint and alliance formation. In most cases, the restrainer sets up the alliance in response to a general concern about provocative policies or the potential for such policies by the restrainee. The formation of the alliance sets up a mechanism (the alliance) by which the restrainer hopes to rein in the restrainee in the future, if necessary. In the case of the ROK and the United States, the United States offered the alliance in response to a specific set of ROK policies intended to disrupt the armistice talks that the United States hoped would succeed. The formation of an alliance was an explicit quid pro quo offered by the United States to get the ROK to drop specific polices.[47]

On April 3, 1953, Pyun Yung Tai, South Korea's foreign minister, told the United States that the ROK wanted a pact in exchange for supporting the armistice. On April 14, U.S. representatives in South Korea suggested to Washington that the United States offer an alliance to placate Korea, but Secretary of State John Foster Dulles and President Eisenhower wanted to avoid a pact.[48] Later in the summer, on June 23, the alliance remained one of four ROK conditions for accepting the armistice.[49]

The United States and the ROK moved through three stages, starting with the U.S. unwillingness to sign an alliance. In the second stage, Washington accepted the idea of an agreement but the two sides disagreed about the timing of the negotiations and implementation. In the third and final stage, the United States consented to South Korea's timetable for accepting an alliance prior to the conclusion of the armistice. The United States, the dominant member of the United Nations Command (UNC), first tried to gain ROK cooperation on armistice issues without offering a security pact, but this proposal failed to sway President Syngman Rhee and other leaders.[50] Thus on May 30, 1953, top U.S. officials accepted that they would have to offer a pact, and they did so on June 6. But the two sides were still split about the timing: Eisenhower offered to formulate the pact after the armistice was signed, but Rhee demanded that the agreement come first.[51]

The shift in U.S. policy toward offering a security pact came as a result of ROK policy—its demand for a security pact and threats to undermine the move for an armistice—rather than as a result of any change in the threat posed by communist forces. In fact, the offer came at a time when communist and UNC negotiators had nearly agreed on an armistice deal as they moved toward the deescalation of the conflict. Dulles summarized the U.S. shift that resulted from South Korean pressure: "But to get an armistice took great sacrifices on our part. . . . We did not promise . . . to give a security pact because we wanted to. The South Koreans have always wanted one and we have refused until now."[52]

Why did South Korea want a security pact? ROK leaders saw a pact as the second-best choice after true unification of the peninsula under ROK rule. First, if the ROK was going to have to accept a non-unified Korea, it needed some assurance on its post-armistice security; a U.S.-ROK alliance would provide such security. Second, Rhee had long pledged to the Korean public that he would oppose an armistice that lacked unification under his rule. Thus for domestic political reasons, he needed a face-saving formula to cover his apparent retreat from that position. A defense pact would provide that cover.[53]

The ROK had a number of military options if it wanted to scuttle the armistice talks. Rhee repeatedly threatened to go it alone and fight the communists without U.S. or UNC support (a "march north"); to withdraw the ROK forces from the UN command; and to prematurely release North Korean prisoners. Koreans rallied in support.[54] Rhee may have made these threats assuming that the United States would have to back him up, though U.S. officials considered a withdrawal from Korea, as noted below. As one U.S. official characterized it, the ROK could disrupt the UNC and the armistice talks by independently attacking the communists, refusing UNC orders, or taking hostile action toward the UNC forces.[55]

Even as the United States and the ROK were talking about a deal, Rhee took provocative steps. On June 7, 1953, he issued "extraordinary security measures," recalled South Korean officers from U.S. training schools, and increased propaganda favoring a unilateral military move.[56] More dramatically, on June 17–18, Rhee ordered the release of thousands of North Korean prisoners of war (POWs). POWs and repatriation procedures had been a central point of contention in the armistice talks, so the release was a major challenge to the Communist side and could have greatly damaged the prospects for a negotiated settlement. Rhee wanted to delay the conclusion of the armistice talks until after a U.S.-ROK alliance was agreed on.[57]

In order to stop renegade ROK military actions that would have ruined the chances for a political deal to end the war, U.S. officials considered several options, including toppling Rhee's regime and taking over the ROK government, withdrawing U.S. forces from Korea, and offering the ROK a bilateral security pact. After rejecting the first two options, Washington offered the ROK a security pact in exchange for moderation and cooperation on the armistice issues. Rhee and Walter S. Robertson, U.S. assistant secretary of state, met for two weeks. In exchange for the pact, the United States asked for assurances that the ROK would "refrain from opposition to and agitation against an armistice," cooperate in the implementation of an agreement, and keep ROK forces under the operational control of the UNC.[58] "If the final issue between Rhee and ourselves appears to be whether or not we give him a security pact," Admiral Donald Duncan noted, "it might well be worth giving Rhee such a pact in order to keep him in line."[59] In a joint statement issued after the Dulles-Rhee consultations, the ROK pledged "to take no unilateral action to unite Korea by military means for the agreed duration of the political conference."[60]

Ultimately, in mid-July, the ROK accepted the trade-off. Although other factors also affected the ROK decision, the security agreement was an important one.[61] The two parties signed a bilateral alliance, and despite continued noise from the ROK about its displeasure with the armistice agreement signed on July 27, 1953, South Korea took no additional steps to enact a military policy that would circumvent or undermine the armistice. To further sharpen the limits of U.S. obligations and reiterate U.S. opposition to unilateral ROK military moves, Congress inserted an additional understanding, which South Korea accepted: "nor shall anything in the present Treaty be construed as requiring the United States to give assistance to Korea except in the event of an armed attack against territory which has been recognized by the United States as lawfully brought under the administrative control of the Republic of Korea."[62]

One could argue that U.S. policy in this case was not alliance restraint but rather the offering of incentives by one party, the United States, to promote negotiations. However, these two categories are not mutually exclusive. A given interaction could fit both the definition of alliance restraint and a different category of negotiation incentives or rewards. The incentives might be the means by which the restrainer achieves its goal. Furthermore, unlike some international negotiations, in this case the ROK made explicit threats and took specific actions in the military realm in June 1953. So the security pact was more than just a reward to

Korea for accepting the armistice agreement; simultaneously, it was the use of inducements to prevent further military provocations.

The United States wanted South Korea to accept the armistice. Fearing that Rhee would use military policies to prevent the armistice, the United States offered a material incentive, a bilateral security pact. The case involved not only alliance restraint but also negotiations brinksmanship. Nevertheless, the U.S. motivation for forming the alliance is consistent with a restraint explanation.

United States–Taiwan (1954)

As with South Korea, the United States at first resisted the idea of an American-Taiwanese alliance. But U.S. officials came to believe that an alliance with the nationalist Chinese, the Kuomintang (KMT), would give Washington the ability to rein in KMT forces and prevent a KMT provocation of mainland communist China. Once the treaty was signed, U.S. officials had to worry that a treaty intended to restrain the KMT could lead to KMT adventurism.

The Mutual Defense Treaty was signed on December 2, 1954; related letters with explicit restraining provisions were signed on December 10, 1954. Eisenhower blocked Secretary of State Dulles's attempt to include an explicit pledge to protect the coastal islands in the treaty.[63] Instead, Article VI stipulated that the treaty protections applied to Taiwan and the Pescadores and "will be applicable to such other territories as may be determined by mutual agreement."[64] In his letter, Dulles stated that the use of force by either party from Taiwan, the Pescadores, or some U.S. areas "will be a matter of joint agreement," and neither party could remove jointly held military "elements...from the territories described in Article VI to a degree which would substantially diminish the defensibility of such territories without mutual agreement."[65]

Congress inserted additional stipulations to limit U.S. obligations under the treaty and to "releash" KMT leaders. The U.S. Senate Committee on Foreign Relations noted that the treaty did not modify the legal status of Taiwan and the Pescadores, that the United States would support Taiwan only in cases of self-defense, and that Senate approval would be required for an expansion of the territorial coverage of the treaty.[66] These clauses all sought to rein in the grand ambition of the nationalist Chinese to harass and even retake the Chinese mainland.

For the Eisenhower administration, a treaty with Taiwan met several needs: deterring mainland China from attacking Formosa, pacifying U.S. groups, maintaining Taiwan's pro-American orientation, and restraining Taiwan. On the U.S. domestic front, it allowed the president to appease the right-wing members of the Republican party, who vehemently opposed communist China and were in favor of an aggressive policy to confront the communists. Also, although the United States did not embrace the Republic of China's goal of invading the mainland, it usually did not rule out this objective entirely because it feared alienating Taiwan and thereby weakening the alliance. If the United States had explicitly rejected liberation of the mainland as a nationalist goal, the Republic of China (ROC) might have defected from the alliance.[67] In late 1954, in U.S. discussions about the possibility of asking the nationalists to remove their military forces from the offshore islands, Eisenhower worried that as a result Chiang Kai-shek, the nationalist leader, could "quit us cold."[68] For a similar reason, the United States also may have dropped demands making the withdrawal of ROC military forces from the islands of Quemoy and Matsu a quid pro quo for signing the defense treaty.[69]

But the treaty also gave the United States a chance to restrain Taiwan. The United States did not support a nationalist invasion of the communist mainland.[70] Robert Divine explains, "By insisting on restraining Chiang Kai-shek, the President protected himself against the danger of automatic involvement in one of the generalissimo's military adventures."[71] If domestic needs meant that Eisenhower had to accept some tie to the KMT, U.S. officials tried to make sure the tie would help rein in Taiwan's leaders. According to one later writer, "the exchange of notes constituted, in effect, a 'releashing' of Chiang Kai-shek's forces."[72] Another observer agrees:

> From Washington's perspective the most desirable feature of the treaty was that it provided Americans with increased control over Nationalist actions. Dulles offered Chiang a simple bargain: in exchange for a mutual security pact, the Generalissimo must renounce his dreams of returning to the mainland by force. The Nationalists would have to pledge themselves to limit operations against the mainland only to those approved by the United States and to abandon any invasion attempt or other activity that might lead to war.[73]

The treaty "negotiated with Taiwan was as much about restraining one's ally as about deterring on its behalf."[74]

The 1954 treaty sharpened the pre-Eisenhower American dilemma of supporting and restraining the ROC at the same time: "So in taking the Nationalists under the American wing again, the Truman administration built a nest in which to not only protect and succor but also closely monitor its fledgling protégé."[75] U.S. officials were concerned that the ROC would use the treaty to draw the United States into a war with communist China (the People's Republic of China [PRC]), so they insisted on several protective provisions: "U.S. leaders feared that once the United States was obligated by treaty to come to Taiwan's assistance, Taipei might provoke a conflict with the PRC by initiating large-scale offensive operations against the mainland or by stationing large concentrations on Jinmen and Mazu [Quemoy and Matsu], thereby triggering a Communist attack against those islands."[76] After the treaty was drafted, Dulles told Eisenhower that the treaty "stakes out unqualifiedly our interests in Formosa and the Pescadores and does so on a basis which will not enable the Chinese Nationalists to involve us in a war with Communist China."[77] But "despite their strong pro-KMT, anti-CCP rhetoric, Eisenhower and Dulles nonetheless feared that Chiang would try to draw the United States into another Chinese civil war."[78]

In the 1958 islands crisis, U.S. policy was a mix of support and restraint.[79] U.S. policymakers were suspicious "that the ROC had deliberately acted so as to increase the probability of a military clash between PRC and US forces."[80] At a meeting on September 1, 1958, as the second islands crisis was just under way, Dulles reported that Eisenhower "expressed some annoyance over what he considered to be Chiang's pressure to get us involved."[81] Just over a month later, Eisenhower "spoke with considerable heat about continuing to have to do what Chiang Kai-shek wanted us to do. He then said he was just about ready to tell Chiang Kai-shek where he (Chiang Kai-shek) got off."[82] In September 1958, Eisenhower reported being told by the U.S. secretary of defense "that Chiang's refusal to do so [to leave the disputed islands] was a reflection of his hope of promoting a fight between the United States and the Chinese Communists as a prelude to a Chinese Nationalist invasion of the mainland."[83] A State Department official reported that "there are disturbing signs of... [ROC] efforts to get the U.S. involved in a nuclear war with Red China" and noted the need for U.S. pressure "to keep the GRC [Government of the Republic of China] under control."[84] Dulles surmised that many Taiwanese officials viewed the crisis "as a golden opportunity for recovering the mainland as the outcome of a war between the U.S. and Red China." Chiang has always "shown good faith," Dulles added, but "this sentiment pervades the thinking of many people on Taiwan."[85] On September 25, 1958, General Charles P. Cabell, deputy director of Central Intelligence, told the U.S. National Security Council that the nationalists were engaged in provocative actions "in violation of their pledged word to us."[86]

As highlighted in this case, two allies may be motivated to join together for contradictory reasons. Even as the United States hoped the treaty would help rein in the Republic of China, the ROC hoped to use it as a lever to compel Washington to support an offensive aim, the invasion of the Chinese mainland: "Friction did arise during both the Eisenhower and Kennedy administrations over Chiang's determination to attack the People's Republic and force the United States into a war to recapture the mainland."[87] That such a war never happened is due, in part, to U.S. restraint.

In sum, the United States tried to restrain the Republic of China by offering certain treaty protections. The U.S. fear of nationalist Chinese provocations led to an American policy of restraint. The tool the United States hoped to use to achieve that restraint was an alliance.

Egypt-Syria (1964, 1966)

In 1964, Egypt brought together the Arab states under the Arab summit system, which lasted for almost two years. Cairo arranged this multilateral political and security alliance to rein in Syria and prevent the execution of a plan to confront Israel over its water diversion project. Egypt's efforts to form a multilateral alliance were not a direct response to a heightened Israeli threat. Egypt feared Syria's *reaction* to the Israeli threat and formed the alliance more to control the Syrians than to balance against Israel.[88]

Egypt and Syria, along with the rest of the Arab world, saw Israel as their enemy. Even before the summit meetings, there was little doubt that Egypt would come to Syria's aid in the event of another Arab-Israeli war.

Rising popular concern over Israeli progress on water diversion and "repeated urgings" by officials of the Arab League led to a meeting of Arab chiefs of staff in December 1963 that set the stage for a restraining alliance. Fred Khouri says that according to published reports, the chiefs agreed to a plan of "strong" military action. The plan was to be submitted to the Defense Council for final approval.[89] Khouri writes that the Arab chiefs of staff "supported Syria's call for the use of military power, if necessary, to compel Israel to halt her water diversion efforts."[90] More generally, Yair Evron notes the growing pressure exerted by the Syrians on Arab governments over the Israeli water project.[91]

But Egypt did not want to get in a military confrontation over water. Just before the meetings, on November 23, 1963, the Syrian vice-president, Ahram Maurani, proposed to Nasser that the Arabs use force to block Israel's water diversion plans. Nasser's answer suggested Egypt did not support this approach: "Ahram, my brother, and what would happen if Israel bombed Damascus?"[92]

The decision of the Arab chiefs of staff forced Egypt's hand and set the stage for a restraining alliance. Although the Israeli military threat to the Arab side did not change during this period, the chiefs' action meant that war was a distinct possibility. Those opposed to war, such as Egypt, would need to step in or risk being dragged along. Khouri says Nasser and other Arab leaders realized that the weakness of the Arab armed forces, intra-Arab fighting (e.g., in Yemen) and tension, and the possibility of Western intervention undermined this plan. "President Nasser therefore requested an urgent meeting of all the Arab heads of state to check the grave trend towards a war on Israel which had developed within the Arab world and to seek and agree upon some nonmilitary course of action which might placate the angry Arab masses."[93] Evron concurs: "In order to create some united Arab position about this 'threat' and at the same time restrain Syria, Nasser came around to the idea of Arab summit meetings." He adds, "There was a pressing need to restrain them [the Syrians] in order to prevent them from throwing him [Nasser] headlong into an unwanted war."[94]

Nasser faced a dilemma, and the summit approach provided a way out. On the one hand, Egypt did not want war and argued that the Arab forces were not ready to confront Israel. A defeat at the hands of the Israelis would be a blow to Egyptian prestige, and Egypt would end up paying a large share of the war's human and financial costs. On the other hand, Nasser did not want the loss of face that would inevitably result from being seen as the state that vetoed a confrontation with Israel. This, too, would not be good for Egypt's leadership and standing in the Arab world.

The summit meeting, then, emerged as a policy that would not undermine Egypt's military or political position. Rather than take the heat for rejecting the Syrian-led call for using force to stop Israel's water diversion activities, Nasser could spread the responsibility across all the Arab states. At the same time, the summit provided links that would allow Egypt to share in the credit for any Arab counterdiversionary water policies that were actually implemented. For instance, if Amman proceeded with a plan to divert water, Egypt would be able to share the spotlight under the rubric of summit resolutions calling for such Arab diversions.[95]

What were the results of the first summit, in January 1964? At the summit, only Syria's Amin al-Hafiz wanted war or at least the use of force to stop Israel's diversion of the Jordan.[96] General Ali Ali Amer, Egypt's chief of staff, was appointed head of the Unified Military Command, "which would draw up plans for coordinating the power and strategy of all Arab armed forces."[97] The summit did not call for any immediate military action, and an Egyptian, Amer, was now coordinating any war efforts.

The summit also sought to divert the tributaries of the Jordan River, a move that was seen by moderates as a way to head off Syrian calls for stopping, by force, Israeli diversion efforts. The Arabs may have hoped to divert the Banyas and Hasbani rivers. "The decision to divert the Jordan was reached as a kind of compromise between the cautious Nasserite and the breast-beating Syrian approaches."[98] Later, in March 1966, Wasfi Tell, Jordanian prime minister, told *Al-Rai Al-Amm*, a Kuwaiti newspaper, that the Arab water diversion and establishment of the Palestine Liberation Organization "are preventive aspects. There was no discussion [at the summits] on any active measures."[99]

As a result of the summit, Syrian calls for a confrontation with Israel were muted. Khouri concludes that the January 1964 summit "precluded any immediate threat of an armed conflict between the contending [Arab and Israeli] parties."[100] He adds: "The most decisive conclusion reached at the summit meeting was to try to frustrate Israel's water diversion plans, not by using armed force, but by preventing as much water as possible from reaching Israeli territory through Arab diversions of the Hasbani, Banyas, and Yarmuk Rivers. At the summit meeting, only the Syrians apparently pressed strongly for military action."[101] Malcolm Kerr concurs: "The most important need of the moment had not been the diversion of water but the diversion of the Syrian government from any hope of immersing Gamal 'Abd al-Nasir in war or embarrassment."[102] UN and Western officials believed that the summit had eliminated any imminent risk of war by rejecting the idea of using military power to stop Israeli water diversion efforts.[103] According to Khouri, Israeli leaders saw the results of the first summit as "a face-saving scheme to justify their [Arab] failure for not carrying out their threats to force Israel to halt her project," but other historians disagree, suggesting that Israel was concerned that the first summit was a sign of an Arab push for war against Israel.[104]

At the second summit meeting, in Alexandria in September 1964, Syria continued to advocate the use of force against Israel but was again blocked. Attendees disagreed on the timetable of Arab (water) diversionary efforts and the coordinated military policies. However, Syria's desire to use force against Israel was again rebuffed at Alexandria. Instead, in the military arena, the heads of state agreed to continue plans to divert water rather than directly disrupt Israeli water diversion efforts; start work on projects in Jordan that would not provoke Israel and thus could avoid a premature Arab-Israeli military confrontation; and grant General Amer the power to position Arab armies in front-line states in the event of war with Israel. Arab plans included "embarking on immediate work for the Arab projects for the exploitation of the waters of the River Jordan and its tributaries." In their statement, the leaders also put Israel on notice: "any aggression against any Arab state will be considered aggression against all the Arab countries, and will be repelled by them all."[105] A few months after the second summit, Nasser stated that "we succeeded...in agreeing on the diversion of the River Jordan sources."[106] After the second summit, Israel protested and threatened but took little action because it was unsure if the Arab states would implement these decisions.[107] On May 31, 1965, Egypt rejected a Syrian call for the removal of the United Nations Emergency Force, a UN peacekeeping mission stationed in Egypt's Sinai Desert in the aftermath of the 1956 Suez War.[108]

The summit framework grew weaker in 1965 even as a third summit was held at Casablanca in September. Almost a year later, on August 5, 1966, the Arab League officially informed members that the next summit was postponed indefinitely,[109] and Syria returned to the offensive. On August 15, 1966, Israel and Syria engaged in a major military confrontation over the Sea of Galilee. Syria claimed the battle was part of its new offensive strategy against Israel. Syria "would not confine herself to defensive action but would attack defined targets and bases of aggression within" Israel.[110] On the same day, *Radio Damascus* explained "the strategy which Syria is now following in facing the state of aggression is a change from the position of defence to the position of attack."[111] Syrian president Nureddin Atassi claimed on August 20, 1966, that the United Arab Republic (Egypt) and Syria had agreed to coordinate military measures.[112] In resolutions released on October 31, 1966, at the end of the Ba'th party conference, Syrian officials said that postponing military action against Israel until the Arab forces were superior was a "treacherous" policy; they thus rejected Nasser's favored approach.[113] Instead, the party resolutions called for "a people's liberation war...to liberate Palestine, overthrow reactionary regimes and eliminate foreign influences."[114]

Egypt again reacted to Syrian moves by trying to use an alliance to restrain Damascus. According to Kerr, Egypt was "clearly disturbed at the Syrians' recklessness but no longer able to invoke the consensus of the summit to restrain them." Nasser "invited [Syrian] Prime Minister Zu'ayyin to Cairo and on 7 [*sic*] November signed a treaty of mutual defence. By this means he would at least bind Syria to advance consultation in the future."[115] Another source suggests a similar Egyptian calculus: "Observers in Cairo and other Arab capitals thought that President Nasser, who led the Egyptian side at the talks, might have obtained a promise in return for Egyptian help in the event of an attack that Syria would not provoke serious incidents with Israel."[116] Anthony Nutting also says Nasser supported a defense agreement to rein in both the Syrians and the Fatah guerrillas.[117] Evron agrees that Egypt wanted to restrain Syria and deter Israel, but he contends that Egypt failed on both counts: it was unable to extricate itself by leaving the pact for fear of jeopardizing its standing in the Arab world.[118] Israeli officials were uncertain whether the pact signaled restraint or Arab aggression.[119]

Months later, on May 5, 1967, Nasser sent his prime minister to Damascus to issue a warning that "our agreement for mutual defense will apply only in the event of a general attack on Syria by Israel. No merely local incident will cause us to intervene."[120] Within days, however, the escalation between the Arab states and Israel was taken to new heights as an erroneous Soviet warning about Israeli troop concentrations, the mobilization of Egypt's military forces, the withdrawal of UN peacekeepers, and the Egyptian closure of the Strait of Tiran to Israel-bound shipping brought the region to the brink of war. On June 5, 1967, Israel attacked Egypt and crushed the Egyptian armed forces within days.

Although the term *alliance* is not the only way to characterize the Arab summit and the Egyptian-Syrian tie, the relationship meets the definition of alliance presented in chapter 1. Two features in particular are important: the establishment of a unified military command and the pledge to respond to an attack by Israel on any one of the parties to the summit. Egypt and Syria had a shared interest in confronting Israel, and the summits clearly focused on security cooperation. The unified command suggested this was not a fleeting agreement but rather an effort to build some lasting institutional linkages.

This case supports the idea that some countries form alliances in order to restrain their new partners. Egypt used the alliance to rein in Syria.

Conclusion

In three cases in this chapter, restraint was at least as important as a threat from an adversary in explaining the formation of an alliance: United

States–South Korea, United States–Taiwan, and Egypt-Syria. Both threat and restraint were convincing parts of the explanation in the Anglo-Japanese case. In a fifth case, the Austro-German alliance of 1879, restraint was the second factor behind Germany's interest in precluding Austria from allying elsewhere. In a sixth case, NATO, the U.S./French/British desire to keep Germany down (restrained) was probably secondary to the desire to address the Soviet threat to the West (although France may have been more concerned about Germany than about the Soviet Union).

This is not to suggest that threat theory is either secondary in general or unrelated to the issue of restraint. As noted, a threat from a mutual adversary often makes restraint necessary for a member of an alliance which fears that its ally might provoke the existing threat. To restate an earlier claim, state A forms a formal alliance with state B ostensibly against C not because of any new threat by state C but because A fears that its soon-to-be ally (B) will act recklessly, provoke C, and drag A needlessly into a war of states A and B against state C.

But even if external threats play a role, the importance of the dynamic between the allies should not be underestimated. The study of alliance formation has often been fixed on how states react to external parties, but the intra-ally dimension of alliance formation is equally important, and alliance restraint is one of several dynamics that emphasize this dimension. Control, restraint, tethering, and efforts to ally in order to promote more aggressive policies all are first and foremost about the parties to the alliance rather than their adversary. Motivations of protection and control for alliance formation merit inclusion in the study of alliances.

3

Anglo-American Relations
and Alliance Restraint

What explains the success or failure of alliance restraint? An assessment of Anglo-American relations in the 1950s helps evaluate the power and norm-based explanations. In four U.S.-British case studies, the normative explanation of policy coordination is not supported. On the power side, the mere holding of an advantage in capabilities does not determine success. A more powerful ally must be willing to mobilize its power resources, whether that means to go it alone and rebuff a restraint attempt or to sanction and induce to achieve restraint success. This chapter, as well as chapter 4, turns to alliance management, or how decisions are taken by allies.

The four cases provide a combination of success/failure and strong and weak restrainer/restrainee. In 1951, Britain rejected military intervention in Iran as a result of U.S. opposition. The United States threatened to withhold backing if an Anglo-Iranian fight drew Soviet forces into Iran. In 1954, the United States rejected military intervention in Indochina as a result of British opposition. Given congressional demands for burden sharing, the Eisenhower administration rejected unilateral intervention on behalf of France. In 1954–1955, Britain failed to restrain the United States with regard to Formosa (Taiwan) and the offshore islands crisis. Washington was willing to go it alone. In 1956, Britain intervened in Egypt despite U.S. opposition but then withdrew under intense U.S. economic pressure; the Suez case, then, is an example of failed alliance restraint followed by successful restraint.

The Anglo-American cases undermine the normative explanation based on policy coordination in three ways. First, the cases highlight the fact that consultation and coordination are not one and the same. Despite extensive consultations, Britain and the United States did not coordinate policy in 1954–1955 (Formosa) or 1956 (Suez). Second, the explanation predicts that allies either come to an agreement to go forward with the policy or agree to drop it. Yet in 1954–1955, the United States brushed aside British objections, as did Britain in 1956 with regard to Egypt when the roles were reversed. Even in the cases in which restraint succeeded, coercive arguments were more important than a persuasive or cooperative norm. Third, deception played an important role in both 1951 and the first part of the Suez war. In both cases, Britain tried to circumvent U.S. objections by hiding its true policy.

Power was useful but only under certain conditions. The more capable ally, the United States, prevailed only when it *mobilized* its power resources. When the United States, as a restrainer, threatened to withhold support against Soviet forces in 1951, Britain was restrained. When Washington relied only on rhetoric in 1956, Britain intervened in Egypt. On the other side, Washington was willing to move unilaterally regarding Formosa and thereby rely on its own power base, but not in the case of Indochina in 1954. In the latter case, the unwillingness to go it alone meant British restraint was successful.

Given these findings, why did the United States mobilize its power in some cases but not others? Four factors affected that decision. First, when acting as the restrainer, the more powerful state, must be aware of the restrainee's policy. Yet in both 1951 and 1956, Britain considered how to deceive Washington. In 1951, London considered portraying the intervention in Iran as an anti-communist move rather than a colonial and commercial intervention. In 1956, Britain and France left the United States in the dark in late October so as to avoid an American restraint attempt, and U.S. officials themselves started to fear that they were not being told something. In the last few days before the war, Washington did not have the opportunity to mobilize its power resources because it was not aware of the war's imminence.

Second, the disunity of decision makers on both sides is sometimes a factor. In 1954, the split between Congress and the Eisenhower administration created space for Britain to be the decisive actor in the crisis. Britain was able to restrain the United States because congressional leaders demanded British support for intervention in Indochina. Absent the split among American elites, this restraint would not have been possible.

In 1956, leadership differences might also have been one of the reasons the United States sanctioned Britain only after the Anglo-French intervention.

Third, the more powerful state's hierarchy of national security objectives affects each restraint decision. In 1951, the United States was unwilling to risk war with the Soviet Union to protect British oil interests in Iran so it threatened to withhold U.S. capabilities should Britain need them against the Soviets. In 1954, Britain refused to join the United States in military action in Indochina because the two allies had different security priorities; British leaders saw the war in Indochina as a dangerous diversion from the central European front in the war against communism. The same difference affected the 1954–1955 argument over defending Formosa.

Fourth, when the United States was the restrainer, it considered bringing its resources to bear in order to develop an alternate pathway to fulfill Britain's needs. In 1951, the United States reinvigorated the diplomatic pathway through the efforts of an American envoy and thus stayed the British hand for a time. In 1956, the United States tried but failed to organize an international response. Washington was willing to devote some American resources to reverse Nasser's nationalization of the Suez Canal, but the multilateral effort did not materialize.

Anglo-American Relations

Throughout this period, U.S. power capabilities were much greater than those of the United Kingdom. In the early and mid-1950s, Washington spent 9–10 times as much on defense, the U.S. gross national product was 7–8 times greater, and both the U.S. population and the U.S. military (total military personnel) were 3–4 times larger than in the United Kingdom.[1] By 1951, the United States had 640 nuclear weapons, a figure that had ballooned to 4,618 by 1956. In contrast, Britain's first nuclear weapon came in 1953; by 1956, Britain had 15.[2]

The Anglo-American alliance has deep roots. The two countries were allied together in World Wars I and II, though in each case Britain was engaged in directly fighting the enemy before the United States. They shared an interest in seeing Germany defeated in both world wars, and the American lend-lease program provided massive aid to England in the early phase of World War II. In the aftermath of the war and with the start of the Cold War, Britain and the United States again joined together, this time under the umbrella of the North Atlantic Treaty Organization (NATO).[3] NATO emerged from the signing of the North Atlantic Treaty on April 4, 1949. The members of the multilateral alliance pledged to come to one another's aid in the event of an attack. London and Washington have also built an extensive infrastructure of security cooperation: consultation and regular meetings, shared technology, military exercises, joint planning, burden sharing, missile deployment, and the like. Whether or not Britain could deter great-power adversaries with its own nuclear force, it is also protected by the U.S. nuclear umbrella. The Anglo-American relationship has long been known as the special relationship, and the military links are paralleled by deep cultural and economic ties.[4] Leaders on both sides appear to believe that the alliance, having lasted for decades, will continue for the foreseeable future.

The United States Restrains Britain in Iran, 1951

In July and September 1951, U.S. opposition stopped British military intervention in Iran. The United States, the more powerful ally, succeeded because it threatened to withhold support that Britain needed to go forward with the use of force. The United States also worked to restart the diplomatic pathway, and this effort was especially helpful in holding Britain back in July.

In 1951, the British government became directly involved in a confrontation between the government of Iran and the private, British company that controlled Iranian oil, the Anglo-Iranian Oil Company (AIOC). After several years of failed negotiations between the government of Iran and the AIOC, Iran began to move forward with the nationalization of its oil industry in 1951. The British government favored a negotiated resolution of the crisis but was willing to use force if talks broke down and nationalization moved forward at the expense of the AIOC.

The United States repeatedly sought to dissuade Britain from using force to resolve its dispute with Iran. On May 11, U.S. officials advised Oliver Franks, British ambassador to Washington:

> With respect to implied threat in proposed Brit note of serious consequences in event Iranian refusal to negotiate, which instruction to Amb interprets as involving possible eventual use of force, US would recognize right of Brit to evacuate Brit citizens whose lives were in danger. Open Soviet intervention in Iran or seizure of power in Tehran by Communist Govt, would, of course, also create situation where use of force must be

considered. US would, however, have grave misgivings with respect to use of force in absence above conditions or, in case of danger to Brit citizens, to extension of use of force beyond evacuation. Dept noted that Brit Govt has made no firm decision in this matter and would expect Brit Govt, as they offer, to discuss matter with US Govt before any such decision is made.[5]

In Washington on both May 16 and 17, U.S. officials cautioned the British against using armed force to resolve the oil dispute.[6] On May 18, Dean Acheson, U.S. secretary of state, again warned the British not to use force, and "he stated flatly that we would not support such a course."[7]

Not only was restraint the official U.S. policy, but the United States also considered the possibility of not backing a unilateral British decision to use force. This is a crucial point because it left open the possibility that Britain would not have U.S. support at either the United Nations or against the Soviet Union. On June 28, President Harry Truman approved NSC 107/2, an updated statement of policy toward Iran:

> Although assurances have been received, the United States should continue to urge the United Kingdom to avoid the use of military force in settling the oil controversy. The entry of British troops into Iran without the consent of the Iranian Government would place British forces in opposition to the military forces of Iran, might split the free world, would produce a chaotic situation in Iran, and might cause the Iranian Government to turn to the Soviet Union for help. However, should the lives of British subjects in Iran be placed in immediate jeopardy by mob violence, the United States would not oppose the entry of British forces into the danger area for the sole purpose of evacuating British nationals on the clear understanding that this would be undertaken only as a last resort and that the British forces so introduced would be withdrawn immediately after the evacuation was completed. In the event of a British decision to use force against the advice of the United States, the situation would be so critical that the position of the United States would have to be determined in the light of the world situation at the time.[8]

This policy differs from previous U.S. policy that promised the British "benevolent neutrality."[9]

In September, the United States continued to argue against British intervention.[10] On September 10,[11] Acheson, U.S. diplomat Averill Harriman, and British foreign secretary Herbert Morrison discussed Iran. Acheson told Morrison:

> It was the hope of the United States Government that His Majesty's Government would not proceed to any military measures except (i) to save British

lives which were in danger; (ii) in the event of a communist government taking over; The United States Government would view with grave concern the taking of military measures against an Iranian Government which still was under the Shah and which was not communist.[12]

The United States had consistently supported only these two types of intervention, repeatedly objecting to British options that were designed to safeguard British oil interests in Iran. According to U.S. minutes of the same meeting, Acheson warned Morrison that although Washington would "render general support to the British," the retention of a non-communist Iran "would best be achieved if the U.S. retained its freedom of action and did not become associated in the Iranian mind too closely with British policy."[13]

Truman's reply to a letter of September 25 from British prime minister Clement Attlee reinforced U.S. opposition to the possible use of force in response to Iran's issuance of the eviction order for the few hundred remaining British technicians at the oil facilities at Abadan, Iran. On September 27, British officials read what by then must have been familiar American language: "I am glad to note from your communication that you recognise the very grave consequences of using force to maintain the British staff at Abadan because, as you know, this Government could not consider support of any such action."[14] Truman suggested that a more detailed response to Attlee would follow, but the most important message had been delivered. Though circumstances on the ground were shifting, the United States remained firmly opposed to military intervention as a means of reversing Iranian policy.

In addition to restraining Britain, the United States sought to use its diplomatic power to reinvigorate British-Iranian negotiations. One British diplomatic mission, led by Basil Jackson, vice-chairman of the AIOC board, departed Tehran without success on June 21, 1951. After failing to prevent the mission from departing, Truman and Acheson proposed sending a U.S. representative, Averill Harriman, to restart negotiations. At the same time, the British government wavered with regard to intervention. Throughout July, the British military was ready to intervene, but the politicians went back and forth.

Harriman eventually succeeded in restarting talks, and the resultant British delegation to Iran, the Stokes mission, lasted through much of August. The U.S. development of a diplomatic alternative temporarily stopped the use of force. As Hugh Gaitskell, chancellor of the exchequer, explained: "President Truman decided to send Harriman and we had to hold our hand."[15]

When diplomacy once more failed to resolve Anglo-Iranian differences, the British again moved toward military intervention but refrained from doing so because of U.S. opposition. On September 27, the British cabinet acquiesced to its U.S. ally:

> It was, however, the general view of the Cabinet that, in light of the United States attitude as revealed in the President's reply and as previously outlined by [Acheson] in a discussion with the Foreign Secretary on 13th September, force could not be used to hold the refinery and maintain the British employees of the Anglo-Iranian Oil Company in Abadan. We could not afford to break with the United States on an issue of this kind.[16]

The cabinet minutes do not give further explanation, but several factors were discussed during this period. If Britain intervened in Iran, British officials wanted both U.S. diplomatic support at the United Nations and U.S. assistance to block Soviet counterintervention in northern Iran.[17] The U.S. intelligence community also feared that British intervention could spark a Soviet invasion: "There is a serious possibility that the landing of British troops in southern Iran, for whatever reason, would be taken by the USSR as a pretext for sending its troops into northern Iran."[18] The loss of Iran could have a domino effect: "Moreover, the Near East nations are strategically interdependent; the loss of such countries as Greece or Iran to the USSR would greatly complicate the defense of the remainder of the Near East [defined as from Greece to Iran]....At present, Iran is the Near Eastern country which is most critically vulnerable to the USSR."[19] Since the end of World War II, British officials had also come to depend on the United States in the Middle East more generally and did not want to risk undermining this strategic partnership by intervening in Iran against U.S. wishes.[20]

Britain considered several forms of deception during this period, clear evidence against a normative explanation for restraint success or failure. In early June, Attlee and other top British officials sought to recast military intervention in a way that might overcome U.S. objections: "We must at all costs avoid getting into the position where we could be represented as a capitalist power attacking a nationalist Persia. Rather we should endeavour to arrange things so that our apparent position was one of supporting a legitimate Persian government against either Russian invasion or communist provoked civil war."[21] By redefining the objective as combating communism in Iran, the British believed they could win U.S. support for intervention or at least circumvent U.S. opposition.[22] Had British officials stuck with a policy of deception, they would have demonstrated one of the reasons that more powerful states do not always mobilize their power resources in a restraint dispute: they are not aware, or at least not fully aware, of what their weaker ally is doing.

In late September, when Britain bowed to U.S. opposition for the second time, British officials pretended that they were always planning on avoiding the use of force rather than attribute the change of heart to the U.S. stance and intra-alliance pressures. British leaders quickly began to couch their decision in different terms, acting as if the resort to the UN Security Council (UNSC) was their favored choice in order to uphold the rule of law and the UN charter. For public relations, the UN charter, not American opposition, precluded the use of force.[23]

Both British and U.S. officials noted the risks of a policy of restraint. One concern was about the relationship between the allies themselves; a second concern was how this disagreement might help Iran in its row with Britain.

The issue of blame and alliance tensions often surfaced. Holmes, the number two U.S. official in the U.S. embassy in London, feared that not supporting the British would lead them to blame the United States:

> I wld like to add a final note of caution. There is a strong feeling in [British] govt circles at the present time that the issue in Iran has been finally joined and, under these circumstances, that their friendliest and staunchest ally shld show its hand firmly and unequivocally in support of them. I fear very much that if the feeling becomes prevalent in Labor circles that we have failed them in their hour of need, some Laborites will, in order to explain their own failure, feel compelled to place blame on US. To my mind it wld be most unfortunate if any US-UK divergency on this issue were publicly aired in this pre-election period. I am not citing this as the principal reason why I feel we shld support the UK at this time, but I think it has an important bearing on the situation and should be kept constantly in mind.[24]

His message implied that an Anglo-American split would also be bad for Attlee's Labor government in the October 1951 general elections. When Acheson sent Holmes instructions for speaking to the British foreign secretary, Acheson noted that the tone was "designed to avoid unnecessary irritation" to Britain.[25] As a result of differences over Iran, Loy W. Henderson, U.S. ambassador-designate to Iran, worried about a "wide divergence" between the United States and Britain on "our approach towards present world problems."[26] Franks, the British ambassador, told U.S. officials that "the impression had been created in London that the more the U.K. gives the more she will be requested" to give by the United States. Franks "felt Anglo-U.S. relations had reached a dangerous posture."[27] But all these concerns did not stop the United States from pursuing a policy of restraint toward its ally.

British officials' displeasure was also connected to their belief that the U.S restraint efforts represented a failure to reciprocate support—support allies were justified in expecting. Morrison wrote Acheson that they had worked together to resolve a number of difficult issues: "In several of these a settlement has been reached by our going a considerable way to accept the American view. In dealing with this question of Persian oil, where we find ourselves in grave difficulties, we need your wholehearted support."[28] With the failure of the negotiations the United States had orchestrated between Britain and Iran in August (on top of the failure in June), the British felt they had earned U.S. support: "They expect the United States to give its full and unqualified support to a 'strong' British policy in Iran."[29] Britain had twice done what the United States had requested, and now it was time for the Americans to follow the British lead. In early October, after Britain had rejected the use of force due to U.S. restraint, London expected the United States to offer full support for the British appeal to the UNSC. When the United States failed to do so, the U.S. ambassador summarized the British view: "They are hurt and bewildered at this attitude of their main ally."[30]

This is strong evidence against the existence of a norm of policy codetermination. The British expected the two allies to follow each other's lead harmoniously, but the United States refused to do so with Iran. The result was tension in the alliance.

The British also felt that such a split would embolden their adversary, Iran. Morrison wrote Acheson:

> One of our main difficulties in dealing with this intractable problem has arisen from a belief persistently held by many Persians that there is a difference of opinion between the Americans and the British over the oil question and that America in order to prevent Persia being lost to Russia, will be ready to help Persia out of any difficulties which she may encounter as a result of the oil dispute. Influential and friendly Persians themselves have told us this, and stressed that it is an important factor in encouraging Dr. Mossadegh's present intransigence.[31]

A similar viewpoint was expressed by the British after U.S. involvement in the dispute in mid-1950.[32]

Why did the United States withhold support from Britain in this case? Why did it move beyond rhetoric and threaten a material move? The main American motivation for restraining Britain reflected an Anglo-American disagreement about the priority of different security objectives. The United States was concerned lest Iran fall into Soviet hands, and protecting Britain's commercial interests was less important than the Cold War battle. A position paper prepared for talks with Britain was clear: "The maintenance of Iran as an independent country aligned with the free world is our primary objective."[33] George C. McGhee, assistant secretary of state for Near Eastern–South Asian–African Affairs, later explained: "We treated Iran like any country that was threatened by a communistic takeover."[34] British leaders not only cared more about protecting British access to and control of Iranian oil, but also viewed differently the effect of military intervention on Soviet power in Iran and the Middle East. While Washington argued that British military intervention would increase Soviet influence, London contended that the use of force would preserve the British position in Iran and thereby block the possibility of Soviet expansion.

Although the United States was sympathetic to Britain's concerns about Iranian oil, Washington was unwilling to allow the oil issue to serve as an opening for Soviet control of Iran. After meeting with Franks on May 11, U.S. officials told the U.S. embassy in Iran that the Abadan refinery was of great value to Britain and "is worth considerable calculated risk on our part even to extent of jeopardizing our own position in Iran, in assisting Brit and Iranians in coming to satisfactory terms." However, "it is not worth risk of complete break between Iran and West or setting into motion chain of events which could lead to communist seizure of Iran Govt or Russian intervention."[35] During late September, as Britain decided how to respond to Iran's expulsion order, Air Chief Sir William Elliot, chairman of the British Joint Services Mission (Washington), called on Robert Lovett, U.S. secretary of defense. Lovett challenged Elliot, noting what better tool could be put into the hands of the Kremlin than for the British to put troops in."[36]

In his May 31 letter, Truman warned Attlee about the dangers:

> I am also acutely aware that it is essential to maintain the independence of Iran and the flow of Iranian oil into the economy of the free world.... I know that you are fully aware of the serious implications of this explosive situation. I am sure you can understand my deep concern that no action should be taken in connection with this dispute which would result in disagreement between Iran and the free world. I am confident that a solution acceptable both to Great Britain and Iran can be found.[37]

The U.S. ambassador to Iran, Henry F. Grady, expressed similar concerns to the State Department. U.S. and U.K. policies are different, he wrote to McGhee, and British policy may lead to a "disaster" in Iran. Grady explained:

> I make this personal appeal to you and through you to Secretary in hopes that we keep in mind overall problem of Iran, remembering that altho oil question is basic, it is not everything. We must make every possible effort to keep this country from slipping behind Iron Curtain. To do this at least one of the great western democracies must maintain a position of basic friendliness for Iran. Otherwise, it will have no place to look for friendship and assistance except to Russia.[38]

Although oil was important, the United States should not lose sight of its higher objective.

These American concerns were codified in U.S. policy by the National Security Council. The first policy statement (NSC 107), approved by the president on March 24, noted that a noncommunist Iran was important to U.S. security, but it did not contain an explicit call for Britain to refrain from the use of force to resolve the oil dispute.[39] The updated and expanded version (NSC 107/2), approved by the president on June 28, explained the U.S. interest in a noncommunist Iran in greater detail. The loss of Iran would threaten Western security in the Middle East and South Asia; deny access to Iranian and possibly Middle Eastern oil; make Western lines of communication more vulnerable to Soviet threats; weaken the prestige of the United States in the area; and be "one in a series of military, political, and economic developments, the consequences of which would seriously endanger the security interests of the United States." British intervention could push Iran into the Soviet camp.[40]

Standing against aggression was also mentioned by one U.S. official in late September. After all the United States had done in opposing aggression around the world, if the Americans now supported British military intervention, "we shall stand before world stripped of all pretense to idealism and obviously guilty of grossest hypocrisy." As a result of the principled American stand, "we have thus far been able to rally most nations of world." The Department of State replied that in substance, this cable represented U.S. views.[41]

Early in the Anglo-Iranian crisis, Morrison, the British foreign secretary, understood correctly the American concerns. He explained: "The Americans, who have been for some time critical of our policy in Persia and are obsessed with the danger of Persia falling under Communist domination, would be likely to oppose any suggestions of coercive action, or the threat of it, on our part."[42]

The U.S. position implicitly embraced fears of war escalation as well. In one scenario for the loss of Iran to the Soviet camp, British military intervention would spark a Soviet counterintervention, which might then lead to global war if the United States was unable to "localize" the war (as called for by secret NSC policy statements). Thus the United States feared not only the outcome of Britain's favored course of action—Iran going communist—but also the dangers stemming from how that negative outcome could come about.

Britain Restrains the United States in Indochina, 1954

In the spring of 1954, the United States rejected military intervention in Indochina because Britain opposed the policy. British opposition was decisive because U.S. elites were split over the exact nature of U.S. military intervention. The U.S. Congress demanded that the Eisenhower administration gain allied participation. Although the United States was militarily capable of intervening on its own, U.S. elites were unwilling to do so. The lack of elite consensus in Washington meant that the United States would not bring its power resources to bear unilaterally; Britain's opposition mattered.

When France asked Washington for military support during the decisive battle at Dien Bien Phu in Indochina, U.S. secretary of state John Foster Dulles proposed on March 29 an ad hoc coalition for military intervention, United Action.[43] However, at an April 3 meeting with Dulles, congressional leaders made it clear that they would support United Action only if Britain agreed to participate. On April 11–12 and April 25, Britain declined to offer its support for United Action and instead hoped the East-West talks at Geneva, scheduled to open on April 26, would yield a compromise settlement on Indochina. The United States did not form United Action.

Congress did not give the administration a blank check for action in Southeast Asia and instead presented several stipulations. Most important, Congress expected the administration to act as part of a multilateral effort; in essence, this meant the United States could intervene only if Britain would join the U.S. effort. Members of Congress asked variants of the same question: "Where do the British stand?"[44]

On April 3, Dulles and Admiral Arthur W. Radford, chairman of the Joint Chiefs of Staff, met with eight congressional leaders.[45] Dulles and Radford had hoped Congress would move first and give Dulles support before he went to the allies, but that was not the case:

> Neither Eisenhower nor Dulles differed fundamentally with the congressmen on the form intervention ought to take, but the conditions did tie their hands by virtually eliminating any possibility of unilateral intervention, an option that they had not entirely ruled out. The conditions weakened Dulles's position with allied leaders by requiring the allies' commitment prior to action by Congress, an order the administration would have preferred to reverse. Most important, they made collective intervention dependent on British support and French concessions, each of which would be difficult to obtain.[46]

Eisenhower and Dulles may have hoped to persuade London to intervene in Indochina by demonstrating a united congressional–executive branch front, but instead they were faced with the reverse—needing to convince the British in order to get congressional support. Dulles had gone into the meeting willing to act with or without allied support.[47] This set the stage for the British reaction to determine the outcome.

The United States twice asked Britain for support for United Action, and Britain blocked the U.S. policy on both occasions. Dulles went to London from April 11 to 13, and the two sides agreed to a joint statement on Indochina and other matters: "Accordingly we are ready to take part, with the other countries principally concerned, in an examination of the possibility of establishing a collective defense, within the framework of the Charter of the United Nations, to assure the peace, security and freedom of Southeast Asia and the Western Pacific."[48] But it soon became clear that they disagreed as to what this meant. When Dulles invited British ambassador Roger Makins and diplomatic officials from other prospective participants to a meeting about forming United Action, British foreign secretary Anthony Eden cried foul. Historians disagree as to whether Eden or Dulles was to blame for this crucial misunderstanding of the communiqué, but the bottom line was that the two sides interpreted its key clause differently.[49] To Britain, it meant that after the upcoming Geneva peace conference, talks could commence on a lasting security organization but not on an ad hoc coalition for intervention in Indochina. Britain opposed United Action, thus thwarting Dulles's plan.

On April 24, the United States pressed London for a second time, to no avail.[50] The British cabinet officially rejected the U.S. request on April 25.[51]

Eisenhower later noted the importance of the British decision on April 25: "This ended for the time being our efforts to find any satisfactory method of Allied intervention."[52]

Deception and misunderstanding played an important part of the story. If norms of policy coordination prevailed, one would have expected the two sides to deal with each other on a level playing field for an informed alliance decision on the contested policy, United Action. Yet Eden and Dulles had an acrimonious split over what they agreed to in London on April 11–13. Eden characterized the problem: "Americans may think the time past when they need consider the feelings or difficulties of their allies. It is the conviction that this tendency becomes more pronounced every week that is creating mounting difficulties for anyone in this country who wants to maintain close Anglo-American relations."[53] Later Britain suspected the United States wanted to use British support for United Action and the fight against communism in Southeast Asia as cover for U.S.-launched direct air intervention at Dien Bien Phu.[54] Rather than a respectful relationship in which the mere mention of an objection leads to the shelving of United Action, this British fear of U.S. deception suggests a wary (and typical) alliance relationship in which both sides suspect the other is trying its best to pursue its own interests.

Furthermore, the United States tried to circumvent British objections and proceed with United Action, a clear sign it did not consider British objections the final word. Dulles tried to set up United Action using Australia and New Zealand and ignoring Britain; on May 19, 1954, Eisenhower stated publicly that he might agree to send U.S. Marines even without British involvement. Perhaps down the road Australia and New Zealand would lobby or compel Britain to join, but either way this suggests a desire to ignore and overcome Britain's opposition. As it turned out, Australia and New Zealand were not eager to join, and the plan was never implemented.[55] The United States tried to circumvent British objections in other ways too, such as Dulles's overture to the Soviet Union and a request for British moral support (only) for United Action.[56]

In early June 1954, U.S. leaders finally accepted that Indochina would be partitioned into communist and noncommunist parts, thus signaling the end of United Action and the effort to form a multilateral coalition to save all of Vietnam from communism.[57] Time and time again, British opposition to United Action blocked the U.S. proposal. According to Anthony Short, "from practically all the papers and studies that have been published on the subject of American intervention at Dienbienphu, one conclusion stands out: if Britain had agreed, the United States would have engaged in some form of intervention in Vietnam in the spring or summer of 1954."[58]

The impact of restraint on the primary Anglo-American adversary, the Soviet Union, was mixed and mostly concerns the Geneva talks just after Britain blocked United Action. At different times both Britain and the United States tried to work *with* the Soviets during the Geneva talks. Evelyn Shuckburgh, Eden's private secretary, was critical of Eden for straying from the American side at the Geneva talks; he felt Eden was trying to be a mediator rather than a loyal Western ally.[59] Dulles tried to use the Soviets against Britain and France. At the start of the Geneva conference, Dulles asked Soviet foreign minister V. M. Molotov if expanding the invitation list would allow the United States to circumvent the French objection to delegations from Vietnam, Laos, and Cambodia; suggested that such delegations should receive U.S.-Soviet guidance; and recommended broader U.S.-Soviet thinking about the conference's outcome.[60] The last suggestion might have opened the door to an array of topics. Molotov offered no response of substance. Gardner claims Dulles was thinking that if "he could get things straight with his main adversary, he could go about dealing with America's allies from a position of strength."[61] Later in the talks, Walter Bedell Smith, U.S. undersecretary of state, reported that Moscow was trying to take advantage of "the deadlock in Western capitals."[62]

Why did Britain restrain the United States?[63] Britain had a number of reasons for opposing United Action, including differences over both the allied objective and the policy in question. But much of Britain's opposition probably flowed from the different strategic assessments of Indochina in London and Washington. London simply did not believe Indochina was crucial in the war against communism and was unwilling to risk war and a loss of focus of the Western allies in order to save all of Vietnam from communist rule. In understanding why Britain opposed United Action, one can also gain insight into British interests in Southeast Asia and beyond.

Britain attached less strategic significance to Indochina, and much of its other discomfort with United Action probably stemmed from this fact. Whereas the United States feared that the loss of Indochina would, like falling dominoes, lead to the loss of other Southeast Asian and Asian states to the communist camp, Britain believed that even with part or none of Indochina, the NATO allies and their Asian partners could establish a defensible line against Soviet and Chinese-sponsored thrusts. In Britain's eyes, Indochina was expendable. In this case, British officials rejected the domino theory.[64]

Britain was concerned about excess efforts to save Indochina in part because of what it might mean for the Western defense of other, more important areas. Resources expended to defend Indochina would take away from the defense of such areas as Malaysia, Australia, New Zealand, and Japan. This was true of British resources, but London also worried about France's preoccupation with Indochina.[65] The war in Indochina was hurting the French effort in the defense of Europe. France's NATO units were "dangerously understrength."[66]

One way, then, to look at London's major reasons for opposing United Action flows from the initial observation that Britain, unlike the United States, believed little harm would be done by the loss of some or all of Indochina to communist control. Better to lose Indochina (or part of it) and strengthen allied defenses in the rest of free Southeast Asia than insist on all of Indochina and thereby prolong the French-Indochinese war, risk a war with China, and scuttle the Geneva talks. Instead of United Action, Britain favored partition of Indochina at the Geneva talks and setting up—post-Geneva—a regional, NATO-like defense organization for Southeast Asia. It made little sense to draw a defensive line through an area that had already been lost to one's enemy. Britain's approach can be summed up as cutting losses, focusing on what really matters strategically (Western Europe and a more narrow area of Asia), and avoiding an unnecessary war (including both direct British entry into Indochina and a larger war with China). From London's perspective, United Action broke all three of these rules.

U.S.-British *policy* differences over the Geneva talks and partitioning Indochina were symptoms of this difference over *goals* (or security priorities) in Southeast Asia. Britain was willing to accept the partition of Vietnam and thus saw Geneva as an excellent vehicle for resolving the conflict. Britain did not want to implement any policy before Geneva that might undermine the talks. The United States long opposed partition even into late April.[67] Just before meeting with Dulles in mid-April, Eden and the French ambassador agreed that talk of a regional defense pact should wait until after the Geneva Conference.[68] Whereas partition not only accepted the existence of the Vietminh but also legitimated the communist Vietnamese control of northern Vietnam, United Action aimed at picking up where the French left off and trying to fully defeat the Vietminh. One policy sanctioned the Vietminh whereas the other still aimed to eradicate the Vietminh. This was a policy difference, but it was based on fundamental differences over the Western allies' defensive perimeter in Asia. Britain was willing to accept the communist Vietnamese. Washington wanted to avoid a "who lost Vietnam?" debate. British policy—supporting the Geneva talks, accepting the idea of partition, opposing United Action—forced the United States to admit, yes, at least for now, we have lost part of Vietnam to the communists.

Britain's fear that United Action would lead to unwanted war included three interrelated pathways to conflict: the introduction of British combat troops in Indochina, a U.S.-led war with China, and the use by the United States of nuclear weapons. Britain did not want to join a ground war and thought the commitments implied by United Action made such a possibility more likely. On April 13, after meeting with Eden, Dulles wrote Eisenhower that "the British are extremely fearful of becoming involved with ground forces in Indochina."[69] In addition, Britain feared that United Action might be designed to launch an attack on China.[70] Though U.S. officials argued that China would stay out of an allied attack on Indochina, some British leaders feared that intervention in Vietnam would ultimately lead to a communist attack on the British homeland.[71] British prime minister Winston Churchill thought the intervention would be ineffective "and might well bring the world to the verge of a major war."[72] At the April 7 British cabinet meeting, Eden also expressed fear of a wider war.[73]

British leaders also feared that any conflict might escalate and lead to nuclear war. Although the United States may not actually have seriously considered using nuclear weapons against Vietnam, general U.S. policy left Britain with the impression that nuclear weapons might be under consideration, especially if fighting in Indochina led to an all-out war. Dulles emphasized the general role of nuclear weapons (massive retaliation) and thereby alarmed the British in a press conference on December 29, 1953, and in a major policy address on January 12, 1954. Ironically, Washington thought the idea of using nuclear weapons would cause its allies to stay the course.[74] According to one scholar, the United States favored the use of nuclear weapons if the People's Republic of China intervened in Indochina but would have needed congressional approval and the cooperation of European allies.[75] A later scholar argues that British fears were unfounded: "In light of what we now know from Communist sources, it seems unlikely that either the Russians or the Chinese would have risked a world war for the sake of the Vietminh."[76]

The nuclear angle raises an important question about alliance restraint: to what extent did U.S. officials internalize prior or anticipated British objections to the use of nuclear weapons and, as a result, refrain from even proposing the idea? A clear answer to this question would contribute to studying how much restraint can occur even without a policy discussion and formal restraint attempt. Dulles knew that Britain feared that the United States would use nuclear weapons against China, but we do not know how much, if at all, this affected his decision making regarding the possibility.[77] In early April, two U.S. officials discussed Admiral Radford's idea of using tactical nuclear weapons in Indochina. One objected on the grounds that French and British officials would oppose the use of nuclear weapons.[78]

At home, Britain would have had a hard time selling British involvement in the war in Indochina. Domestic opposition seemed to revolve around the idea of sending British ground forces. The British people were not in favor of suffering casualties to defend France's hold on Indochina. Shuckburgh, Eden's private secretary, later wrote: "A war for Indo-China would be about as difficult a thing to put across the British public as you could find."[79] Shuckburgh asserted that Eden felt the British government would fall if it went along with the U.S. policy for intervention.[80] Dulles characterized Eden's position less drastically. He cabled the State Department that in his meetings with Eden, the foreign secretary told him "that there is real problem of UK parliamentary and public opinion; [and] that any implied commitment for involvement in the Indochina war would be intensely unpopular."[81] Further evidence is needed to assess whether British officials were genuinely concerned about domestic opposition or whether they felt this was an argument against supporting United Action that the United States would understand and accept.

Britain Fails to Restrain the United States in Taiwan, 1954–1955

In late 1954 and early 1955, Britain failed to restrain the United States in its relations with Taiwan. Britain pursued a number of policies aimed at reducing the likelihood of a conflict between the communist Chinese mainland and the nationalist Chinese on the island of Formosa (Taiwan). From the perspective of alliance restraint, probably the most important British effort was to get the United States to totally exclude Taiwan's offshore islands, Quemoy and Matsu, from the U.S. pledge to protect Taiwan and the autonomy of the nationalist Chinese government based there. British officials were rebuffed by the United States, even though the United States did not go as far as Taiwanese leaders would have preferred.

In September 1954, intense fighting between communist and nationalist Chinese forces brought the issue of the offshore islands to the forefront of Anglo-American relations. Since the nationalists had lost the mainland to the communist Chinese, Chiang Kai-shek's nationalist forces had been confined to the island of Formosa, later known as Taiwan. In addition to the larger island of Formosa, the pro-American nationalists controlled several smaller islands and outcroppings, including Quemoy, Matsu, and the Tachens. The nationalists used these islands to harass the mainland and claimed that the islands were indispensable.

The British were concerned the clashes might spark U.S. intervention and even a nuclear conflict. They favored abandoning the offshore islands. British officials sought to convince the United States of the merits of range of steps that would lead, they thought, to deescalation. London wanted a general cease-fire as well as U.S. pressure on Taiwanese leaders to get the Kuomintang (KMT) to stop using Formosa "for offensive purposes against China."[82] The United States rejected most of these British suggestions.

On December 2, 1954, the United States and Taiwan signed a Mutual Defense Treaty, as well as related letters on December 10. In defining the scope of the U.S. security commitment to Taiwan, the treaty neither explicitly mentioned the offshore islands nor explicitly ruled them out. When, in late November 1954, Britain learned of the likely treaty text, British officials sought to restrain the United States by calling for a modification in U.S. policy; Britain wanted the offshore islands explicitly left out of the treaty.

Although one potential objection in this case is that U.S. leaders were not united, both Dulles and Eisenhower sought treaty language more favorable to Taiwan than that advanced by Britain. Dulles advocated the explicit inclusion of the offshore islands in the treaty's security guarantee. Eisenhower did not want the islands to be mentioned. Eden sought the explicit exclusion of the offshore islands in the treaty's security guarantee.[83] Dulles advanced his inclusive position but ultimately bowed to pressure from President Eisenhower. However, even the language that was acceptable to Eisenhower implied too much of a U.S. commitment to the islands from the British perspective.

The Eisenhower administration also received high levels of congressional support, as demonstrated by the lopsided votes in favor of the Formosa Resolution. The resolution, passed in January 1955, asked for congressional authorization for U.S. action to defend, if necessary, Formosa, the Pescadores, and "closely related localities and actions which, under current conditions, might determine the failure or the success of such attack." It passed 410–3 in the House and 83–3 in the Senate. A Senate amendment to exclude Quemoy and Matsu was defeated 74–13.[84]

British efforts to limit the U.S. commitment to Formosa continued in 1955. In a letter to Eisenhower on February 15, 1955, Churchill, the British prime minister, proposed a three-part policy that would include the evacuation of all the offshore islands, including Quemoy.[85] On March 8, 1955, Eden, British foreign secretary, took a similar approach when he publicly urged a nationalist withdrawal from Quemoy and Matsu in exchange for a communist no-invasion pledge for Formosa. "Such a suggestion," Eisenhower later wrote, "more wishful than realistic, in the light of our past experiences, I simply could not accept."[86]

Despite these British proposals, the United States never modified its support for the KMT, as the British would have liked. One scholar notes, "In the crisis over Quemoy and the Matsus in early 1955, Churchill was completely unable to influence Eisenhower on a policy which the British considered to be extremely dangerous."[87] The Anglo-American disagreement over the offshore islands continued until May 1955, when the crisis deescalated, largely due to actions by the Chinese themselves.

The United States and Britain shared a concern but disagreed about the best means to address it. Both worried that the KMT would act too aggressively and spark an unwanted war with mainland China. The United States, however, also worried about deterring mainland China from a major assault on Formosa. Eisenhower explained to Churchill: "We are doing everything possible to work this situation out in a way which, on the one hand, will avoid the risk of war, and, on the other hand, preserve the non-Communist position in the Western Pacific."[88] Perhaps because Washington was trying to balance deterring China and restraining Taiwan, the United States sought a defense treaty worded in such a way that it could be read to favor both deterrence and alliance restraint.

In revealing why the United States was willing to act unilaterally and mobilize its own power resources in the face of British opposition, this case points to the same difference as the dispute over Indochina in 1954. The United States fundamentally valued the preservation of noncommunist East and Southeast Asia much more than Britain. For Britain, these issues were of secondary concern. Eisenhower's comment to Churchill is revealing as well in terms of the link to "the Western Pacific." The United States, which bordered the Atlantic and the Pacific, was a great power on both oceans. In that sense, East and Southeast Asia are closer to U.S. national interests than they are to British ones even if mileage-wise they are not any closer to the United States than to the British Isles.

The Suez War, 1956

a. The United States fails to stop British intervention in Egypt
b. The United States forces Britain to accept a cease-fire and then withdrawal from Egypt

The Anglo-American alliance during the Suez War (1956) provides one example of restraint failure and one example of restraint success. The United States failed to stop British military intervention in Egypt because Washington failed to mobilize its power resources and, though probably less important, elite (U.S.) support for restraint was less than 100 percent. Once the war started, the United States used economic pressure related to oil supplies and currency support to force Britain to accept a cease-fire and then, soon thereafter, the withdrawal of British troops from Egypt.

On July 26, 1956, President Gamel Abdel Nasser of Egypt nationalized the Suez Canal, which had been owned by an Anglo-French company. Britain wanted to reverse the nationalization by force. At a secret meeting in Sèvres, France, on October 22–24, 1956, Britain, France, and Israel agreed to an invasion of Egypt. The plan was for Israel to invade first. Britain and France, in the guise of separating the Egyptian-Israeli combatants, would then intervene and capture the canal. As planned, Israeli armed forces moved into Egypt's Sinai Desert on October 29. The Anglo-French ultimata to Egypt and Israel were issued on October 30, and Egypt rejected the call to withdraw from the canal zone. In the evening of October 31, a few hours later than originally scheduled, British bombers began attacking Cairo airfields. On October 31 (7 P.M. EST), Eisenhower went on television and radio and opposed the Anglo-French intervention.[89]

The United States actively tried to restrain Britain (and France) by preventing military intervention in Egypt. The United States repeatedly emphasized three interrelated ideas that formed the basis of U.S. policy from the nationalization until Anglo-French intervention: Washington favored diplomatic action, opposed the use of force, but did not rule out the use of force as a last resort.

In late July 1956, U.S. officials told Britain of American hesitancy to reverse the nationalization by force. The State Department suggested that "the question of eventual military intervention does not seem to arise. It would depend on developments. For the present we believe it should be relegated to the background."[90] After a July 31 meeting at the

White House which rejected the use of force, Eisenhower sent a letter to British prime minister Eden emphasizing U.S. opposition to British military intervention. The president acknowledged "that eventually the use of force might become necessary" but emphasized that "the step you contemplate should not be undertaken until every peaceful means of protecting the rights and the livelihood of great portions of the world had been thoroughly explored and exhausted." Eisenhower went so far as to note the "unwisdom" of even contemplating the use of force at that time.[91]

In September, U.S. officials clearly and repeatedly stated opposition to British military intervention. On September 2, Eisenhower wrote to Eden that "American public opinion flatly rejects the thought of using force, particularly when it does not seem that every possible peaceful means of protecting our vital interests has been exhausted without result." The president could "not see how a successful result could be achieved by forcible means."[92] At a press conference on September 5, the president emphasized the diplomatic route: "The United States is committed to a peaceful solution of this problem."[93] In response to a broad argument by Eden of the similarity between Hitler, Soviet expansionism, and Nasser, and the need for military intervention, Eisenhower sent a second note to Eden on September 8, claiming that the "result you and I both want can best be assured by slower and less dramatic processes than military force." Though the president acknowledged that eventually force might be the only option, he argued that "to resort to military action when the world believes there are other means available for resolving the dispute would set in motion forces that could lead, in the years to come, to the most distressing results."[94] On September 12, Eden told the House of Commons that the failure of the Suez Canal Users' Association (SCUA)—a diplomatic/maritime idea meant to resolve the crisis—might lead to other steps by the Western governments. Yet the next day, Dulles told a news conference that the United States was not planning on shooting its way through the canal if Egypt blocked the canal by force.[95]

A similar pattern of U.S. warnings continued in October. On October 5, Eisenhower told Makins of strong American opposition to the use of force. The same day, Dulles told British foreign secretary Selwyn Lloyd and French foreign minister Christian Pineau that the United States did not rule out force "as an ultimate choice" but thought it would be a "fatal mistake"; he also called the resort to force a "desperate measure" and a "disaster."[96] On October 22, Dulles cabled the U.S. ambassadors in London and Paris and asked whether they should reiterate the strong presidential opposition to the use of force and to explain that "the views of the President and myself on this point are basic and fundamental and I do not see any likelihood of their being changed after [the] election."[97]

Dulles sought to restrain U.S. allies by dragging out the diplomatic options until the enthusiasm for confronting Nasser had dissipated.[98] On July 31, he told a meeting of the president and top U.S. officials that U.S. policy was aimed at "gradually deflecting their [the allies'] course of action."[99] When Dulles returned on August 3 from his first trip to London, he and Allen Dulles, the head of the Central Intelligence Agency, agreed that "the job is not done yet—just a cooling off period." On August 10, Secretary of State Dulles was quite clear with Dag Hammarskjold, the UN secretary general: "I said that I certainly thought the more delay there was the less likelihood there was it [force] would be invoked." On August 18, Dulles told Dmitri Shepilov, the Soviet foreign minister, that when Dulles had conceived of holding an international conference on the Suez issue, he had hoped it would calm Britain and France, as had in fact happened; Dulles earlier told congressional leaders that Britain and France had held back because of the conference.[100] On September 6, Dulles told the president that he thought "the passage of time was working in favor of some compromise." That same day, he told congressional leaders that Egypt had rejected the proposals of the First London Conference. As a result, the United States "must find further steps to postpone the U.K. and French use of force."[101] Eisenhower reiterated this viewpoint at the NSC meeting on October 12: "if the United States could just keep the lid on a little longer, some kind of compromise plan could be worked out for a settlement of the Suez problem. Time and time alone will cure the disease; the only question was whether we could be sure of the time."[102]

Dulles believed that if the United States hoped to prevent British/French intervention, Washington needed to offer some policy alternatives.[103] On September 8, Dulles spoke with Eisenhower: "I said I was not sure either [that the SCUA would work] but that I felt we had to keep the initiative and to keep probing along various lines, particularly since there was no chance of getting the British and the French not to use force unless they had some alternatives that seemed to have in them some strength of purpose and some initiative."[104] C. Douglas Dillon, the U.S. ambassador to France, also sought alternatives and at one point cabled the State Department that "we will have to develop some sort of agreed concrete action in the economic field in order to ensure that military action does not follow an unsuccessful debate in the UN."[105]

A month later, on the issue of a debate on the Suez crisis in the UN General Assembly, Dillon said he assumed "that once Assembly is in session it would supply strong moderating influence."[106] One gets the sense that U.S. officials hoped to line up enough nonmilitary options to prevent military intervention from ever being the only available choice.[107]

Thus the late summer and early fall of 1956 were filled with the development of multiple diplomatic efforts, one after another. Dulles's trip to London in early August laid the groundwork for the First London Conference, which led to the unsuccessful Menzies mission to Cairo.[108] As this first major effort was failing, Dulles conceived of the SCUA, and Eden publicly presented the SCUA on September 12. The Second London Conference led to the formation of the SCUA even as Britain and France were turning to the UN Security Council. Dulles was annoyed that without consulting him, they went to the UNSC immediately after the SCUA was agreed on. Yet he may also have been annoyed that two diplomatic tracks were working at once; this condensed the diplomatic efforts rather than drawing them out, as would have been the case if the UN appeal had begun only if and when the SCUA were to fail. In the second half of October, as Britain and France decided on military intervention, the United States worked with the UN secretary general to bring Egypt, France, and Britain together—possibly in Geneva—to negotiate along the lines of the UNSC Resolution 118 of October 13, the unanimous resolution that laid out six principles for the control and administration of the canal.

With some exceptions, British officials heard the U.S. policy: restraint.[109] On August 1, Lloyd told the cabinet that Dulles had "made it clear that the United States Government would strongly deprecate any premature use of force" to restore international control of the canal.[110] In his diary, William Clark, Eden's press secretary, "at first sight" characterized Eisenhower's letter of September 2 as "an absolute ban on our use of force."[111] Of the same letter, Eden told the cabinet that Eisenhower expressed "his disquiet at the prospect that the United Kingdom and France might have in mind to take military action before all the possibilities of securing a peaceful settlement had been finally exhausted."[112] On September 9, Makins, the British ambassador to the United States, cabled London that there "is no support in the United States for the use of force in the present circumstances and in the absence of further clear provocation by Nasser." He added that "a go-it alone policy of military intervention would obviously deal them [U.S. officials] a body blow."[113] Two days later, when the British cabinet discussed possible options if the Menzies mission failed, Lloyd said the United States was "strongly opposed" to proceeding at once with military action. Walter Monckton, minister of defense and an opponent of military intervention, told the ministers he was wary of acting without U.S. support and approval.[114] In his memoirs, Eden himself notes that at one Dulles-Lloyd meeting in October, Dulles stated U.S. opposition: "[Dulles] declared that he was with Britain on every point, except the use of force. Even force he did not rule out as an ultimate resort, and he once more recognized our right to maintain the threat of using it. Nevertheless, he felt that to employ force in the immediate future would be a mistake, since in his view Nasser's position was deteriorating."[115]

Perhaps most important, doubts were expressed on the eve of British military intervention. At the October 25 cabinet meeting, an unidentified cabinet member feared the "lasting damage" that would be done to Anglo-American relations. Moreover, there "was no prospect of securing the support or approval of the United States Government." But the cabinet decided to go ahead with the plan for military intervention.[116] At the next cabinet meeting, however, the ministers considered whether to approach the United States to seek support for Anglo-French intervention. They also noted a crucial economic point: "Our reserves of gold and dollars were still falling at a dangerously rapid rate; and, in view of the extent to which we might have to rely on American economic assistance, we could not afford to alienate the United States Government more than was absolutely necessary."[117]

Before Anglo-French intervention in Egypt, the United States neither threatened Britain if London ignored U.S. warnings nor suggested a possible penalty such as U.S. economic pressure. In fact, the only material U.S. policy was *helpful* to Britain: the United States warned the Soviets not to attack Britain and France in defense of Egypt.[118]

Among U.S. leaders, support for a policy of restraint was not absolute. Although the overall message was one of restraint, the United States sent some contrary signals. As noted, the United States offered Britain some cover from the Soviet Union. In addition, in August the United States told Britain "it would permit emergency purchases of military equipment as long as there was no publicity."[119] Near the height of the crisis, on October 30, Dulles said he did not want Britain to go under financially. This may explain why Dulles never threatened economic punishments; he may not have believed in using the economic club on Britain. (The same day, in contrast, Eisenhower told Dulles he did not want to help Britain and France with dollars.)[120] Furthermore, even after Britain intervened, Eisenhower and Dulles were still willing to stand aside as long as Britain and France accomplished their task quickly. When London and Paris delayed and drew out the time frame of intervention, Washington started to pressure them more heavily.[121]

In late October, the U.S. allies stopped consulting with Washington. They had decided on a course of action, and it was not one of which the United States would approve. On October 18, Dulles expressed his concerns to his brother, Allen Dulles: "[Foster Dulles] does not think we have really any clear picture as to what the British and French are up to there [the Near East]. He thinks they are deliberately keeping us in the dark."[122] On October 26, Secretary Dulles cabled the U.S. embassy in London and noted, "We are quite disturbed here over fact there is apparently a deliberate British purpose of keeping us completely in the dark as to their intentions with reference to Middle East matters generally and Egypt in particular. We have had no high-level contacts on any of these matters with British Embassy for a week."[123] He reiterated his concerns to the Paris embassy on October 29, referring to the "almost complete blackout of information from French and British with us regarding Middle East matters."[124] The French prime minister, Guy Mollet, was frank about the need to keep the United States in the dark: "If your government was not informed of the final developments, the reason . . . *was our fear that if we had consulted it, it would have prevented us from acting.*"[125] No norm of policy coordination was in operation.

After the intervention, when the United States was loud and clear about the penalty it would (and did) impose, Britain agreed to a cease-fire and then withdrawal. History was run twice, once without a stick and once with one. In this second phase, U.S. economic pressure led to a cease-fire, as can be seen in both the memoirs of key British participants (Harold Macmillan, Lloyd, R. A. Butler, Monckton) and the judgments of several later scholars. The reality was that the United States controlled the international financial institutions and the flow of oil from the Western Hemisphere, and Britain needed access to both. The timing of the policy shifts is also strong evidence: the U.S. refusal to provide economic support, followed by British acceptance of the cease-fire, much back-and-forth but continued U.S. economic pressure, British agreement to a full withdrawal, and then the lifting of the economic sanctions.

The available U.S. documentary evidence mostly details the U.S. decision to withhold oil supplies until the U.S. allies agreed to withdraw from Egypt. At a meeting on November 4 (9:30 a.m. EST), the United States decided not to activate the emergency oil committee, for two stated reasons. Not only would it look bad to be acting with Britain and France now, especially in the eyes of African and Asian states, but also "it was felt that one of the best cards we had to bring the British and French to take a constructive position was the way we handled the oil matter. If we rushed into cooperation with them, we would perhaps be giving away a vital card."[126]

U.S. officials refused to address Britain and France's oil needs in order to compel the two allies to withdraw from Egypt. At the National Security Council (NSC) meeting on November 8, the secretary of the treasury, George M. Humphrey, argued that U.S. action on oil should wait until "British and French evidenced compliance with the orders of the United Nations." The NSC decided that, in Eisenhower's words, "this Government officially should keep out of the oil supply problem until we were assured that the cease-fire was in effect." In policy terms, this meant that the use of the Middle East Emergency Committee (MEEC) to coordinate oil supplies during the crisis would be delayed: "When a cease-fire has been arranged in Egypt and when the UN police force is functioning in Egypt, [the United States will] consider putting into operation the plan of action of the Middle East Emergency Committee."[127]

At the next NSC meeting, on November 15, the United States still did not activate the MEEC. U.S. officials noted that they had already authorized the shipment of oil from Venezuela to Europe but that not enough tankers were available. In holding off on the MEEC, they expressed concern about several issues: the reaction of Arab states; advising U.S. oil companies in courses of action that might violate U.S. antitrust laws; and being seen as rescuing Britain and France.[128]

On November 25, Herbert Hoover Jr., U.S. undersecretary of state, expressed his fear that the United States would be blamed for the worsening oil situation in Europe, especially as winter approached. When pressed to start the MEEC, Eisenhower reiterated U.S. policy: "The President recalled that we have held up this measure until the invading powers accepted immediate withdrawal of their troops."[129] Nevertheless, Eisenhower agreed to set the MEEC in motion and soften U.S. policy: "[The draft public statement] should take account of our requirement for prior compliance by the British and French with UN resolutions, or at least a prior commitment on compliance, but should focus on the idea that we are acting to help all the other European countries which, through no fault of their own, have suffered as a result of the closing of the Suez Canal."[130] On November 26, Hoover cabled Winthrop Aldrich, U.S. ambassador to Great Britain, that the United States needed "concrete evidence of more substantial withdrawal" before resuming consultations with Britain and France. However, he added that it was not necessary for the evacuation to be completed prior to renewed consultations.[131]

On November 29, the United States learned that Britain would comply with the UN resolutions and withdraw. The British cabinet agreed to withdrawal after it was promised U.S. support and a UN pledge to clear the canal with "all available equipment."[132] On November 30, the NSC freed up oil for Britain, activated the MEEC, and took several fiscal steps to help shore up the British pound.[133] The Anglo-French withdrawal was completed on December 22, though Israeli forces remained in Egypt until early March 1957.

Britain agreed to a cease-fire and withdrawal because the United States withheld both oil and support for the British pound. Reserves of the pound were falling, and the United States refused to allow fiscal support until Britain agreed to the cease-fire.[134] Britain's only alternatives were to devalue the pound and end its role as an international reserve currency, place import restrictions, or take some other drastic economic measure at home. Only the United States had the financial resources, International Monetary Fund leverage, and access to oil supplies to satisfy Britain's economic needs.

The most important evidence that U.S. economic pressure determined British policy comes from Harold Macmillan's memoirs. As the British cabinet met, Macmillan tried and failed to secure either a temporary loan from the United States or approval to draw from Britain's quota at the International Monetary Fund (where the United States had the controlling votes): "Accordingly I made the necessary soundings. I telephoned urgently to New York; the matter was referred to Washington. It was only while the Cabinet was in session that I received the reply that the American Government would not agree to the technical [IMF] procedure until we agreed to the cease-fire."[135] Lloyd, the foreign secretary, later claimed that this economic pressure determined Macmillan's outlook: "Also before the Cabinet met, I had spoken to Macmillan, who said that in view of the financial and economic pressures we must stop." Lloyd added that Macmillan "strongly advocated" accepting the cease-fire during the cabinet meeting itself.[136] Others who support an economic explanation include Lloyd himself, Alistair Horne (one of Macmillan's biographers), Diane B. Kunz (citing Macmillan), and Richard Betts; they all reject the major alternative explanation that a Soviet threat forced Britain to back down.[137] Butler, known by his initials, RAB, agreed. According to Butler, just after he became acting prime minister because Eden was ill, Humphrey called: " 'Rab,' he said, 'the President cannot help you unless you conform to the United Nations resolution about withdrawal. If you do that, we here will help you save the pound.' This was blackmail. But we were in no position to argue. I gave him assurances."[138] Monckton, the minister of defense, agreed: "I have always thought that the decisive point was reached when Mr. Macmillan was of opinion that the United States would make our financial position impossible unless we called a halt."[139]

Britain had nowhere else to turn when Washington refused to provide oil or support for the pound. Washington controlled access to oil supplies in the Western Hemisphere, the main alternative for Britain, France, and Western Europe when oil shipments through the Suez Canal came to a halt: "Deprived of petroleum, England and France had no choice but to give in."[140] Washington held a controlling share at the IMF and could thus block British efforts to draw down its IMF quota in order to bolster its currency reserves at home. Only Washington could decide whether to waive the annual British payment on its postwar loans from the United States and thereby save Britain a portion of its currency reserves.

As a result of a report commissioned by the North Atlantic Council (NAC) a few months before the Egyptian nationalization of the Suez Canal but discussed a month after the Anglo-French military intervention in Egypt, NATO foreign ministers had the opportunity to air their concerns about greater alliance consultation. At this post-Suez meeting in December 1956, Lloyd told ministers of other NATO countries that consultation had to have limits: "If consultation proposals mean every member given right to criticize and obstruct every decision, not much will be accomplished. But consultation can be favorable if it looks toward a desire of sharing responsibility. Recognized, however, this may raise some doubts in members' minds about desirability consultation." Dulles agreed: "If adopting report means U.S. will do nothing in world without consulting NAC [North Atlantic Council], this will lead to confusion, misunderstanding and descrimination [sic]." Although Dulles acknowledged the importance of consultation, he noted that sometimes the United States had to consult with other, non-European states first and that "timely and effective" action might preclude consultation. He highlighted the significance of advance consultation "in case quick action later required." Both Lloyd and Dulles explicitly linked their comments to the inevitable clash between global and Atlantic commitments and interests.[141]

Dulles was also aware that the British might try to leave the United States no choice but to support them. This is strong evidence against the idea of policy coordination. He characterized Britain in this light: "He

[Dulles] recalled that the British went into World War I and World War II without the United States, on the calculation that we would be bound to come in. They are now thinking they might start again and we would have to come in again."[142] On October 17, he worried that differences over the Suez Canal Users' Association implied Britain expected U.S. support: "But never has it been suggested that US would be expected to go along blindly with concept to which it has never agreed and import of which never explained but which seems [to] involve danger of leading us into war or at least supporting a war which has been judged by President to be morally unjustifiable and practically imprudent."[143] On the eve of the war, Dulles cabled Dillon, U.S. ambassador to France: "Under circumstances it is unlikely US will come to aid of Britain and France as in case of First and Second World Wars where they were clearly victim of armed aggression."[144]

The United States was aware that a policy of restraint has certain dangers, and Washington sought to avoid such pitfalls. Some officials worried that too much restraint could signal to Egypt that the threat was not credible. Washington also considered how such family squabbles might look in Moscow. How would America's adversary react to a split among the allies? Does such a split strengthen one's adversaries? The United States also risked being seen as a scapegoat by its allies. Restraint may create a responsibility trap in which a restrainee comes to hold the restrainer responsible for the outcome of a disputed policy whether or not the military policy in question goes forward. In a similar vein, the policy differences could have negative implications for the future relations of the alliance members.

Washington was also aware that too much restraint might embolden Egypt by suggesting that nothing stood behind the U.S.-led diplomacy. In other words, U.S. officials were acquainted with the British and French argument that Egypt would accept a negotiated settlement only if the threat of force was on the horizon.[145] In his October 5 meeting with Lloyd and Pineau, Dulles told them to keep their forces in being because "it should be made clear that if good faith UN efforts fail, force may become a permissible alternative to be considered."[146] One danger in threatening force, of course, is that the adversary may call the bluff and then the cost of restraint and non-use of force may be higher.

U.S. officials debated how American adversaries would perceive the split among the three Western allies. On October 6, Hoover told the president that Egypt was trying to split the United States from its allies.[147] Britain feared that U.S. restraint would strengthen the Soviet-Egyptian relationship.[148] In a Special National Intelligence Estimate (September 5), U.S. analysts suggested that Moscow would use Anglo-French military intervention to "exploit opportunities for causing friction among the Western allies."[149] Dulles admitted the United States sometimes modified plans to preserve a show of allied unity.[150]

U.S. officials discussed whether or not to hide the allied split from the Soviet Union. Charles Bohlen, U.S. ambassador to the Soviet Union, argued that Washington should hide the split because knowledge of Western divisions would embolden the Soviets and foster greater opposition to the West.[151] By not hiding the split, Dulles countered, the U.S. policy of restraint could serve as an example to the Soviets.[152] Ultimately, Bohlen only hinted at the split at a meeting with Soviet premier Nikolai Bulganin; a few days later, Dulles told Soviet foreign minister Dmitri Shepilov that the United States would offer moral support and possibly more tangible support despite the Western disagreement.[153] Dulles later complained to Eisenhower that while the United States was restraining its allies, the Soviet Union was encouraging Egypt in the direction of greater belligerence.[154] Posturing sometimes occurs around restraint as states use restraint efforts to send messages to parties other than the restrainee.

U.S. officials also considered what the impact of a restraint policy might be on present and future alliance relations. Washington worried that the United States would be blamed by Britain and France if things turned out poorly. In general in the eyes of the restrainee, does the restrainer become responsible for the outcome if restraint succeeds?[155] The French seemed to believe so at Suez, and the United States feared being seen as a scapegoat.[156] Criticism may be inevitable given the effort to play a moderating role.[157] Eisenhower disagreed with Britain and France, but he also did not want to "alienate our friends."[158] Even if the United States wanted to explore other policy options, Dulles assured Macmillan that "the United States is not going back on its promise to support the French and the British."[159] At a meeting with Lloyd and Dulles, Pineau suggestively raised the possibility that the split over Suez would destroy NATO. He added that the "temporizing tactics of the US alarm us."[160] Some U.S. officials expressed concerns that the United States might use up all its influence with Britain and France.[161] Just as an ally may tire of repeatedly playing the role of the restrainee, it is worth clarifying whether officials tend to see restraining influences as a finite commodity. Do states suffer from restraint fatigue? Nevertheless, Eisenhower feared a war more than a split among the allies; a split "would be extremely serious, but not as serious as letting a war start and not trying to stop it."[162]

The United States tried to prevent Anglo-French intervention in Egypt for a range of reasons, although only three were mentioned frequently and in many settings. Washington feared that military intervention against Nasser's Egypt would provoke an Arab nationalist backlash against the West in the Arab and Islamic worlds. It worried that intervention might create an opening for greater Soviet involvement in the region. The Americans also did not want to appear to support aggression and colonial intervention in the face of UN and world opinion that thought otherwise.

The possibility of an Arab backlash concerned the Eisenhower administration. Early in the crisis, the United States thought Western opposition to an international conference to resolve the dispute would arouse the Arab and Muslim worlds.[163] More broadly, the use of force would turn the peoples of the Middle East, Asia, and Africa against the West, Dulles told Pineau and Lloyd.[164] Henry A. Byroade, U.S. ambassador to Egypt, argued that intervention would actually fuel Nasserism.[165] On August 30, Dulles told Eisenhower (who agreed) that military intervention would turn the Mideast and Africa against them, create "bitter enemies," and result in a loss of Western influence for a generation if not a century.[166] A high-level intelligence assessment argued that intervention "would provoke a violent anti-Western popular reaction throughout most of the Arab world." Over time, the report continued, the "violent manifestations of popular emotionalism would gradually subside," but "popular anti-British and anti-Western feelings throughout the area would remain at a high pitch for a protracted period." Intervention would intensify resentment of the West.[167]

In Washington's eyes, British intervention would also facilitate Soviet penetration of the Middle East. On August 12, Eisenhower told a congressional delegation that "there shouldn't be much doubt but what the Soviet will fish in troubled waters."[168] On August 30, Dulles linked the anti-Western tide that would result from military intervention to Soviet prospects in the third world: "The Soviet Union would reap the benefit of a greatly weakened Western Europe and would move into a position of predominant influence in the Middle East and Africa."[169] The same intelligence assessment mentioned earlier echoed these sentiments: "The political and moral appeal of the USSR...would almost certainly increase greatly....On the whole, the Arabs would become more susceptible to Soviet influence."[170] It concluded that "throughout the underdeveloped areas of the world, this deepened suspicion and resentment of the West would provide new opportunities for the Communist powers."[171]

The Soviet threat against Britain, France, and Israel on November 5, 1956, exacerbated the American fear of growing Soviet involvement in the Middle East. On the one hand, the United States did not believe the Soviet Union would directly intervene in Egypt or against Western forces in Europe and thereby start a general war. The Joint Chiefs of Staff doubted the Soviets would take military action.[172] On November 6, a Special National Intelligence Estimate, developed by the various agencies in the American intelligence community, also determined the Soviets were unlikely to attack. The United States decided not to release this estimate to the British.[173]

On the other hand, American officials were concerned that the Soviets might use Anglo-French military intervention as an excuse for meddling in the region. The Soviets might send arms, volunteers, or advisers and offer diplomatic support in an effort to woo Arab states, especially if those states were alienated or threatened by the Western bloc.[174] Washington believed ending the intervention would reduce the likelihood of Soviet efforts in the Mideast.[175] Eisenhower, writing to Eden just after their midday phone call on November 6, asked the prime minister to accept the cease-fire resolution without condition "so as not to give Egypt with Soviet backing an opportunity to quibble or start negotiations." The United States wanted British compliance with the UN resolution to avoid "developments of [the] greatest gravity."[176] Much of the U.S. focus was on Syria and the possibility of Soviet support. On November 5, Hoover told the president of "his great concern over the situation in Syria, and the possibility of the USSR sending forces, volunteer or other, into Syria."[177] The next morning, Eisenhower authorized reconnaissance flights over Syria and Israel.[178]

U.S. officials were discussing economic pressure to force Anglo-French compliance even before the Soviet threat of November 5, but the Soviets' move probably hurried along the U.S. timetable. According to Kunz, the threat strengthened the American determination to force British and French compliance "lest they give the Soviet Union an opportunity to intervene in the Middle East."[179] Herman Finer takes a stronger line and claims the threat caused the United States to use fiscal pressure against Britain and France, but the evidence that U.S. officials considered such pressure even before the Soviet threat was issued undermines such a direct causal story.[180]

The United States took several steps on November 6 to increase the readiness of U.S. forces, but the notes of the meeting at which this decision was made have not been found.[181] It was probably a response to the Soviet threat the day before, and may also have been part of a reaction to Soviet moves in Hungary, though the timing fits better with the Soviet threat against Britain, France, and Israel on November 5.

Eisenhower was clear that he viewed the Soviet Union, not his NATO allies, as the primary threat to U.S. interests. As the president told Dulles and Hoover, "The Bear is still the central enemy."[182] Unknown to the British, on November 1 Eisenhower told the National Security Council that the idea that any U.S. action would result in fighting with Britain or France was "simply unthinkable." He could accept the imposition of moderate sanctions against them, but he would not abandon Britain and France.[183]

Britain's proposal would violate norms against aggression and undermine the United Nations. World public opinion would be outraged, Eisenhower wrote Eden, by an immediate resort to force. It would violate the UN charter.[184] At one point, Eisenhower suggested writing to Eden that if Britain used force without exhausting all diplomatic options, "the United Nations organization would be badly weakened and possibly destroyed." Dulles cut this line.[185] But when Dulles met with Pineau and Lloyd on October 5, he made the same argument: "The use of force in violation of the Charter would destroy the United Nations. That is a grave responsibility."[186] In the Tripartite Declaration (1950), the United States had pledged to help victims of aggression, and in an initial discussion of the Israeli invasion, Eisenhower said that "we must make good on our word."[187] The notes of this October 29 meeting on the Israeli invasion suggest that Eisenhower was very concerned (and angered) by Israeli aggression, the possibility of having been double-crossed by Britain and/or France, and the violation of the Tripartite Declaration.[188]

U.S. officials also cited domestic checks, such as congressional opposition and U.S. public opinion, on the Eisenhower administration's support for military intervention. American public opinion would be outraged by an immediate resort to force, Eisenhower wrote Eden on July 31.[189] Dulles argued there was not public support for the use of force, and Congress would not approve such an action.[190] Eisenhower wrote to Eden that Congress was highly unlikely to grant authority even for lesser measures of support and that U.S. public opinion rejected the use of force, "particularly when it does not seem that every possible peaceful means of protecting our vital interests has been exhausted without result."[191] At one point, Eisenhower mentioned (and Dulles agreed) that military force would mean West European use of Western Hemisphere oil supplies and, consequently, U.S. domestic controls on oil consumption.[192]

Washington was concerned that the conflict in Egypt could escalate, spread, and possibly drag the United States to war. An attack on Egypt might lead Israel to attack Jordan.[193] A top U.S. diplomat warned Eden that "forceful methods might release chain of events which could be disastrous to whole world."[194] Given the possible impact of military intervention on East-West relations, Dulles told Makins "there would not be enough forces to send troops to put out all the fires which might start once hostilities in Egypt began."[195] On August 30, Eisenhower told the NSC that the United States could hope to "prevent the enlargement of the war if it actually breaks out."[196]

Through much of this period, the United States agreed that Nasser's Egypt needed to be deflated, but Washington preferred a gradual process to weaken or topple Nasser. When Eden and Dulles met on September 20, Dulles told the British prime minister that "the United States fully agreed that Nasser should not come out ahead [from nationalization]."[197] On September 25, Dulles told Macmillan that economic and political measures would be more effective than military ones in "diminishing Nasser's prestige."[198] On October 2, Eisenhower told Dulles he thought Nasser should be deflated by the development of alternative Arab leadership rather than through overt or covert military action.[199] Part of this difference probably turns on the fact that the United States saw cracks in Nasser's facade whereas France and Britain believed Egypt's leader was only growing stronger.[200] At one point, the United States considered economic sanctions against Egypt as a way to co-opt Britain and France and avoid military intervention.[201]

These factors did not all operate in isolation, as a few examples demonstrate. U.S. officials believed the success of Soviet activities in the Middle East would be affected by the image the United States projected regarding the United Nations and aggressive interventionist policy. If Western Europe's economy became weaker as a result of Anglo-French intervention, the United States would have to bear a larger share of the West's burden, affecting both domestic and international (Cold War) issues. Being dragged into the war or forced to come to the aid of the former colonial powers Britain and France would only deepen the negative reaction Arab states would have to the West, including the United States.

Given these many influences, the key question is why the United States declined to mobilize its power resources prior to the intervention but did so rapidly afterward. In light of how U.S. officials viewed the strategic environment, it seems likely that the anomaly is why the United States did not mobilize its resources before the intervention rather than why it did mobilize them afterward. The available evidence suggests that the United States would use material means to stop Britain. One possibility is that Dulles himself was the obstacle. As of November 3, he was sick and not participating in U.S. decision making during much of November when the United States sanctioned Britain.[202] He may have been personally opposed to going beyond restraint rhetoric with such a close ally; as indicated earlier, he did not want Britain to go under financially. This is evidence for the normative explanation and demonstrates the relevance of leadership unity on alliance restraint questions. Alternatively, Dulles may have thought the British had promised to consult before resorting to arms.[203]

A second possibility is that British deception worked. The United States never had the chance to threaten materially because it was kept in the dark in the closing days of October 1956. As one later observer points out, "Between October 3 and 29, Washington naturally was told nothing."[204] As we have seen, the French prime minister noted that this lack of communication was an intentional strategy to prevent the United States from blocking military intervention. Although this comment is technically accurate, it still leaves one wondering why the United States had not mobilized its power, or threatened to do so, in the months of discussion about British options.

A third possibility is that the Soviet threat on November 5 either changed or hastened U.S. policy. Although this explanation is theoretically plausible, the available evidence neither confirms nor undermines it.

Conclusion

In examining the success or failure of restraint attempts, the cases in this chapter provide greater support for a power-based explanation than for a policy coordination explanation. The more powerful state, the United States, got its way when it mobilized its power resources, as in the second part of Suez in 1956 and with Formosa in 1954–1955, or at least threatened to do so, as in Iran in 1951. When the United States did not mobilize its power resources, with Indochina in 1954 and in the first part of the Suez crisis, merely being the more capable ally was insufficient. Power mobilization determined the outcome of the alliance restraint efforts. Britain and the United States showed few signs of coming to an agreement about policy outcomes or coordinating their policy. In 1951 and 1956, British deception played a prominent role and thereby further undermined the normative explanation.

4

American-Israeli Relations and Alliance Restraint

The United States has frequently tried to modify Israeli military policy. Sometimes Washington has not been successful. Although the United States is by far the more powerful player, it failed to restrain Israel in three of the seven examples mentioned in this chapter. Furthermore, rather than accept the counsel of its partner, Israel has often defied the United States and deceived Washington. A normative alliance commitment to policy coordination does not explain the U.S.-Israeli cases. Only when the United States was willing to mobilize its power resources was it able to restrain Israel. A power advantage alone is insufficient if the powerful state relies on rhetoric but is unwilling to use its material capabilities to achieve restraint.

This chapter considers seven Israeli military policy questions in which the United States opposed Israel's position. The United States failed to stop Israeli nuclear proliferation in the early 1960s, failed to prevent an Israeli attack in 1967, and failed to stop an Israeli invasion of Lebanon in 1982 because Washington refused to mobilize its power resources. In each case, the United States failed to use carrots or sticks to stop Israel and/or failed to use U.S. power to ensure that a policy alternative favored by the United States came about to satisfy Israel's needs. When the United States succeeded in restraining Israel before the 1973 Arab-Israeli war, Israel knew that launching a preemptive strike in defiance of the United States might mean the loss of U.S. aid and arms. In 1977, the United States forced Israel out of Lebanon after a minor incursion by threatening to terminate further arms deliveries. During the 1991 Gulf War, the United States used a mix of carrots, sticks, and an alternative policy. In 2000 and 2005, the potential loss of aid and then military sanctions led Israel to cancel two arms sales to China.

These cases point to several important factors for understanding when a restrainer will mobilize its power resources. First, it must be aware of the restrainee's policy, but potential restrainees often deceive even their allies.[1] Awareness is a necessary but not sufficient condition. To state the obvious, it is difficult, though not impossible, to block a policy of which one is not aware. In the 1960s, Israel was not open with the United States about its pursuit of nuclear weapons. In 1977, Israel told the United States it had left Lebanon but U.S. satellites suggested otherwise. In 1982, Israel misled the United States about the extent of its planned invasion of Lebanon. (Even many Israeli leaders were not informed of Defense Minister Ariel Sharon's plans to drive to Beirut.) In 2004–2005, Israel may also have tried to hide its agreement to upgrade Chinese military drones by calling it a mere refurbishment. Yet in 1973 and 1991, the United States and Israel openly discussed the military policies in question, a preemptive Israeli attack on Egypt and Syria (1973) and Israeli intervention against Iraqi SCUD missile launchers. Of course, a potential restrainer that is aware of the policy still may choose not to mobilize its power resources, as was the case with the United States in 1967.

Second, disunity among the leadership of the restrainer about whether to restrain is often correlated with an unwillingness to mobilize power resources. The argument is not that disunity causes restrainers to avoid mobilization but rather that the two often go hand-in-hand. One also observes the reverse: unified support for restraint and power mobilization. In 1973, Henry Kissinger and Richard Nixon both opposed an Israeli preemptive strike; similar unanimity occurred in 1991. In contrast, in 1982, Ronald Reagan, Alexander Haig, and some other officials were more sympathetic to the Israeli perspective than previous American administrations and, in particular, were sensitive to Israeli self-defense needs. They opposed an Israeli invasion, but only to a point. In 1967, a modicum of American disunity was present but involved more peripheral officials, as Lyndon Johnson and many others favored reining in Israel. There were no signs of American disunity in the early 1960s over Israeli nuclear proliferation even though the United States did not mobilize its power resources.

Disunity on the restrainee side may matter as well. The 1973 war, for example, is viewed in two ways: in one interpretation, some Israeli leaders were swayed by American pressure while others, such as General David Elazar, were not. But in another perspective, some Israeli leaders, such as Prime Minister Golda Meir, assumed the Arab side would not even attack and thus were wary of preemption. Bowing to American demands was a useful argument for settling an existing internal debate. Israeli leaders also embraced multiple viewpoints in 1991. I am skeptical that one can disentangle these two chicken-and-egg possibilities and instead favor a different position: there is an important interplay between domestic disunity at the elite level and the success or failure of restraint. Even if the restrainer's efforts are valid because of domestic fractures, the fact that they helped restraint succeed at the end of the day is still an important finding.

Third, the hierarchy of national security priorities of the more powerful state shapes decisions on power mobilization. Whether to mobilize is tied to how the resource mobilization would affect higher priorities than the restrainee's contested military policy. In the first several cases in this chapter, the American concerns about a real or potential Israeli policy were secondary to two U.S. Cold War concerns: the Soviet Union and/or Vietnam. Power mobilization vis-à-vis restraining Israel was weighed in light of whether it would strengthen the Soviet Union, escalate the Cold War, or even be possible in light of the deep U.S. commitment to Vietnam.[2] In the early 1960s, John Kennedy feared that power mobilization to restrain Israel, which would have meant a U.S. security guarantee for Israel, would spark an escalatory Soviet response. In 1967, U.S. involvement in Vietnam limited the range of U.S. options—unilateral options were off the table—with the result that Johnson felt he needed congressional and foreign support for military action to break the Egyptian naval blockade of Israel. When that was not forthcoming, the U.S. effort fizzled and U.S. restraint was only rhetorical. In 1973, the Nixon administration worried that allowing Israel to launch a preemptive attack would undermine détente with the Soviet Union and the balance of forces in the Middle East; thus, in 1973, Cold War needs meant the United States should and did mobilize power resources to prevent an opening Israeli strike. The 1991 Persian Gulf War came after the Cold War had ended, but it again showed that the higher U.S. security interest would prevail. With the United States fighting a war against Iraq, the decision to mobilize resources to restrain Israel was an obvious one. Keeping Arab partners on board against Iraq as part of winning the war meant using multiple material instruments to keep Israeli forces on the sidelines. In 2000 and 2005, holding off China and protecting Taiwan trumped the economic needs of the Israeli defense industry.

This third argument builds on Abraham Ben-Zvi's view of the American-Israeli tie in terms of patron-client relations.[3] Ben-Zvi highlights the way the Cold War gave clients such as Israel extra leverage because the two patrons, the Soviet Union and the United States, were so desperate to win the battle for allies. He is right to emphasize how the U.S.-Israeli relationship was embedded in the larger Cold War framework for American decision makers. At the same time, one needs to account for the possibility that other Cold War interests, based on other American alliances, regional security considerations, direct U.S.-Soviet relations, and the like, could trump the American need to hold onto Israel in any given case. Keeping Israel as an ally and managing the Arab-Israeli conflict were two of many Cold War needs, so how the U.S.-Israeli relationship would play out in any given case depended on what other aspects of the Cold War came into the picture; support for Israel was not a dominant or unidirectional factor. Whereas in 1967 Cold War concerns undermined or limited the U.S. restraint effort, in 1973 the desire to block Soviet meddling propelled the U.S. policy of alliance restraint.

This chapter's close look at U.S.-Israeli relations also points to the fact that not all contested policies are of equal importance in restraint cases. A belief that Israel's survival may have been at stake in 1967 was different from a debate about a small Israeli incursion into southern Lebanon in 1977. Future research may lead to greater exploration of the impact of this variation in policy type.

American-Israeli Relations

Throughout the decades covered in this chapter, American power capabilities were far greater than Israeli ones. In 1961, for instance, the United States spent 360 times as much on defense, the U.S. GNP was 172 times larger, the U.S. population was 82 times greater, and the United States had almost 37 military personnel for every Israeli one. By 1982, the gaps had narrowed, but they were still tremendous: 44 times as much on defense, a GNP that was 135 times larger, a population that was 57 times greater, and almost 12 military personnel for every Israeli soldier.[4] Although Israel developed a nuclear bomb by about 1970, the United States also had a massive advantage in nuclear weaponry.

The American-Israeli politico-military relationship evolved over time. In the early 1960s, it was not a formal alliance, but Israel and the United States were aligned in the Cold War. The first exchange of advanced military arms came with the Kennedy administration's sale of Hawk missiles to Israel.[5] Weapons sales intensified after the 1967 war; President Lyndon B. Johnson lifted the Middle East arms embargo and by late 1968 had agreed to sell Israel fifty advanced F-4 Phantom jets.[6] The American arms resupply effort drew particular attention during and after the 1973 war. U.S. policy during the war in 1973, including a $2.2 billion arms resupply, showed that Israel needed the United States for more than just deterring the Soviets.[7] Some argued Israel could not "take care of itself."[8] U.S. aid increased dramatically as part of the Egyptian-Israeli peace process in the mid-1970s. By 1980, Israel received about $3 billion annually in economic and military assistance.

In both 1967 and 1973, the United States took military action to ensure that the Soviet Union did not intervene in the Arab-Israeli wars. On June 10, 1967, Johnson responded to a threatening Soviet hot-line message by turning the U.S. Sixth Fleet toward the Syrian coast. Later that day an Arab-Israeli cease-fire went into effect, defusing the superpower crisis. On October 24, 1973, the Soviet Union warned the Nixon administration that if the United States did not work with the Soviets to make the cease-fire stick, Moscow "should be faced with the necessity urgently to consider the question of taking appropriate steps unilaterally." The United States responded by raising the alert level of U.S. forces worldwide. The next day, UNSC Resolution 340 called for a cease-fire, and this time it worked. Again, the superpower crisis quickly ebbed.[9] Not surprisingly, the Arab-Soviet side considered Israeli-U.S. relations an alliance.[10]

The United States also received some benefits. Israeli wars against Soviet-equipped Arab armies gave the United States important evidence of how American weapons might perform against the Soviets if the Cold War ever turned hot. After the 1973 war, for example, Israel and the United States cooperated in examining captured Soviet equipment.[11] In 1958, the United States appreciated Israeli support during crises in Jordan and Lebanon. One author argues that this episode "planted the seed of the U.S.-Israeli alliance."[12] In September 1970, Israel helped the United States prevent a Syrian takeover of Jordan. This example was especially significant because Israel expressed its willingness to launch air and ground strikes against Syrian forces, no minor decision on Israel's part.[13]

Israel's willingness to act on U.S. requests during the Jordan crisis in September 1970 solidified the relationship and led to much higher levels of U.S. assistance to Israel. President Nixon "was deeply impressed by the determination shown by the Israelis at a time when America's formal allies had quit on him." More broadly, the crisis "demonstrated to [Nixon and some of his advisers] in a concrete and dramatic fashion the value for the United States of a strong Israel."[14] The crisis, William Quandt writes, brought American-Israeli relations "to an unprecedentedly high level."[15]

The stronger ties were also reflected in dramatic increases in U.S. aid for Israel, which had already grown in the aftermath of the 1967 war. For fiscal years 1968–1970, Israel received $140 million in military credits. For fiscal years 1971–1973, the total jumped to $1.145 billion.[16] Nixon approved a $90 million arms deal on October 15.[17] In late October 1970, Prime Minister Meir came to Washington seeking more support. The Nixon administration promised $500 million, and Nixon signed the supplemental appropriation on January 11, 1971.[18] In late 1971, Nixon promised Israel Phantom jets and Skyhawk fighter bombers.[19]

Israel and the United States have signed several strategic agreements. In 1971, a few weeks after U.S.-Israeli cooperation during the Jordan crisis, the two sides signed a memorandum of understanding in which the United States pledged to help "Israel to enhance its military self-sufficiency."[20] In 1974, as part of the Egyptian-Israeli disengagement agreement known as Sinai I, Israel and the United States signed a separate ten-point memorandum pledging U.S. support for Israel.[21] On September 1, 1975, they signed a Memorandum of Understanding with several noteworthy provisions:

- The United States Government will make every effort to be fully responsive...on an ongoing and long-term basis, to Israel's military equipment and other defense requirements, to its energy requirements and to its economic needs.
- Israel's long-term military supply needs from the United States shall be the subject of periodic consultations between representatives of the U.S. and Israeli defense establishments, with agreement reached on specific items to be included in a separate U.S.-Israeli memorandum....The United States will view Israel's requests sympathetically, including its request for advanced and sophisticated weapons.
- In view of the long-standing U.S. commitment to the survival and security of Israel, the United States Government will view with particular gravity threats to Israel's security or sovereignty by a world power. In support of this objective, the United States Government will in the event of such threat consult promptly with the Government of Israel with respect to what support, diplomatic or otherwise, of assistance it can lend to Israel in accordance with its constitutional practices.[22]

All these provisions emphasize the long-term or continuing nature of the strategic relationship. Another Memorandum of Agreement accompanied the Egyptian-Israeli peace treaty in 1979 and spelled out further "defense cooperation."[23] An additional Memorandum of Understanding was signed on November 30, 1981. The agreement called for strategic cooperation and joint military exercises, and it set up an organizational framework to discuss military issues. Israel is not in NATO or formally under the U.S. nuclear umbrella, but the joint security cooperation and infrastructure is extensive. In December 1981, the United States announced a "temporary suspension" of the agreement because of the Israeli annexation of the Golan Heights on December 14 (Israel extended Israeli law and jurisdiction). But this action did not change the underlying dynamic, and the suspension was lifted in 1983.[24] On October 29, 1983, President Reagan signed National Security Decision Directive 111, which focused on strategic cooperation and, the Department of State's undersecretary for political affairs told Israel, meant, "We like Israel and want to establish the closest relationship."[25] The United States and Israel formed a Joint Political Military Group, and in 1984 they began joint military exercises. On April 21, 1988, they signed a five-year Memorandum of Agreement that noted "that Israel is currently designated ... as a major non-NATO ally of the United States." This status gives Israel access to a range of military and financial programs. The renewable agreement reaffirmed the "close relationship" between Israel and the United States.[26]

In the area of rhetorical evidence, Eisenhower laid the groundwork for tighter American-Israeli relations. Though the conventional view of the Eisenhower administration among Israel's supporters is one of tension and disagreement, Eisenhower took some steps toward Israel. On July 25, 1958, in the aftermath of Israeli help with a crisis in Jordan, the president wrote to Israeli prime minister David Ben-Gurion and stated that Israel could "be confident of United States interest in the integrity and independence of Israel."[27] The United States, officials pledged, would extend protection to Israel if it came under communist attack, just as Washington had done for Jordan and Lebanon.[28] During discussions about how to deal with Arab nationalism, a report of the National Security Council Planning Board of July 29, 1958, noted the "special U.S. relationship with Israel, both historical and present."[29] Still, the Eisenhower administration did not think of the protection of Israel as a fundamental American objective in the region. It was not listed as a "primary" objective in "U.S. Policy Toward the Near East," a document adopted by the National Security Council on October 30, 1958.[30]

From Kennedy onward, the special relationship continued to deepen. On December 27, 1962, President Kennedy told Golda Meir, then Israeli foreign minister:

> The United States…has a special relationship with Israel in the Middle East really comparable only to that which it has with Britain over a wide range of world affairs. But for us to play properly the role we are called upon to play, we cannot afford the luxury of identifying Israel—or Pakistan, or certain other countries—as our exclusive friends, hewing to the line of close and intimate allies (for we feel that about Israel though it is not a formal ally) and letting other countries go.

He added: "I think it is quite clear that in case of an invasion the United States would come to the support of Israel."[31] Shlomo Aronson claims that "Kennedy gave Foreign Minister Meir the first American executive promise to guarantee Israel's boundaries." Kennedy later offered Prime Minister Levi Eshkol a similar statement.[32] As president, Kennedy "pledged nineteen times his support for Israel's security in case of an Arab attack."[33] President Johnson himself felt supportive of Israel, as he later wrote in his memoirs: "I have always had a deep feeling of sympathy for Israel and its people, gallantly building and defending a modern nation against great odds and against the tragic background of Jewish experience."[34] The top pro-Israeli lobbyist in Washington, Isaiah Kenan, later called him a great friend of Israel.[35] Nixon and Kissinger repeatedly called Israel an "ally." In 1970, Kissinger told the Israeli ambassador to the United States, Yitzhak Rabin, that Washington was "fortunate in having an ally like Israel."[36] According to a later analysis, "Nixon's presidency dramatically deepened and broadened" the special relationship between the United States and Israel.[37] In the midst of the 1973 war, Israeli prime minister Meir publicly thanked the United States: "Friendship of US, its people and its govt, has always been dear to us and is particularly dear to us in these times of tribulation."[38]

In terms of the essential elements of an alliance, Israel and the United States were allies by the 1970s and arguably after the 1967 war, even if they lacked a formal defense treaty. Already in the early 1960s, they had a *shared interest* in minimizing Soviet influence and keeping the Arab parties under control, with the United States seeing the Arab issue more as a function of the Soviet one, and Israel seeing the Soviet angle more as a function of the Arab one. The *exchange of benefits* started in the 1960s; Israel got more, but as shown in the 1970 Jordan crisis, Israel also contributed to U.S. national interests.[39] If arms sales are a sign of *security cooperation,* then such cooperation started in the early 1960s and intensified after 1967. Leaving aside arms, in both 1967 and 1973 Washington took military steps to defend Israel vis-à-vis the Soviet Union. Joint military exercises did not arrive until the 1980s, but several memoranda describe security cooperation. The *specific written obligations* of the 1970s and 1980s gave the alliance a more formalized foundation. The *expectation of a continuing relationship* is harder to judge, but as early as 1962 some U.S. officials privately recognized the "strength and enduring quality of the United States' relationship with Israel."[40] Note also the language of the 1975 agreement quoted earlier, the renewable nature of the 1988 agreement, and the comments of presidents starting with Kennedy in 1962.

What does this trajectory mean for the cases? The 1961–1963 nuclear proliferation case came before the alliance took deep roots, but the two parties were aligned or informally allied by that time.[41] The 1967 case is on the cusp, a time when the alliance was being hardened. By 1973, and certainly 1977, 1982, 1991, and 2000/2005, the United States and Israel were allies. To the extent that the tightness of the alliance might affect the nature and effectiveness of restraint, we need to be on guard for possible differences between the first two and last five U.S. Israeli cases.

Both sides debated the merits of closer military ties, and the Israeli debate is further evidence for this book's proposition of the relevance of alliance restraint. States are aware of the potential restraining element of alliances and thus may seek to avoid such alliances so as to avoid the restraint effect. On the American side, some policymakers worried that close ties with Israel would harm important U.S. relationships with Arab states, especially oil-exporting ones.

On the Israeli side, some policymakers feared closer ties with the United States because they did not want to become dependent on an external power for survival or be obligated to coordinate security policy. For example, in early 1954, Prime Minister Moshe Sharett was asked by his staff: "Supposing the Americans say, 'Let's make a pact and Israel will become a base like Greece' what will our answer be?" In response, Sharett indicated he was neither prepared nor "interested" in offering bases to the United States. He added: "We are also opposed to her humiliating military supervision...it would mean the increase of dependency on the United States and the decrease of our independence." In mid-1954, he rejected the hypothetical idea of a U.S. public guarantee of Israel's security, in part because it "would constrain Israel's own freedom to act independently when she gauged her own local interests to be threatened." (Israel soon changed its mind due to Western agreements with Arab states.) Israel's military establishment opposed a "binding connection" with the United States for fear it would "curtail Israel's freedom of action." Ben-Gurion wanted a deal with the United States but felt that retaining the ability of independent military actions was Israel's top priority.[42] The American airlift during the 1973 war, Ariel Sharon later wrote, reinforced his concern about the dangers of too much dependence on the United States. Moshe Dayan drew the opposite conclusion from the war and sought closer ties.[43] Former U.S. secretary of state Dean Rusk later commented: "It is my impression that Israel was never interested in such a treaty [of alliance] because that would imply an obligation upon Israel to try to coordinate its policy with us."[44]

These Israeli concerns have important theoretical implications. First, it meant that Israelis did not look toward an alliance with the United States as an opportunity to facilitate a more adventurous foreign policy. Whereas one could argue that Taiwan felt ties with the United States would provide a security cushion and thus the possibility of riskier policies, several Israeli leaders focused on the prospect of less room for maneuver in the event of an American-Israeli security agreement. Second, U.S.-Israeli cases provide a hard test for alliance restraint. Given the Israeli tendency toward self-reliance, both in theory and in practice, the ability of any outside power to stop military policies will be harder than in a typical alliance relationship.

In sum, it is simultaneously true that the United States and Israel were developing stronger and stronger military ties over time; that some Israelis resisted the idea for fear of being restrained by the United States; and that the two sides have a close relationship that nonetheless has room for even deeper military ties. Israel welcomed material support, but it wanted no strings attached.

The United States Fails to Stop Israeli Nuclear Proliferation, 1961–1963

The United States was unable to restrain Israel's nuclear program. In trying to stop Israel, the Kennedy administration (1961–1963) faced a difficult task because key Israeli leaders saw developing a nuclear deterrent as vital to Israel's security. Nevertheless, the administration might have succeeded if it had mobilized U.S. resources. This would have meant either sanctioning Israel for noncompliance or proposing a quid pro quo: Israeli nuclear nonproliferation in exchange for an American security guarantee. Instead, President Kennedy saved his most threatening language for specific aspects of the U.S.-Israeli dialogue concerning the Israeli nuclear facility at Dimona rather than the general issue of Israeli proliferation. This case is an example of a more powerful state that fails to restrain because it fails to mobilize its power capabilities. The United States did not offer Israel a full-fledged security guarantee because it feared such an offer would lead to stronger Arab-Soviet ties and would tilt U.S. policy toward Israel, thereby undermining the prospects for an Arab-Israeli settlement.

This case does not address the entire history of Israel's pursuit of nuclear weapons, which was not complete until the late 1960s. But focusing on the Kennedy administration allows us to look at alliance restraint in a distinct period when U.S. policy still could have made a difference to the outcome without exacting an unreasonable cost from either party.

On a rhetorical level, Kennedy officials told Israel that the United States opposed Israeli nuclear proliferation. On February 3, 1961, Assistant Secretary of State G. Lewis Jones informed the Israeli ambassador that the "proliferation of nuclear weapons was absolutely anathema to the United States."[45] When Kennedy and Ben-Gurion met on May 30, 1961, at the Waldorf-Astoria, the U.S. president told the Israeli prime minister that "it was important for the United States that it did not appear 'that Israel is preparing for atomic weapons.'"[46] On December 27, 1962, Kennedy met with Israeli foreign minister Meir. "We are opposed to nuclear proliferation," he told her.[47] In a mid-May 1963 letter to Ben-Gurion, Kennedy again stated his position: "I am sure that you will agree that there is no more urgent business for the whole world than the control of nuclear weapons."[48]

But this American policy of restraining Israel on the nuclear question was not backed up by any material threats or inducements. One later scholar refers to the "non-coercive pattern" of Kennedy's policy. Another notes that "Israel never really had to choose between Dimona and Washington."[49] With one exception (inspections), Kennedy's statements do not contain any reference to material sanctions or coercion.

In spite of the rhetoric, the only tangible U.S. threat was related to the specific issue of inspections of Dimona rather than to the overall issue of Israel's development of nuclear weapons.[50] The first U.S. visit, as the Israelis preferred to call the inspections, took place in 1961. By the spring of 1963, however, Kennedy was tired of Israel's resistance to setting up a regular schedule for the inspections. In a May 18, 1963, letter to Ben-Gurion and then in a July 5, 1963, letter to Israel's new prime minister,

Levi Eshkol, Kennedy wrote that Israel's pursuit of nuclear weapons could jeopardize the U.S. "commitment to and support of Israel."[51] However, near the end of August, Eshkol defused the mini-crisis by satisfying Kennedy on the issue of Dimona inspections.

Throughout this period, Israeli officials misled the United States about Israel's nuclear objectives. The Eisenhower administration, according to a memorandum written by Kennedy's secretary of state, Dean Rusk, had received "categoric assurances" from Ben-Gurion that Israel was not developing nuclear arms.[52] Israel, Ben-Gurion told Kennedy at the Waldorf-Astoria in 1961, was seeking inexpensive nuclear energy to help with water desalinization. Ben-Gurion introduced an important qualification, however: "There is no such intention now, not for 4 or 5 years. But we will see what happens in the Middle East.... Maybe Russia won't give bombs to China or Egypt, but maybe Egypt will develop them herself."[53] At the Kennedy-Meir meeting in December 1962, "Mrs. Meir reassured the President that there would not be any difficulty between us on the Israeli nuclear reactor."[54] Meir herself, however, "had long feared" that Ben-Gurion's deception of the United States would harm bilateral relations.[55] The following April, using what would become Israel's favored way of characterizing its nuclear program, Shimon Peres told Kennedy that "we will not introduce nuclear weapons to the region, and certainly we will not be the first."[56]

How should one evaluate the balance of interests in this case, given that a nuclear bomb could ensure Israel's survival? Although one could suggest that Israel was unrestrainable on this question of national survival, the record indicates that Israel could have been restrained had the United States been willing to offer a formal security guarantee. A nuclear bomb and a security pact with the United States could have served the same function of guaranteeing Israel's existence. In short, if Washington had been willing to mobilize its power resources to pursue an alternate policy, restraint of Israeli nuclear proliferation was possible though not certain.[57]

As Ben-Gurion told the Israeli cabinet on May 5, 1955, he saw two ways to guarantee Israel's survival: "Our security problem could have two answers: if possible, political guarantees, but this is not up to us. But on what depends on us, we must invest all our power, because we must have superiority in weapons.... All those things that have to do with science, we must do them." For Ben-Gurion, "science" meant a nuclear weapon.[58] The interchangeability between an American guarantee and a nuclear weapon is suggested by Ben-Gurion's protégé, Peres, who told the French in November 1956, just after the Suez war, "I don't trust the guarantees of others.... What would you think if we prepared our own retaliation force?"[59] Some other Israeli officials, such as Moshe Sharett (prime minister 1954–1955), strongly favored a military alliance to ensure Israel's continued existence.[60] As late as May 12, 1963, Ben-Gurion asked Kennedy for a formal commitment to come to Israel's defense if Israel were attacked. Kennedy had offered public support for Israel during a press conference on May 8. During the same period in which Kennedy was threatening Israel over the inspections issues, the president gave the idea of a formal pact serious consideration.[61] But ultimately, he rejected it, officially informing Israel on October 2, 1963.[62] Ben-Gurion believed a nuclear weapon would protect Israel's existence, but a pact with the United States—something within U.S. capabilities—would have done the same.

Why did the United States consider but reject the idea of an explicit security guarantee, thus declining to mobilize its resources to try to head off the Israeli nuclear program? The United States knew Israel wanted "a full-fledged alliance, with all the trimmings."[63] Furthermore, the United States was well aware that Israel was trying to leverage restraint on the nuclear question to get such a guarantee: "[the] Israelis regard Dimona inspection as a bargaining card on security guarantee."[64] The CIA concluded that Israel would develop nuclear weapons if it did not have a U.S. security guarantee.[65] Israeli nuclear nonproliferation would only come at a price.

Opposition within the U.S. government to a security guarantee or deeper military ties was led by the State Department and the Joint Chiefs. The State Department feared that "new United States arrangements with Israel could result in comparable Soviet-Arab ties, bringing the Soviets back in, probably in a more permanent and damaging fashion." Soviet entry might be coupled with an arms race. Kennedy's "primary aim" was to "block Russian influence" in the Middle East.[66] Moreover, working with Arab states rather than provoking them by moving even closer to Israel would best promote Israeli security.[67] In 1962–1963, most U.S. officials believed Arab-Israeli balance was a prerequisite for conflict resolution that would ultimately be in the American and Israeli interest. While Washington privately assured Israel, it refrained from a public tilt. At a pivotal meeting of top officials on July 23, 1963, Kennedy decided to put off the security guarantee for fear of helping the Soviets: "We should wait on the security guarantee question. We should point out to the Israelis that the May 8 [1963] statement is as far as the President can go without inviting the Soviets into the Middle East."[68] Kennedy conveyed this position to Israeli prime minister Eshkol in a letter of October 2, 1963. The letter embodied the central arguments against a security guarantee that had been offered inside the U.S. bureaucracy.[69]

Domestic interest groups probably did not influence Kennedy's policy, though Kennedy likely knew that pressuring Israel on any issue would not be popular with American Jewish voters. Kennedy pursued both nuclear nonproliferation and his own reelection in 1964, objectives that could have conflicted on the question of Israel's nuclear program.[70] Rusk mentioned the issue to Kennedy, suggesting that the president assess "the extent of Congressional and other pressures for a security guarantee to Israel."[71] But a later historian concludes otherwise: "On the nuclear issue, Kennedy was not much interested in what the American Jewish community thought." One of his aides, Mike Feldman, who looked after the interests of both Israel and American Jewry, "was often out of the loop on Dimona."[72] In studying the domestic angle, we need to be clear about what aspect of the question might have been affected by interest group politics. In this case, domestic voices would be more likely to undermine a call for pressure (coerce Israel) than to bolster a call for offering a carrot (a U.S. security guarantee).

One important caveat is relevant here. Despite the fact that this case took place more than forty-five years ago, the highly sensitive nature of Israel's nuclear proliferation means that much information on the Israeli side is still classified. It is possible that the U.S. effort had some effect concerning which the evidence remains hidden. For instance, Israel has limited its program in two ways: it has not conducted a nuclear test, and it does not acknowledge possessing nuclear weapons. We do not know if either of these limits was influenced by U.S. pressure, so it remains possible that this case of American restraint failure covers an American success that will come to light only in the long view of history.

The United States Fails to Stop the Israeli Attack, 1967

The United States tried to stop Israel from going to war against Egypt and Syria in May and early June 1967. Although the U.S. effort had some initial success, the effort to restrain Israel ultimately failed, and Israel attacked on June 5, 1967. The effort failed because despite the fact that the United States opposed the idea of war, Washington declined to mobilize its capabilities to pressure Israel. Furthermore, the United States refused to commit to a unilateral (or near-unilateral) American show of force to break the declared Egyptian blockade of the Strait of Tiran. The preferred American option, a multilateral effort to counter Egypt's blockade, was time-consuming and, by early June, was slowed by the hesitance of many potential participants. The United States relied on rhetorical tools to restrain Israel, but they proved insufficient on their own to prevent the war.

The immediate crisis began when Egypt moved more forces into the Sinai Peninsula on May 14, 1967. The Egyptian move was a direct response to a Soviet warning to Egypt on May 13 that Israel was massing forces on the Syrian border and to an escalating war of words between Israel and Syria. The Soviets may have learned of an Israeli cabinet decision on May 7 to "launch a limited retaliatory strike if Syrian-sponsored border incursions continued."[73] On May 18, the UN secretary general ordered the UN peacekeepers in Sinai (the UN Emergency Force) to withdraw in accordance with a request to do so from the host country, Egypt. The most important step, however, was Egypt's closure of the Strait of Tiran on May 22–23 to ships bound for the Israeli port of Eilat; the closure blocked tankers with much of Israel's oil supply.[74]

Both before and after the closure of the strait, U.S. policy was to restrain Israel. On May 15, the United States "urge[d] restraint" on Israel.[75] On May 17, President Johnson sent a telegram to Israeli prime minister Eshkol: "In this situation, I would like to emphasize in the strongest terms the need to avoid any action on your side which would add further to the violence and tension in your area. . . . I cannot accept any responsibilities on behalf of the United States for situations which arise as the result of actions on which we are not consulted."[76] The American ambassador to Israel cabled home on May 19: "I have put to them in strong terms importance they keep their nerve and not do anything in their anxiety to heat up the situation further."[77] The May 22 closure of the strait was especially important given that, according to the Israeli ambassador in Washington on May 20, "GOI [government of Israel] has also noted U.S. injunction Israel not move unless Egyptians take action to close straits."[78] On May 25, Secretary of State Rusk told Britain's foreign secretary, "We were making it clear to the Israelis they shouldn't count on our support if they moved on their own."[79]

The general U.S. policy was a policy of restraint, as it always was, according to former U.S. ambassador to Israel Samuel Lewis.[80] Richard B. Parker counts "at least nine high-level messages to Israel telling it not to start the fighting." Parker concludes: "Neither Johnson nor the people around him had interpreted Johnson's attitude as permissive."[81] In later years, both Ephraim Evron, who met with Johnson during the crisis and was the number two Israeli official at its embassy in Washington, and Meir Amit, the head of Israel's Mossad (counterintelligence service), stated in public that restraint dominated U.S. policy in May–June 1967.[82] According to Rusk, "Johnson emphatically urged the Israelis to stay their hand."[83]

Initially, the U.S. policy worked, and Israel was restrained. In light of the closure, the Israeli cabinet met on May 23 to consider going to war. Israel decided not to attack at that time because of U.S. warnings and the possibility of an alternative solution to the crisis.[84] On May 26, Rusk explained the decision to Johnson: "In our conversations with [Israeli foreign minister Abba] Eban last night, he made clear that Ambassador Walworth Barbour's intervention on May 23 held off a preemptive strike."[85] Eban used a similar explanation with Secretary of Defense Robert S. McNamara: "Mr. Eban said the Israeli Cabinet had met just before his trip and the decision was made to fight rather than to surrender to a blockade in Aqaba; Israel would not try to live on one lung. It had delayed thus far in striking because of President Johnson's urgings and because Ambassador Barbour had spoken of another alternative to surrender or war, namely, that the maritime nations would keep the Straits open."[86]

The key to securing continued Israeli restraint was the success of one of two alternatives for breaking the blockade other than Israeli action: U.S. action or multilateral action. At the end of the day, Washington rejected the former and failed at, or at least took too long at, the latter. When pressed by Justice Abe Fortas on May 26, Johnson rejected the first option, a U.S. display of force: "The President asked whether Mr. Fortas meant we would enforce the passage of an Israeli vessel with our men and ships. Mr. Fortas answered that we would use whatever force necessary. The President said he did not believe he was in a position now to say that."[87] On June 3, Johnson wrote Eshkol, "Our leadership is unanimous that the United States should not move in isolation."[88] As Quandt notes, "Unilateral U.S. action was ruled out without much consideration."[89] The second option, however, was supported by the United States and could have led to Israeli restraint, as Eugene Rostow, undersecretary of state for political affairs, explained to the president and others on May 26. Eban, Rostow said, "felt that if there were some hope that an international group would keep the Straits open, this would be sufficient to stay Israel's hand."[90] On May 25, Eban told Rusk restraint could happen: "He said that when he returned to Tel Aviv it was important that he be able to state that something concrete was being done about the Strait situation. If there was nothing concrete to say Israel would feel alone. If on the other hand, international action were instituted, Israel would 'harmonize' its effort with the others."[91]

Eban came to Washington and met with top U.S. officials on May 25–26 to gauge the seriousness of the alternatives to war. During his visit, U.S. officials continued to urge restraint and claimed the multilateral flotilla was being seriously pursued. Rusk warned Eban on May 25 that "preemptive action by Israel would cause extreme difficulty for the United States."[92] Before Johnson met with Eban, Rusk suggested that the United States propose a multilateral flotilla rather than allow an Israeli show of force. One option, he noted, was "to let the Israelis decide how best to protect their own national interests, in the light of the advice we have given them: i.e., to 'unleash' them. We recommend strongly against this option."[93] Johnson's famous words were spoken to Eban on the evening of May 26: "At the same time, Israel must not make itself responsible for initiating hostilities. With emphasis and solemnity, the President repeated twice, Israel will not be alone unless it decides to go it alone."[94] Eban pressed Johnson: "I would not be wrong if I told the [Israeli] Prime Minister that your disposition is to make every possible effort to assure that the Strait and the Gulf will remain open to free and innocent passage?" Johnson answered "yes."[95] In Johnson's eyes, however, every effort did not include "the one thing that might have kept [Israel] from acting on its own—a firm guarantee to use force if necessary to reopen the strait."[96] The night of the meeting, Johnson told others he thought it had gone very well: "They came loaded for bear, but so was I! I let them talk for the first hour, and I just listened, and then I finished it up the last 15 minutes. Secy McNamara said he just wanted to throw his cap up in the air, and George Christian said it was the best meeting of the kind he had ever sat in on."[97]

Instead of unleashing Israel, Rusk favored working with the British on the flotilla idea. The United States worked diplomatically to organize a multilateral flotilla, the Red Sea Regatta.[98] The flotilla was envisioned as the third stage in a process that started with UN action, was followed by a maritime declaration on the rights of innocent passage, and, if necessary, ended with the assertion of those rights in an international flotilla.[99] Also, after Eban's visit, the United States continued to urge restraint.[100]

After Eban reported back to the cabinet, Israel again decided to postpone fighting because it preferred a U.S.-led effort to break the Egyptian blockade. Yitzhak Rabin, the chief of staff, later wrote that Eshkol received a warning from Johnson "against going to war and specifically urging us to permit the United States to explore all political avenues. Under the impact of this message, the cabinet decided to wait two or three weeks, in deference to Johnson's request."[101] On May 28, the American ambassador reported that Israel decided "to postpone military action for few weeks in favor of continuing effort to ascertain whether diplomatic activity can solve crisis."[102] Again, the cabinet acted on the basis of U.S. policy: "[Israeli ambassador to the U.S.] Harman said GOI decision had been taken on basis Israeli reliance on President and with emphasis on time factor."[103] When Israel believed the United States would exercise its power in the form of a multilateral flotilla to break the blockade, the Israelis were restrained. On May 30, for instance, Eban told a U.S. official that Israel "is relying on US-UK plan for international force to provide decisive capability."[104]

Throughout these tense weeks, the Johnson administration, more focused on Vietnam than Israel, was mindful of the constitutional and congressional processes that would be necessary to secure support for U.S. intervention in the Middle East. U.S. officials frequently mentioned these domestic constraints to Israeli officials and others as qualifiers to strong U.S. support for Israel during the May–June crisis.[105] The Pentagon, in particular, was concerned about any use of force above and beyond Vietnam, and as a result, many military leaders were not in favor of either a unilateral (U.S.) or multilateral show of force.[106]

Some U.S. officials were aware of the limits of the U.S. restraint effort. In the absence of an iron-clad American promise to open the strait and, in a related sense, to use force if necessary, the United States was unlikely to convince Israel to stay its hand indefinitely. The United States had a limited time frame for action (which, given the Israeli attack on June 5, turned out to be a week shorter than U.S. officials expected).[107] On May 30, Evron told the United States it had "about 10 days."[108] On June 1, Richard Helms, head of the CIA, met with "a senior Israeli official" (probably Amit) and noted that "my visitor had hinted that Israel could no longer avoid a decision." On June 2, Helms reported about the meeting to the president and "added my own conviction that this visit was a clear portent that war might come at any time, with no advance warning."[109]

Israel quickly came to the conclusion that the flotilla idea was moving too slowly, and Israel would need to take action on its own.[110] Meir Amit, the Mossad chief, visited Washington from May 31 to June 2. On June 1, Amit met with McNamara, who gave a vague answer on the flotilla's progress and did not explicitly urge restraint.[111] More generally, Amit had the sense from intelligence and military sources that the flotilla would not come into being.[112] He later paraphrased Helms's warning to him: "There is no task force.... There is no armada of 'maritime powers' and there is no constructive plan of action."[113] On June 2, Ambassador Harman met with Rusk and "said the test of the Strait must be made in the course of next week. Secretary Rusk replied that the test would take place seven to nine days after a decision was reached." The U.S. transcript of the meeting supports the perception that the flotilla idea was moving slowly. The transcript also suggests that activity at the United Nations, originally presented to Israel as a fruitless option needed only to build political support for the flotilla, would drag on for days and push the flotilla even further into the future.[114] Prime Minister Eshkol was sold: "Meir Amit's report from Washington had relieved Eshkol of his lingering qualms; he felt that Israel had been given the go-ahead."[115] Less central U.S. figures (Justice Abe Fortas and UN ambassador Arthur Goldberg) also encouraged Israel to act on its own.[116] On June 1, after hearing about a meeting between Fortas and Evron, Eban felt Israel no longer needed to be restrained.[117] In addition to problems with the flotilla, Israel feared that other diplomatic efforts might allow Egypt to lock in gains from the May crisis, an outcome Israel wanted very much to avoid.[118]

While Johnson still talked to Israel about restraint, some U.S. officials internally argued that the flotilla policy was having problems and might not work at all. In a letter to Eshkol on June 3, Johnson repeated his earlier language: "Israel will not be alone unless it decides to go alone."[119] Johnson's letter was noted at the crucial Israeli Ministerial Defense Committee meeting on June 4.[120] As noted, neither Secretary Rusk nor McNamara opposed restraint.[121] In contrast, Charles Yost, who was working at the State Department but was sent to Egypt, cabled to Washington as to why the flotilla would not reverse Egypt's closure of the strait. Only the unilateral American use of force could do so, but Yost opposed such a move; it was not in America's interest, he wrote.[122] Yost demonstrated that the United States would have to mobilize its power resources in order to undo the blockade and thereby prevent an Israeli attack on Egypt. More important, he made clear that he did not think such a U.S. show of strength was the best course of action.

Scholars have frequently suggested that divisions among U.S. policy-makers undermined the restraint effort. Although the many voices were relevant to the outcome, they were less of a factor than the U.S. failure to provide a viable and timely alternative to an Israeli attack. Israel wanted to reverse Egypt's May 22 closure of the strait.[123] It saw three options involving the use of force: U.S., international (including the United States), or Israeli. Washington was not interested in the first option, and Israel believed the second one was moving far too slowly—and might not happen at all. For Israeli leaders, this left only one alternative: an Israeli attack on Egypt.

By early June, some U.S. officials had become resigned to the fact that the U.S. restraint effort would likely fail.[124] This was not a policy shift. Rather, it was a reflection of the fact that the United States had done what it was willing to do (different from what it *could* have done in terms of U.S. capabilities), but this would not be enough to satisfy Israel's needs.

On June 3, top Israeli military and political figures met at Eshkol's home. Harman and Amit had reported to Eshkol, Minister of Defense Dayan, and others that "there was no chance of unilateral U.S. action or of successful multilateral action. The conclusion was inescapable: Israel was on its own."[125] At this June 3 meeting, Israel's leaders decided to move for war at the cabinet meeting on June 4.[126]

On June 4, the Israeli cabinet voted to go to war. Dayan argued that Israel should not forfeit the military advantage it would get by striking the first blow. Eban emphasized that "Israel would not be isolated after an armed clash."[127] Only two ministers, both from the small, leftist Mapam party, wanted to allow the United States to continue to try to resolve the strait issue.[128]

Quandt calls U.S. policy a red light that changed to yellow. For Oren, the light changed to green.[129] I think other analogies might state the case more clearly. By early June, the United States had played all the cards it was willing to play and recognized that it had a losing hand. It was not that the color of the traffic light had changed; it was that Israel and the United States stopped thinking the traffic light itself was relevant to the outcome. The United States declined either to use its capabilities to coerce Israel not to go to war or to ensure that an alternative, non-Israeli way of opening the strait worked in a timely fashion.[130] In doing so, Washington sealed the fate of its restraint effort.

It is important to stress that the United States did not use or consider either coercion or material rewards to block Israel from launching a war. Unlike the case in 1973, U.S. officials used only rhetoric in hoping to persuade Israel to change its mind. The United States did not mobilize its power resources to bring about successful alliance restraint.

The balance of interests may also have played a secondary role, though the Israeli leadership's view of whether Israel's survival was at stake is not known for certain. U.S. analysts and officials argued that Israel would win any war; some thought it would be close and taxing whereas others foresaw a major Israeli victory.[131] As Johnson told Eban on May 26, "if Israel is attacked, our judgment is that the Israelis would lick them."[132] The Joint Chiefs thought Israel would win in ten days, as did the CIA until it lowered its estimate to seven days.[133] The Israeli military concurred, according to Parker.[134] In contrast, Michael Brecher concludes that many Israeli leaders feared for the state's existence.[135] Richard Helms, director of Central Intelligence, later speculated that "the glum Israeli projection was meant to influence foreign opinion and that more balanced evaluations of the situation were restricted to Israeli government officials."[136] If Israeli leaders thought Israel's survival was at stake in 1967, that would be another reason why U.S. restraint failed.

In his memoir, Rabin, then Israel's military chief of staff, suggests that the Israeli military had serious concerns in terms of the dangerous message that would be sent by a weak Israeli response to Egypt's aggressive moves. Israel's existence was not in immediate danger in late May or early June 1967, but the wrong course would create future difficulties. This view is perhaps a middle ground between the idea that Israel faced no threat and the idea that its immediate survival was at stake. A few hours after Israel learned of Egypt's closure of the Strait of Tiran, Rabin quotes Aharon Yariv, head of Israel's military intelligence during the war: "It's no longer just a matter of freedom of navigation. If Israel takes no action in response to the blockade of the straits, she will lose her credibility and the IDF [Israel Defense Forces] its deterrent capacity. The Arab states will interpret Israel's weakness as an excellent opportunity to threaten her security and her very existence." The Egyptian moves were testing Israeli strength and resolve. Rabin made a similar point to a skeptical Israeli minister:

> Nasser has presented us with a grave provocation. If we don't face that challenge, the IDF's deterrent capacity will become worthless. Israel will be humiliated. . . . Why bother with a state [Israel] whose neighbors are growing stronger and subjecting it to humiliating pinpricks? We're going to war over freedom of navigation. Nasser has threatened Israel's standing; later on his army will threaten Israel's very existence.[137]

Israeli military doctrine had relied on strength to deter Arab attack. Israeli military leaders did not want to undermine that approach in response to Nasser's tests of May–June 1967.

Domestic pressure on Johnson from pro-Israeli Americans was not the decisive factor in determining U.S. policy during the May–June crisis. Pro-Israeli groups wanted the Johnson administration to support Israel during the crisis. Abe Feinberg, a leading member of the American Jewish community, said Johnson was "in constant touch" with him and Prime Minister Eshkol.[138] On May 23, according to one U.S. official, "there was tremendous pressure brought on Johnson to get him to come out for Israel."[139] That night Johnson read a televised statement on the crisis, but the statement had been written and approved before the pro-Israeli lobbying of that day. The president repeated the generic U.S. concerns about the security and territorial integrity of all states in the region, but he also directly condemned Egypt's "purported" closing of the strait, calling it "illegal and potentially disastrous to the cause of peace."[140] This condemnation was in line with the Israeli position.

The pro-Israeli effort did not explicitly support or oppose American restraint but advocated a U.S.-led flotilla to break the blockade. Fortas and David Ginsburg, an attorney and friend of Johnson, asked Johnson to break the blockade of Tiran.[141] Moreover, U.S. efforts to restrain Israel and to promote an international effort to break the blockade continued after May 23. It would have been reasonable for Johnson to conclude that pro-Israeli groups would not approve of a material threat against Israel, but no evidence demonstrates whether he or other officials explicitly made such a connection.[142] On June 3, Johnson spoke largely about domestic policy at a Democratic fundraiser in New York City; many in the audience were important members of the New York Jewish community. Johnson added a few unscripted remarks about the Middle East that were quite general, calling for the preservation of peace and the protection of the territorial integrity of all the countries in the region. His comments on the Mideast were "loudly applauded."[143]

One alternate explanation for the U.S. restraint failure is that the United States concentrated on the less serious maritime threat to Israel and did not address the Egyptian military mobilization. In other words, Israel was most concerned about an Egyptian attack as more Egyptian forces moved into Sinai, not the closure of the strait. Israeli statements that have come to light to date do not emphasize this potential disparity. Israeli officials at the time seemed deeply engaged in the naval aspects, though one could argue that that was only in response to U.S. demands. Although U.S. policy did not directly address the Egyptian mobilization, success at breaking the blockade could have relieved the tension and set the stage for deescalating the crisis. If the flotilla idea had gathered momentum instead of floundering, it might have led diplomats to add other policies to prevent war, perhaps including the issue of Egyptian and Israeli military mobilizations.

The United States Prevents Israel from Launching a Preemptive War, 1973

In 1973, Israel considered but rejected the idea of launching a preemptive strike against Egypt and Syria, as it had done in 1967. One major reason Israel opted not to attack first was a series of strong and consistent warnings from the United States against starting the war. According to several accounts, Washington threatened to withhold aid and arms if Israel started the war. At 2 P.M. local time on October 6, 1973, Egyptian and Syrian forces attacked Israel. By the time the war ended, 2,688 Israelis had been killed.[144] The United States successfully restrained Israel from striking first.

The United States had long urged Israel not to preemptively attack Egypt or Syria. According to one former member of the U.S. National Security Council staff, "It is true that [Secretary of State Henry] Kissinger and [President Richard] Nixon had consistently warned Israel that she must not be responsible for initiating a Middle East war."[145] Kissinger "feared that Israel might start a war, and he warned the Israelis that, if they did, they could not count upon American support."[146] After a Palestinian attack on Soviet Jews in Austria transiting to Israel on September 28, 1973, Kissinger warned Israeli ambassador Simcha Dinitz against escalation that might lead to war.[147]

Kissinger himself vehemently denied to his staff that he had urged Israel not to preempt an Arab attack. On October 23, 1973, near the end of the war and just before the U.S.-Soviet crisis, Kissinger met with other senior U.S. officials and spent significant time denying that he or the United States was responsible for Israel holding back: "We had no incentive in the world to tell anyone not to engage in a pre-emptive attack."[148] Kissinger's syllogism was that if the United States did not know of the impending Egyptian-Syrian attack, as it did not, then Washington could not warn Israel against responding. Yet the United States could still have warned Israel in anticipation of a hypothetical war; in other words, if the Arabs mass to attack, do not repeat 1967 and preempt.

In attempting to restrain Israel, the United States threatened to withhold support. U.S. support was vital to Israel because Israel would need U.S. arms to resupply in the event of a war:

> Kissinger's warning [to Mordechai Shalev on October 6, 1973] was not new. It had been his constant refrain for months. Shalev [chargé d'affaires of the Israeli embassy in Washington] knew it by heart. So did Ambassador Dinitz, who was then in Israel to attend his father's funeral. "Don't ever

start the war," Kissinger would admonish them. "Don't ever preempt!" He would then forecast absolute disaster if Israel ignored his counsel. "If you fire the first shot, you won't have a dogcatcher in this country supporting you. You won't have presidential support. You'll be alone, all alone. We wouldn't be able to help you. Don't preempt." It was the kind of warning no Israeli leader could ignore.[149]

On October 7, the day after Egypt and Syria attacked Israel, Dinitz told Kissinger it was a "hard decision" not to strike first. Kissinger agreed: "But it was right. You would have been killed if you had struck first. It's hard enough as it is."[150]

On the Israeli side, Prime Minister Meir, Defense Minister Dayan, and Dinitz all made the connection between Israeli restraint and the availability of U.S. aid for Israel. Saturday morning, October 6, after her chief of staff asked for permission to strike first, Meir responded: "I know all the arguments in favor of a preemptive strike, but I am against it. We don't know now, any of us, what the future will hold, but there is always the possibility that we will need help, and if we strike first, we will get nothing from anyone."[151] The same day, she offered a more succinct version: "Only if we do not preempt can we be reasonably assured the United States will support us."[152] Dayan explained his position at the same meeting: "I rejected the idea of a pre-emptive strike by the Air Force as well as the mobilization of more reserves than were required for immediate defense. I feared that such moves would burden our prospects of securing the full support of the United States."[153] He added: "And if American help was to be sought, then the United States had to be given full proof that it was not we who desired war—even if this ruled out pre-emptive action and handicapped us in the military campaign."[154] After the war, on November 16, 1973, Meir explained Israeli restraint in the same manner on Israeli television: "I think that so far as everything that happened—including the need for equipment and the obtaining of equipment—had the situation not been clear beyond the shadow of a doubt regarding who began hostilities, I doubt whether the vital equipment received in the course of time would have flowed in as it did, as it still continues to do."[155] Dinitz, who arrived back in the United States from Israel on October 7, "immediately went to see Kissinger and told him that the United States was the main factor behind Israel's difficult decision not to preempt. Therefore he felt justified in suggesting that the United States had a special responsibility to its ally in the matter of military resupply."[156]

On October 5, the day before the war, Israeli policy moved in several directions as it became clearer that Egypt and Syria were planning something. Meir promised not to attack first. She relayed the following message to Kissinger: "We wish to assure you personally that Israel has no intention whatever to initiate offensive military operations against Syria or Egypt."[157] Meanwhile, Israel's chief of staff, General David Elazar, urged the prime minister to launch a preemptive strike, but Meir refused because she had the U.S. warnings on her mind. On October 5, "Elazar conferred with Mrs. Meir. He pleaded for permission to call up the reserves, and he urged her to consider 'as a matter of highest priority' a preemptive air strike against Syrian and Egyptian positions."[158] He also took steps to prepare for launching a preemptive attack. At 11 A.M. on October 5, he "canceled all military leaves, warning his staff that a call-up of reserves, meaning the bulk of the Israeli army and air force, was now possible." He also brought General Ariel Sharon back from retirement.[159] Brig. General Benny Peled, either with or without Elazar's permission, prepared the air force for a preemptive strike.[160]

The next morning, just hours before the war, the United States continued to restrain Israel. Kissinger called the Israeli foreign minister, Eban: "Don't preempt!"[161] Just before 7 A.M., Kissinger called Shalev and said, "We would like to urge you not to take any preemptive action."[162] Kissinger then told President Nixon of this call: "I emphasized to him [Shalev] the essentiality of restraint on the Israeli part, and said there must be no preemptive strike."[163]

In Israel that morning, Meir met with Dayan, Minister without Portfolio Israel Galili, former chief of staff Haim Bar-Lev, and Elazar at her home and again rejected Elazar's calls for a first strike. Elazar pressed for a full mobilization of reserves.[164] Meir explained that he also wanted to strike: "Dado [Elazar] was in favor of a preemptive strike since it was clear that war was inevitable in any case. 'I want you to know,' he said, 'that our air force can be ready to strike at noon, but you must give me the green light now. If we can make that first strike, it will be greatly to our advantage.'"[165] But Meir opposed the strike: "Dayan and Mrs. Meir were convinced, however, that such a step would not be countenanced by Israel's main ally, the United States, and they vetoed Elazar's proposal."[166] "How many friends would we have left if we did that?" she asked Elazar.[167] In addition to concerns about the U.S. reaction, Dayan opposed a preemptive attack on military grounds; he feared it would not be effective. Dayan told Meir that Israel could absorb the initial Arab attack.[168]

Meir next met with the U.S. ambassador to Israel, Kenneth Keating, and promised that Israel would not strike first. Keating reported back to the secretary of state very clearly about his meeting on the morning of

October 6: "In answer to my specific question, Mrs. Meir replied without hesitation that Israel would not rpt not launch a pre-emptive attack, noting that Israel would successfully defend itself if attacked, but emphasizing that the GOI wishes to avoid bloodshed."[169] Meir confirmed that she told Keating that Israel would not strike first.[170] Meir may have met with Keating to convey to the United States the sacrifice Israel had made in the name of restraint—and therefore indirectly highlight the reward in terms of aid and political support that it justly deserved.[171]

Keating also suggested the United States would not aid Israel if Israel attacked first. He did so in an indirect manner:

> As a double check, he [Kissinger] instructed Keating to repeat his warning against preemptive action to Mrs. Meir. According to one Israeli source, Keating heightened the general warning with an implied threat. "If Israel refrained from a preemptive strike, allowing the Arabs to provide irrefutable proof that *they* were the aggressors," Keating was quoted as saying, "then America would feel morally obliged to help" Israel. No translation was needed. If Israel struck first, then the United States would feel *no* moral obligation to help. Israel would be alone.[172]

Keating's message was consistent with previous U.S. suggestions that linked refraining from a first strike and continued U.S. support and aid.

After her meeting with Keating on the morning of October 6, Meir met with top Israeli leaders and rejected a preemptive strike for the final time. In doing so, she again highlighted U.S. policy. Meir convened with her kitchen cabinet, which included Deputy Prime Minister Yigal Allon, Dayan, and Minister without Portfolio Galili. Elazar again "pleaded" for "a preemptive strike against Egyptian and Syrian troop concentrations.... The Prime Minister decided that Israel would accept the first blows." Meir refused to put Israel on full alert or call up additional reserves because it was Yom Kippur, she wanted to avoid provoking the Arab side, the moves would be expensive, "but, perhaps most important, she didn't want to go against Kissinger's injunctions."[173] At their meeting on October 7, Dinitz told Kissinger that the Israeli decision had been influenced by U.S. policy: "I told her [Meir] after Keating left, 'Dr. Kissinger had always told me, whatever happens, don't be the one that strikes first. He told this to Rabin too.' She said, 'You think I forgot?'"[174]

Israel considered a preemptive strike against the Arab side but rejected it, largely due to U.S. pressure. The United States made clear that an Israeli preemptive strike would jeopardize U.S. military aid and political support for Israel in the event of war. The dynamic became especially intense on October 5–6, 1973, when the Israeli chief of staff pushed for such a strike, but Meir resisted, fearful of the American reaction. The U.S. restraint effort, backed up by the threat of material nonsupport, carried the day.

Why did the United States mobilize its power resources in 1973? At the most basic level, the United States was planning "a major diplomatic initiative" after the Israeli elections in October 1973.[175] If Israel started a war, especially if it led to an Israeli victory on the scale of 1967, such an initiative might be blocked or delayed.[176] But the question also suggests two broader explanations tied into U.S.-Soviet relations, both in the region and across the globe.

One could argue that Washington warned Israel not to start a war in order to protect détente. After the Nixon-Brezhnev summits in 1972 and 1973, a slight thaw had developed in the Cold War. A war between American and Soviet clients, Israel and the Arab states, respectively, might undermine détente, but a diplomatic process would advance cooperation. If détente was a cornerstone of Nixon-Kissinger policy, and part of the explanation for Nixon's landslide reelection in 1972, one would expect it to be protected and expanded.[177]

Yet détente was already in trouble behind the scenes before the October war. At the June 1973 summit, the Soviets realized how weakened Nixon was by the unfolding Watergate scandal; Nixon's domestic problems damaged his foreign bargaining position and thus the likelihood of deeper U.S.-Soviet cooperation. Also, in May–June 1973, the Soviets had pressed the Americans for a statement of principles on Middle East peace. In Kissinger's eyes, the Soviet proposal was simply a restatement of the Arab line, and the United States repeatedly rejected these Soviet overtures.[178]

More important, both Nixon and Kissinger later wrote that they saw Arab-Israeli peace as a tool by which to *limit* Soviet influence. In spite of détente, they still sought to freeze the Soviets out of the Mideast and advance U.S. interests. According to Nixon, even Brezhnev knew that "if America was able to contribute toward a peaceful settlement of Arab-Israeli differences, we would be striking a serious blow to the Soviet presence and prestige in the Middle East."[179] Both a U.S.-run peace process and a peaceful outcome would be setbacks for the Soviet Union. The conflict with Israel drove the Arab need for Soviet support and arms. Kissinger added: "We were prepared to discuss overall principles with Moscow in consultation with our ally Israel and, for that matter, with Egypt, with which preliminary talks had already started. We were not willing to play for détente in the coin of our geopolitical position."[180] Kissinger "wanted peace, but without Soviet participation."[181]

In short, the Nixon administration saw an opportunity to undermine Soviet influence in a strategically crucial region. If an Israeli preemptive war had the potential to block that opportunity, U.S. officials would be clear with Israel about the need to refrain from such a policy. Ironically, if U.S. officials had understood Anwar Sadat's intentions of using war to jump-start stalled diplomatic talks, they might have realized that having a war and advancing the peace process were not at odds.

That said, the preceding statement might apply only to Sadat's war— the war that actually was—rather than a war launched by Israel, which might have further humiliated the Arab side, as in 1967. As U.S. policy at the end of the war demonstrated, the United States believed it had to avoid another total Israeli victory if it wanted to advance peace and thereby undermine Soviet power and influence. In sum, the U.S. calculation was to restrain Israel to promote Arab-Israeli peace in order to reduce Soviet influence in the Middle East and advance the Western cause in the Cold War.

The United States Stops Israeli Intervention in Lebanon (1977)

In September 1977, the United States successfully pressured Israel to withdraw some forces from southern Lebanon. President Jimmy Carter used explicit material threats to restrain Israel. Advanced technology allowed the United States to overcome Israeli deception, the claim that Israel had already removed its forces from Lebanon.[182]

Israel intervened in a fight between Christian militias, Israel's allies, and Palestinian forces. This action broke Israeli prime minister Menachem Begin's pledge to Carter to consult if Israel was considering any move in Lebanon. In talks in July 1977, Begin had "promised that Israel would never take the United States by surprise [in southern Lebanon]."[183] In September, the United States objected to Israel's use of American-supplied armored personal carriers (APCs). Israel was allowed to use American arms only for "legitimate self-defense," according to U.S. legislation, the Arms Export Control Act of 1976, and Washington argued that this defensive stipulation did not apply to the Israeli intervention in Lebanon.

Israel claimed that it removed the APCs, but U.S. satellite technology indicated that the APCs were still in Lebanon. The United States had just begun receiving real-time satellite feeds, and this technological advance allowed U.S. officials to verify Dayan's promise that the APCs were out. Carter was now doubly upset because he had been defied twice, first by Begin's failure to consult and then by Dayan's claim that the APCs had left Lebanon.

Carter's message to Begin on September 24 was blunt and threatened material consequences if Israel did not comply. The Israeli move violated the U.S.-Israeli agreement on "American military equipment," and "if these actions are not immediately halted, Congress will have to be informed of this fact, and that further deliveries will have to be terminated."[184] When the message was conveyed to Begin, he responded angrily. But when the U.S. diplomat asked Begin what Israel's answer would be to the American request, Begin calmed down, poured two glasses of whiskey, and conceded the point. Israel withdrew the American equipment.

Why did the United States threaten to stop arms deliveries to Israel? In the first year of the Carter administration, U.S. officials were focused on convening an Arab-Israeli summit in order to advance the peace process. For this effort to work, the Arab parties had to trust Washington, even though everyone knew the United States was Israel's ally. Carter feared that the Israeli use of U.S. arms in Lebanon "would undermine his credibility with Arab leaders."[185] This, in turn, would make the conference more difficult to convene.

Israel's military policy in this case was of less overall significance than in the other cases in this chapter, and that might be one reason Israel withdrew so quickly once pressed. Although this case involved Israeli security, it lacked the major-war urgency of 1967, 1973, or 1982. William B. Quandt, a member of Carter's National Security Council staff with responsibility for Arab-Israeli affairs, notes that the fact that this case was of less consequence for Israel might have made Begin more willing to concede at the end of the day.[186]

The United States Fails to Stop the Israeli Invasion of Lebanon (1982)

The Israeli invasion of Lebanon contained two notable examples of restraint failure. First, the invasion, on June 6, 1982, followed a failed U.S. effort to prevent an Israeli attack. Second, on June 9–10, Israel also defied President Ronald Reagan's call for an Israeli-Syrian cease-fire in Lebanon; Israel preferred another day of fighting to solidify its position.

The United States failed to restrain Israel because Washington did not mobilize any resources to threaten or induce Israel. Furthermore, on some issues, Reagan officials did not send a consistent message of restraint. In particular, U.S. secretary of state Alexander Haig did not fully oppose an Israeli military move.

From late 1981, Israeli officials informed the United States of plans for a large-scale invasion of Lebanon that might involve Israeli-Syrian clashes.[187] Ariel Sharon, then Israel's minister of defense, mentioned the possibility of a clash with the Syrians.

Israel's desire to give the United States advance notice may have stemmed from the ex-post U.S. reaction to several unilateral Israeli moves earlier in 1981. After Israel bombed an Iraqi nuclear facility at Osiraq on June 7, 1981, the United States "ordered an investigation of possible Israeli violations of the Arms Export Control Act" because Israel had used U.S.-supplied aircraft for the attack; suspended shipments of four F-16s that Israel had already paid for; and voted in favor of a UNSC resolution condemning the attack.[188] An order for six more F-16s was frozen in July after Israel bombed the PLO headquarters in Beirut on July 17.[189] When Israel extended Israeli law to the occupied Golan Heights on December 14, 1981, Washington suspended the just-signed U.S.-Israeli Memorandum of Understanding on Strategic Cooperation. It was reinstated in 1983.[190]

In general, Washington tried to block an Israeli invasion. The U.S. ambassador to Israel at the time recalls, "For six months, Haig, [Philip] Habib, [Morris] Draper [Habib's deputy], other U.S. officials, and I had urged maximum restraint, cautioned against exaggerating the PLO military threat, railed against the danger of triggering a major war with Syria, and stressed the broader international implications of unrestrained Israeli military retaliation."[191] Reagan wrote to Begin in January 1982, "urging restraint."[192]

The United States also sought a diplomatic solution and called on several interested European countries, including France, Ireland, and Norway. Haig later argued that the "fact that diplomatic alternatives to war existed weakened the will to war."[193]

Secretary of State Haig offered Israel some openings for action, however. Reagan and Haig believed Israel had a legitimate right to self-defense, and Haig's warnings to Israel were not always categorical. In an October 1981 meeting with Begin, he said, "If you move, you move alone. Unless there is a major, international recognized provocation, the United States will not support such an action."[194] Haig used similar terminology in a February 1982 meeting with the IDF's chief of military intelligence and a May 1982 meeting with Sharon.[195] As a former U.S. official and noted analyst of U.S. policy explains, the phrasing left Israel some wiggle room: "To some, that sounded like an invitation to find a pretext to go to war."[196] In general, Haig emphasized three points: self-defense, provocation, and the proportionality of the Israeli response.[197] Ironically, in Haig's memoir the chapter on Lebanon is titled "Lebanon: 'Mixed Signals Bedevil Our Diplomacy.'"[198]

Still, on May 28, 1982, just after the Haig-Sharon meeting at which Sharon claimed Haig signed off on the invasion, Haig "wrote directly to Begin expressing concern over a possible offensive and called on Israel to exercise 'absolute restraint.'"[199] Moreover, Sharon was not concerned with the idea that Haig's view was not representative of other members of the Reagan administration.[200]

In addition, even those who argue that Haig tacitly approved a limited Israeli invasion stopping forty kilometers into Lebanon, as Begin had promised Reagan, agree that neither Reagan nor Haig supported a grand Israeli invasion that took Israeli forces all the way to Beirut—as actually occurred.[201] In terms of this book, then, even if the initial Israeli invasion was not a restraint failure (because, some claim, the United States gave Israel a green or yellow light for a *limited* invasion), the Israeli drive all the way to Beirut was a restraint failure because all U.S. officials agreed that Israel should not launch a full-scale attack.

In addition to a lack of elite consensus in Washington, the United States never threatened ex-ante to do anything to Israel if it invaded despite U.S. opposition. Washington did not mobilize its resources in order to achieve restraint but instead relied only on rhetorical opposition: "Not once did he [Haig] suggest to Begin that the penalty for using United States equipment in such an attack might be the suspension of further military aid."[202] Haig's letter of May 28, for example, "contained no hint of a threat or ultimatum to Israel."[203] More generally, Israel was not told before the war of the few "modest" measures that Washington eventually enacted. Haig later wrote that he "never believed that mere words would restrain Israel."[204]

Once the war started, U.S. sanctions were still quite limited. In internal meetings in the early days of the invasion, Vice President George H. W. Bush and Secretary of Defense Caspar Weinberger suggested the United States should impose sanctions for the offensive use of U.S. arms, but they were blocked by Haig, U.S. ambassador to the United Nations Jeane Kirkpatrick, and CIA director William Casey.[205] In addition, even when, for instance, the United States decided to postpone the formal notification to the U.S. Congress of the sale of 75 F-16s to Israel, the decision was not initially depicted as a penalty for Israel's policies in Lebanon. The Reagan administration suspended a shipment of cluster bombs but allowed the flow of most arms and spare parts to continue.[206]

The United States also failed to attach material conditions to its call for a cease-fire in Reagan's June 9, 1982, letter to Begin. Reagan called for a cease-fire on June 10 at 6:00 a.m. Israel's refusal, Reagan wrote, "will aggravate further the serious threat to world peace and will create extreme tension in our relations."[207] The letter offered no explanation of "extreme tension," however, and made no mention of any penalties.

In a second example of restraint failure, Israel again defied the United States and agreed to a cease-fire on June 11, 1982, only when further Israeli military objectives had been accomplished. Early on June 10, the Israeli cabinet met to consider Reagan's request: "The ministers were in no mood to bow to an American *diktat.*" Sharon told other ministers that Reagan's letter was an "ultimatum, which should not be acquiesced in." Instead of agreeing to a cease-fire on June 10, the Israeli cabinet delayed while Israeli forces in Lebanon continued to advance; the cease-fire went into effect on June 11.[208]

Why did the United States not take material steps with Israel either before the invasion or when the cease-fire was under discussion? I think two explanations are plausible, although the documentary paper trail is not yet available. First, some U.S. officials, most significantly Reagan and Haig, had sympathy for Israel's right to self-defense. Given that sympathy, they might have been reluctant to press Israel too hard and imply that Israel's hands were tied when faced with attacks from PLO forces based in Lebanon. A second possibility is that Israeli deception, or really Sharon's deception, was successful. The United States did not realize Israel was going to pursue an extensive invasion of Lebanon including a drive to Beirut. Had the United States known, it would have acted more aggressively to stop the Israeli move. Israel misled U.S. officials and thereby hampered the U.S. ability to rein in Israel. These two possibilities remain tentative barring further documentary revelations or other information.

The United States Prevents Israeli Attacks on Iraq, 1991

The United States restrained Israel during the 1991 Persian Gulf War. By using positive and negative sanctions, Washington prevented Israel from retaliating against Iraqi ballistic missile attacks. Washington elites sent a consistent restraint message, mobilized U.S. capabilities, and developed an alternative policy (albeit a contested one).

On August 2, 1990, Iraq invaded and occupied Kuwait. The United States built a wide coalition to oppose the Iraqi occupation and feared that Israeli involvement in the war against Iraq might anger Arab members of the coalition such as Saudi Arabia and Syria. If Israel participated, the United States worried, Arab states might abandon the anti-Iraq coalition. As a result, even before the fighting began in 1991, the United States expected that Israel would not participate militarily in the war to expel Iraq from Kuwait.

Before the start of the war in January 1991, the United States and Israel exchanged views at many meetings on the possibility of Israeli retaliation. Israel claimed it would not be restrained by U.S. opposition. In mid-September 1990, both Defense Secretary Dick Cheney and National Security Advisor Brent Scowcroft asked Israel not to hit back. Israeli defense minister Moshe Arens rebuffed them: "I told him [Scowcroft] that if we were attacked we would hit back."[209] In December, Israel's prime minister, Yitzhak Shamir, met with President George H. W. Bush in Washington. Bush asked what Israel would do if hit by missiles. Shamir "told him that we would defend ourselves and that we would consult with him. He understood that I was saying that we would not seek permission to take action."[210] Some have suggested that Shamir agreed not to strike first at this meeting.[211] In January 1991, just days just before the start of the war, Cheney and other U.S. officials frequently repeated the message of restraint.[212]

In the official document laying out U.S. objectives in the war, Bush included the desire to restrain Israel. The president signed National Security Directive 54 on January 15, 1991. He included the objective of precluding the "Iraqi launch of ballistic missiles against neighboring states and friendly forces." NSD 54 also contained a section specifically dealing with Israel: "The United States will discourage the government of Israel from participating in any military action. In particular, we will seek to discourage any preemptive actions by Israel. Should Israel be threatened with imminent attack or be attacked by Iraq, the United States will respond with force against Iraq and will discourage Israeli participation in hostilities."[213] Whether or not Israel was attacked, the United States hoped to restrain Israel.

Once the fighting began, in January 1991, Iraq attacked Israel with ballistic missiles (SCUDs). The missiles did not include nonconventional warheads, as some had feared; they caused some damage but few casualties.

The United States urged Israel not to retaliate: "The Americans pleaded for restraint."[214] Before the war, Israel declined to rule out retaliation, but Shamir committed to "genuine consultation" with the United States.[215] Secretary of State James A. Baker later claimed he spent "most of my energies" in the first days of fighting pushing Israel for restraint.[216]

After the first SCUD attack on Israel, on January 18, 1991 (Israeli time), U.S. officials continued to press Israel not to respond. On January 18, for instance, President Bush spoke with Prime Minister Shamir, informed him that U.S. forces were hunting for the launchers, and said, "I hope you leave it to the coalition to act against Iraq."[217] Bush repeated his message the next day after a second wave of SCUD attacks on Israel. Top U.S. officials traveled to Israel "to hold the Israeli hand," a move that Scowcroft called "probably the deciding factor in dissuading Shamir from retaliating."[218]

On January 19, after the second SCUD attack, Israel was poised to attack, but the United States refused to cooperate. Defense Minister Arens ordered Israeli aircraft aloft and called Defense Secretary Cheney. "Israel's patience is running thin," Arens said, "and it is deeply disappointed with the US failure to stop the missile attacks." Arens requested an air corridor, the identification-friend-or-foe (IFF) codes, and a U.S. effort to get Saudi Arabia to let Israeli aircraft enter its airspace as part of hunting the missiles. Cheney declined; U.S. forces were doing all that could be done. Arens then made the same request of Baker, who also declined.[219] Arens continued pressing U.S. officials as the war continued, including at a meeting with President Bush in Washington on February 11, 1991.[220] On January 23, Shamir formally asked the United States to allow Israeli retaliation.[221] In general, however, Shamir maintained a policy of restraint despite the repeated calls from a handful of ministers to retaliate.[222]

The Israeli cabinet approved Israeli attacks subject to coordination with the United States. When that coordination was not forthcoming because the United States refused to allow operational coordination or to provide Israel with satellite imagery of western Iraq for targeting, Israel's hands were tied. Israel did not want to risk a conflict with U.S. aircraft, a war with Jordan started by Israel's use of Jordanian airspace to reach Iraq, or the collapse of the anti-Saddam coalition. Israel called off individual attack operations several times in late January due to the lack of military and technical coordination with the United States.[223]

Washington relied on a number of positive and negative inducements to ensure that Israel would not fire back or hunt for the SCUDs itself. On the positive side, the two allies established a secure communications link, known as Hammer Rick, which could be used to warn Israel of imminent missile attacks. This information allowed Israel to increase the warning time before missiles struck.[224] The United States also moved Patriot missile batteries to Israel and gave aid to Israel. U.S. diplomats traveled to Israel several times during the crisis and war period. On the negative side, the United States limited Israel's access to real-time data and refused to provide IFF codes that Israeli pilots would need to avoid clashing with U.S. aircraft.[225] Baker later noted, "Our refusal to give Israel the electronic codes was critical to this outcome."[226] The United States also refused to accept Israeli codes.[227]

The United States also tried to provide an alternative to Israeli retaliatory action by promising that U.S. forces would hunt for the mobile SCUD missile launchers in western Iraq. On January 10, 1991, for instance, Cheney spoke with Arens: "I want to emphasize that the targets in western Iraq will be dealt with by the U.S. Air Force, including all targets that could be a threat to Israel."[228]

U.S. forces did pursue the SCUD launchers, but Cheney and General Norman Schwartzkopf, commander of U.S. forces during the war, disagreed over the policy. Schwartzkopf did not want to divert significant U.S. resources from the Kuwaiti theater of operations for SCUD-hunting missions in western Iraq. In practice, this meant that the United States devoted less military effort to stopping the missile attacks than it had led Israel to believe.[229] In this case, the alternative policy offered by the restrainer, the United States, was not a key factor in either securing or undermining Israeli restraint.

In terms of the balance of interests, Israel's survival was not at stake, but the situation could have been quite different. Had the SCUD missiles included nonconventional weapons and/or caused major casualties, Israel might have responded regardless of the U.S. position. As Lasensky notes, luck played a role in that the attacks caused no serious damage.[230] Although Iraq could have armed the missiles with chemical warheads, it was apparently deterred from doing so.[231]

Israel also benefited from restraint in two important strategic ways, but it remains unclear whether these factors influenced Israeli decision makers. For Israel, the Gulf War removed a major threat and the linchpin of the long-feared Eastern front, the idea of an Arab conventional attack on Israel from Jordanian territory. Iraqi forces were always thought to be the key to an attack from the east. As a bonus, Israel did not even have to do the heavy lifting; the United States was taking care of eliminating this strategic threat. The Israeli public, according to Shamir, favored restraint as Israel's "contribution to the erasing of an evil regime."[232] In addition, restraint meant that Israel's "strategic alliance with the US could be strengthened and long-term benefits could be derived."[233] In short, a major enemy would be removed by someone else's forces, and Israel would draw closer to its most important ally (which also happened to be the strongest country in the world).

These two strategic goals point to the general way in which restraint may change the relationships between a state's foreign policy objectives. In this case, the need to retaliate to maintain Israel's deterrent strength could be weighed against a weaker Iraq and a tighter U.S.-Israeli alliance, which were both more likely given Israeli non-involvement or restraint. Once a restraint attempt is made, it may shift the calculus. Absent the U.S. restraint effort, Israel could have pursued all these goals. Once the United States asked Israel to stand aside, however, Israel could not achieve all these objectives simultaneously.

The reason for the all-out American push for Israeli restraint is straightforward. The United States was launching a war involving hundreds of thousands of U.S. soldiers and sought to minimize any perturbations such as an Israeli move that might drive away Arab support for the U.S.-led attack. The failure of the American war effort would be a major blow to U.S. national security in the largest combat operation since the end of the Vietnam conflict. The United States had a very strong national security interest in managing Israeli policy and was willing to mobilize its power resources to make Israel fall into line. The Iraqi invasion of Kuwait affected a vital American interest, the free flow of oil at a reasonable price, and the U.S. stance toward Israel was a corollary of that initial determination. Given conventional Iraqi warheads, the balance of interests favored Washington.

One alternative explanation for the 1991 case is that domestic opponents of the contested military policy, Israeli retaliatory strikes on Iraq, used the restrainer's effort as a tool to win the internal debate about the policy. Such an argument is plausible in the 1991 case, as well as the 1973 case, but it complements rather than undermines the overall argument about power mobilization and the success or failure of restraint. It may suggest another mechanism by which such power mobilization works; in other words, it is not a pure alternative explanation. Inside the restrainee's government, opponents of the contested military policy point to the restrainer's opposition. That argument carries weight precisely because the restrainer is capable of inducing and threatening. External opposition is not ipso facto a powerful argument for internal opponents of the policy. Israeli officials who mention U.S. opposition will have a significantly better chance of winning the argument than if the restrainer had been Micronesia. This possibility that the restraint effort is a domestic political football between contending factions also serves to highlight the role of leadership (dis)unity.

The United States Prevents Israeli Arms Sales to China in 2000 and 2005

The United States has twice restrained Israel over arms sales to the People's Republic of China. In 2000, Israel canceled the sale of the Phalcon, an advanced, airborne early warning system, under U.S. pressure. Although there is no evidence of presidential sanctions against Israel, members of Congress openly discussed cuts to Israeli aid at a time when Israel and the Clinton administration were likely to seek congressional approval for even more American aid as part of the Arab-Israeli peace process. In 2005, Israel dropped a second arms deal, a contract to upgrade Harpy anti-radar drones that Israel had previously sold to China. In this second case, the United States had imposed several military sanctions. In order to avoid future problems, Israel and the United States signed a memorandum of understanding on August 16, 2005, regarding rules and procedures for Israeli arms sales.

In both cases, the United States pressed Israel hard because of the nature of the weapons and the particular recipient, China. The United States has had a long-standing commitment to protect Taiwan, and both weapons sales were seen as a potential help to China should it ever seek to attack Taiwan. Furthermore, many American elites view China as the most likely rising power that one day will be capable of challenging the United States globally. Israeli arms sales that advance China's military modernization are seen in that light, and thus the mobilization of American power to rein in Israel. The United States also claimed that the Harpy case included an element of Israeli deception.

The argument over Israeli weapons sales to China also highlights the fact that some types of restraint may be easier to carry out than others. Although I lump together war, intervention, proliferation, and arms sales, disaggregating the military policies offers some explanatory leverage. As with the 1977 Lebanon example, the stakes for Israel are different when the case involves a billion-dollar arms sale to China as opposed to Arab armies massing for attack on the Israeli border.

By mid-2000, Israel Aircraft Industries (IAI) had nearly completed the upgrade of an Ilyushin-76 with the Phalcon early warning system. The $250 million upgrade for China could have led to work for IAI worth about $2 billion.

However, the United States indicated to Israel that it opposed the upgrade. Secretary of Defense William Cohen and Secretary of State Madeleine Albright both expressed U.S. opposition to the sale to Israeli officials. Cohen told them that "the radar system would greatly heighten the risks faced by United States forces in Asia."[234] U.S. military officials "strongly objected on grounds that the radar could upset the China-Taiwan strategic balance and might threaten U.S. forces in some future conflict."[235] When asked about the sale at a press conference on June 28, 2000, President Bill Clinton himself also expressed concern. Nevertheless, I have not seen evidence that the Clinton administration directly threatened Israel with material sanctions.

In Congress, however, opposition to the sale led to talk of cutting U.S. foreign aid for Israel. The most vocal supporter of such a move was Rep. Sonny Callahan (R-Ala.), chair of the Foreign Operations Subcommittee of the House Appropriations Committee, but he was not the only member who opposed the sale. Rep. Benjamin Gilman (R-N.Y.), a strong supporter of Israel and chair of the House International Relations Committee, explained that the "initial [Israeli] decision to make the sale left a great deal of resentment among [House] members." He added that "people thought they were giving too much of an edge to the Chinese militarily."[236] In late June, the Appropriations Committee voted down a proposal from Callahan to dock Israel $250 million in aid.

Israel likely had enough overall backing in Congress to block any major aid cuts, but the timing made the issue much more about support for increased aid to Israel. By late June, Israel and the United States knew they would soon be headed to a summit with Palestinian leaders, what became the Camp David summit of July 11–25, 2000. Had Israeli and Palestinian negotiators reached a final agreement, Israel would have asked the United States for tens of billions of dollars in aid. Rejecting U.S. pleas about the Phalcon sale to China would have angered Congress, jeopardizing such an unprecedented amount of support. Thus the potential financial damage to Israel was much larger than simply the risk of a $250 million assistance cut.

With the possibility of a peace process aid package in mind, Israeli prime minister Ehud Barak informed Clinton in a letter on July 11, 2000, that Israel was canceling the Phalcon sale.[237] July 11 was the same day

Barak and Clinton began their summit with Yasser Arafat and Palestinian negotiators in order to reach a final Israeli-Palestinian peace agreement. In the letter, Barak wrote that "Israel is currently unable to continue the Phalcon project due to Israel's joint effort with the United States to achieve an historic decision regarding Israel's vital interests in the region."[238]

The second U.S.-Israeli dispute over Israeli arms sales to China began in 2004 after the United States learned Israel was planning to sell China upgrades for Harpy anti-radar drones that Israel had sold to China in the 1990s. From the U.S. perspective, the Israeli sale occurred despite a 2003 American request to Israel to refrain from arms sales to China.[239] In 2004–2005, the United States told Israel to stop the sale of the upgrades, and Israel eventually complied.

Overall, high-level American opposition was based on the same factors as in 2000: "Defense officials are concerned that Israeli weapons will be used against U.S. forces in any conflict with China over Taiwan."[240] Many U.S. officials view China as the top security threat not only in relation to the specific security of Taiwan but also in terms of global American hegemony and the potential rise of a peer competitor. The upgraded drones would pose specific problems: "The aircraft, which have a range of about 310 miles, were considered important because they could destroy radar used to guide the surface-to-air missiles that would be instrumental in Taiwan's defense against potential attacks by Chinese missiles and aircraft."[241] Because of the advanced nature of the upgrades, the drones would have had the ability to destroy radar even if the radar sites were turned off.[242] In short, "the dispute reflects mounting U.S. concerns over China. In recent years, U.S. officials have watched warily as China upgraded its military."[243]

Around March 2005, the United States imposed military sanctions against Israel as a result of the proposed Israeli sale to China. Both Secretary of State Condoleezza Rice and Secretary of Defense Donald Rumsfeld signed off on the sanctions in late 2004 or early 2005.[244] U.S. officials blocked Israeli participation in the development of the Joint Strike Fighter, withheld night-vision and other high-tech equipment, and suspended other military programs and development projects.[245] Even Douglas Feith, a strong supporter of Israel inside the U.S. government and then undersecretary of defense for policy, opposed the Israeli sales.[246]

Congress also exerted pressure on Israel. Many of Israel's traditional supporters in the United States opposed the Israeli deal with China.[247]

Proposed legislation targeted Israeli or European firms that wanted to defy the U.S. pressure to cut sales to China: "A version of the fiscal year 2006 defense authorization bill approved by the House May 25 [2005] requires the secretary of defense not to procure any goods or services for five years from any firms that transfer arms to China, a provision that could affect Israel's defense sector, which is one of its largest industries."[248]

Under U.S. pressure, Israel was restrained. By June 2005, Prime Minister Ariel Sharon dropped the arms sales to China and agreed to sign a new agreement clarifying the issue of Israeli arms sales.[249] Israel and the United States signed a memorandum on August 16, 2005 (the document remains classified). It does not allow the United States to veto Israeli sales, but Israel pledged to maintain transparency and consult closely with Washington. Israel also agreed to abide by, but not join, the Wassenar Arrangement on Export Controls for Conventional Arms and Dual-Use Goods and Technologies. Wassenar is a voluntary export-control regime. A statement released on the signing referred to the American-Israeli "strategic alliance."[250] The U.S.-Israeli defense ties limited as a result of the sale would be gradually reinstituted by the American side.

Israeli deception played a central role in the American restraint effort. U.S. officials felt that Israel had tried to pass off the upgrade of the drones as a sale of spare parts, a mere refurbishment rather than an advance in technology and capability.[251] One may speculate that Israeli officials feared just such a U.S. restraint effort if they revealed the true nature of the deal, so they tried not to let the United States know the full extent of the sale. As a result of the deception, the United States refused to deal with certain Israeli defense bureaucrats, including the director general of Israel's Ministry of Defense.[252] In June 2005, Israeli foreign minister Silvan Shalom issued a semi-apology: "If things were done that were not acceptable to the Americans then we are sorry but these things were done with the utmost innocence."[253]

Conclusion

These seven U.S.-Israeli cases demonstrate that a powerful restrainer will prevail with its ally only if it mobilizes its power resources. The United States restrained Israel in 1973, 1977, 1991, and 2000/2005. In each case, Washington used material threats and, in 1991 and the Persian Gulf War, inducements. In 1961–63, 1967, and 1982, the United States failed to restrain Israel. In each case, the United States relied on rhetoric to promote alliance restraint, and in each case the restrainee, Israel, prevailed.

The cases also undercut the normative explanation proposed in chapter 1. Israel and the United States did not coordinate their policies, and Israel often relied on deception to try to avoid American restraint efforts. Deception featured prominently in four of the seven cases: Israeli nuclear proliferation, Israel's intervention in Lebanon with U.S. military equipment, Israel's invasion of Lebanon in 1982, and Israel's arms sale to China in 2004–2005.

Several cases also highlight the importance of the restrainer providing an alternative policy to achieve the same ends. On the issue of nuclear proliferation, the United States decided not to offer an alternative, a U.S. security guarantee. In 1967, one U.S. option (the flotilla) failed, and U.S. officials decided against pursuing a second possibility (unilateral U.S. show of force). In both cases, this contributed to Israel's defiance of U.S. wishes and the failure of the American restraint effort. In contrast, in 1991 the United States implemented an alternative policy, a U.S.-led hunt for Iraq's mobile SCUD missile launchers. Although this alternative was not the primary factor, it helped stay Israel's hand and led to successful alliance restraint.

All the cases in this chapter are examples of the United States restraining Israel. Has Israel ever tried to restrain an American military policy? Israel has tried to stop American arms sales to Israel's Arab adversaries. In these cases, Israel's main instrument was lobbying via its supporters in the United States and Congress. But the overall paucity of Israel-as-restrainer examples, especially on questions of military intervention, might suggest that Israel recognizes that capabilities, not coordination, drive alliance restraint outcomes. It also might be that many U.S. military policies take place in other parts of the world and do not affect Israeli interests. Britain in the 1950s, like Israel, was much weaker than the United States, but it still had global connections and a fresh memory of superpower status and its empire. Nuclear-armed Israel is also more self-reliant in terms of its immediate regional adversaries than Britain was vis-à-vis the Eastern bloc. This meant that Britain could ill afford to let the United States expend precious security resources on secondary concerns in Asia.

In the case of Iraq in 2002–2003, some have argued that Israel warned the United States against intervention or at least occupation and democratization in Iraq.[254] If this view is correct, and some sources have argued strongly for the opposite case, it might be an example of an Israeli effort to restrain the United States.[255] Both arguments might be correct. Israel may have supported toppling Saddam Hussein but opposed a long American occupation and effort to plant democracy in Iraq.

If Israel did, at least in part, try to restrain the United States, it might have believed it could influence U.S. policymakers by making its case on the basis of its own 35-plus years of occupation of an Arab people. Israel also might have aimed to modify, not block, U.S. policy in recognition of the power disparity and the clear American desire to go to war against Saddam Hussein's Iraq. The aim would have been partial, not total, change.

In 2006, the United States did not restrain Israel in its war against Hizbollah in Lebanon. The American decision was a decision not to restrain its ally, Israel, because larger national security objectives dictated that giving Israel a free hand was the best policy. Israeli military action was consistent with U.S. regional policies, including its concern about Iran and its allies, such as Hizbollah. But these fit into larger U.S. goals: the global war on terror and the desire to democratize the Middle East. By taking down Hizbollah, the United States hoped, Israel would help Lebanon's democracy by removing the major obstacle to the consolidation of power under Lebanese prime minister Fouad Siniora. In addition, in American eyes, Israel would be weakening a major terrorist organization.

5

Expanding the Restraint Story

Alliance restraint is a common feature of international relations. The case studies in chapters 2, 3, and 4 support the four findings described in chapter 1. This chapter begins by reviewing the same four findings on alliance formation, alliance management (success/failure), the conditions for power mobilization, and the institutional and other differences between alliance restraint and restraint-like activities in international affairs writ large. Bearing in mind future research on alliance restraint, the chapter then reflects on the potential richness of the historical record surrounding a single event, the 1973 Arab-Israeli War. The next section considers what case studies in bipolar and multipolar international systems might tell us about the current unipolar period, bringing us back to the 2002–2003 debate over the U.S. invasion of Iraq. The concluding section addresses the impact of alliances on international stability.

The Findings

Alliance Formation

Chapter 2 demonstrates that states form alliances to restrain their new partners. Restraint is often not the only motivation, and its importance does not negate the role of threats and similar motives. But in some cases, states form alliances for reasons of control rather than or in tandem with the desire to aggregate capabilities and thereby better protect themselves.

Alliance Management and Power Mobilization

In cases of alliance management, or how decisions are made within an alliance, alliance restraint success depended on the powerful ally's willingness to mobilize its power resources. Whether restrainer or restrainee, the more capable state could prevail if it chose to mobilize its resources either to sanction and induce (as the restrainer) or to go it alone and pay the full costs without alliance assistance (as the restrainee). In 1951, the United States restrained Britain when Washington refused to commit to fighting the Soviets if British intervention in Iran drew in Soviet military forces. In 1954, Britain restrained the United States when the Eisenhower administration needed British support to intervene in Indochina on behalf of French forces, and Britain refused to play along. In 1954–1955, the United States signed a treaty with Taiwan despite British objections to protecting smaller islands in nationalist Chinese hands; Washington could support the treaty with or without London's help. In the second part of the 1956 Suez crisis, U.S. economic pressure forced Britain to agree to a cease-fire and then withdraw its force from Egypt. In 1973, Israel did not launch a preemptive attack against Egypt and Syria in part because Washington warned it might not supply Israel with arms if Israel moved first. In 1977, Israel withdrew its forces from southern Lebanon after the United States threatened to terminate pending arms transfers to Israel. In 1991, the United States used threats and inducements to keep Israel out of the Persian Gulf War with Iraq. In two examples of Israeli arms sales to China, Israel backed down in the face of potential foreign aid problems and, the second time around, in 2005, military sanctions.

In the other cases, the alliance restraint outcome was determined by the opposite tendency, the more powerful state's unwillingness to mobilize its power. In 1956, U.S. rhetorical opposition failed to stop Britain and France from military intervention in Egypt. In 1961–1963, the United States failed to stop the Israeli nuclear program, in part because the Kennedy administration decided against offering Israel a security guarantee. In 1967, the United States did not threaten Israel and tried but failed to organize a multilateral flotilla. The United States rejected the idea of unilateral U.S. action to break the Egyptian blockade. In 1982, efforts to rein in Israel in Lebanon were not accompanied by any threats; U.S. officials who wanted to sanction Israel after the invasion did not prevail.

The case studies in chapters 3 and 4 were useful for assessing whether a norm of policy coordination existed as an example of the kinds of institutional constraints that might limit the influence of the strongest ally. The normative/institutional approach was especially appropriate given that the case studies were of special relationships between Britain and the United States and between Israel and the United States. In both bilateral relationships, this particular normative explanation was lacking. Although there was significant consultation, there was little if any policy coordination. There was little evidence that allies gave up restraint efforts or abandoned contested military policies in order to adhere to a norm of coordination with their friends.

Furthermore, allies often tried to deceive each other with the goal of avoiding or circumventing alliance restraint efforts. In six of the cases in chapters 3 and 4, deceit played a moderate to large role in the restrainee's policies. In 1951, Britain considered ways to recast its proposed intervention in Iran as an anticommunist move so as to win support from Washington. In 1956, Britain and France stopped communicating with the United States in late October so as to avoid further American restraint efforts. In 1961–1963, Israel was not forthright with the United States about its nuclear weapons programs. In 1977, Israel first lied to the United States and suggested it had complied with the U.S. restraint policy, only to be revealed as a liar by new American satellite technology. In 1982, the Israeli minister of defense concealed the extent of Israel's planned invasion of Lebanon not only from the United States but also from many Israeli officials. In 2004–2005, Israel may have misled the United States about an arms transaction with China. States are adaptive, and they seem to respond to the information incentives in the case of potentially punitive policies. If restraint is a danger, allies may suppress information so as to avoid even coming into conflict about the proposed military policy.

This explanation for success or failure based on power mobilization suggests that the key player is the more powerful state. Weak states can prevail only when the powerful ally does not mobilize its resources. If weaker allies can influence that decision—whether to mobilize—they may have more options. That said, the unwillingness or inability of powerful states to mobilize their power is not a rare occurrence.

One alternate explanation is that restrainers mobilize resources only when the threat faced by the restrainee is low. If the restrainee faces a high-level or existential threat, the potential restrainer assumes it will have a hard time succeeding and therefore does not even attempt to restrain. Though one cannot totally rule out this alternative, some evidence undermines it. The British-American cases are not useful in assessing this alternative because none of them dealt with either the defense of the homeland or an imminent nuclear exchange with Soviet forces. But both the 1967 and 1973 wars were arguably about Israel's survival. The United States did not see it that way; in both cases Washington expected Israel to prevail. Yet U.S. policy in the two cases was divergent, as the United States mobilized American resources only in the second case, the 1973 war. In 1991, Iraqi missiles armed with chemical weapons would have posed a grave danger to Israel, but the United States used threats and inducements. So although the intensity of the threat faced by the restrainee is hard to measure precisely, it appears that power mobilization (yes/no) and threat level (low/high) are not strongly correlated.

Explaining Power Mobilization

When do states mobilize their resources in order to restrain an ally? Four important factors are deception, leadership unity, the national security agenda, and the development of substitute policies.

Deception prevents states from restraining or complicates their restraint efforts. As already noted, deception was a moderate to major factor in six of the alliance management cases. Restrainees or potential restrainees will mislead or hide their activities from restrainers or potential restrainers so as to avoid or undermine an alliance restraint attempt. Restrainers have a harder time restraining if they are not aware of a policy to which they would likely object. This seems self-evident, but it is an important obstacle nonetheless.

Unity is also correlated with the mobilization of power resources in order to restrain an ally. The argument is not that this is a causal relationship; the unity is affected by how various leaders perceive the military policy and the larger issue in broader national security terms and whether they feel their survival is at stake. That said, disunity will complicate efforts to mobilize power resources. In 1954, congressional-executive disunity in the United States gave Britain the ability to restrain the United States in Indochina. In 1956, Dulles may have opposed the use of material threats to stop the Anglo-French attack on Egypt. Only when he was out of the loop in November due to illness did U.S. officials embrace a punitive approach toward achieving British compliance. In 1982, all U.S. officials opposed a major Israeli invasion of Lebanon but may have differed on small-scale Israeli attacks. They disagreed about sanctioning Israel after the fact, and those opposed to doing so prevailed.

The unity or lack thereof of leaders also matters for the restrainee. In 1973 and 1991, Israeli decision makers were not fully unified, perhaps easing the ability of the United States to restrain its ally. In contrast, in 1967 all the major Israeli leaders were concerned about the growing Arab threat, even if reports about how likely they assessed Israel's chances for victory remain uncertain.[1] In 1982, Israeli leaders were not on the same page, but it is not clear that U.S. leaders were either.

The most important factor for understanding whether a powerful state will mobilize its power resources is where the alliance restraint attempt fits into its national security framework. If a proposed military policy clashes with some higher security objective, a more powerful restrainer will mobilize its resources to stop it. In 1951, the United States feared that British military intervention could result in a communist Iran. In American eyes, U.S. Cold War concerns trumped British commercial and imperial ones. In 1954–1955, the U.S. need to deter the People's Republic of China and protect America's Pacific flank meant it was willing to defend a broader definition of Formosa than Britain would have preferred. The difference was not vast—neither Washington nor London wanted to unleash nationalist China—but it was enough to lead to different perspectives on the wording of the American-Taiwanese agreement. The United States was willing and able to disregard British sniping and go it alone on the treaty language. In November 1956, the United States used economic coercion with Britain to bring about an end to British intervention in Egypt. To do otherwise would help the Soviets meddle in the region. In 1973, U.S. officials probably perceived that a preemptive Israeli attack would hinder U.S. efforts to achieve Arab-Israeli peace; both the peace process and the hoped-for outcome were a means toward limiting and reducing the Soviet presence in the Middle East. Again in 1977, Israel's intervention in Lebanon might harm U.S. peace efforts. In 1991, U.S. forces were directly engaged in war, and the Israeli desire to fight back against Saddam's missiles was considered secondary. In 2000/2005, Israel's arms sales to China were in areas that might hurt U.S. forces with regard to the American ability to defend Taiwan.

In contrast, in other cases, the powerful ally decided not to mobilize its power resources because to do so would have jeopardized U.S. national security objectives. In the early 1960s, the United States did not offer Israel a full-fledged, public security guarantee because it feared that such an offer would lead to stronger Arab-Soviet ties in response. The Soviet threat and the overall Arab-Israeli framework were paramount, as in other cases, but this time these factors led to a decision not to mobilize U.S. resources.[2] In 1967, members of Congress and military leaders did not favor an American show of force in the Middle East, given the already deep U.S. involvement in Vietnam. This meant a unilateral show of force was out of the question.

A final element in power mobilization is the ability to offer a substitute for the contested military policy. Offering a substitute policy usually means the restrainer must mobilize some aspect of its power resources to threaten or protect its ally, the restrainee. When substitutes failed to materialize or were not offered, restraint was more likely to fail. In 1951, U.S. diplomatic efforts delayed British action, especially in July and August. In 1956, U.S. diplomatic efforts may have delayed British action, but the matter festered for months and diplomatic efforts ran out of steam. In the early 1960s, the United States declined to support an alternative, a full-fledged security guarantee for Israel. In 1967, the United States failed to organize a multilateral flotilla and refused to act unilaterally to break the Egyptian blockade of Tiran. U.S. diplomatic efforts also did not succeed in averting war in 1967. In 1991, the United States succeeded in restraining Israel in part by using American forces to do exactly what Israel wanted to do: to track down Iraqi SCUD missile launchers.

Institutions

How is alliance restraint different from restraint-like efforts in international affairs among non-allies? First, although allies may try to coerce in order to restrain another ally, they do not attack or threaten to use force against their own ally, as would be the case in international relations more generally. This is a crucial distinction since material threats can be an important part of successful alliance restraint. Allies may threaten to throw an ally to the dogs—for example, Britain would be on its own against the Soviets in Iran in 1951—but restrainers do not pledge to join the dogs or, to stretch the metaphor even further, to be the dog themselves. In no case in this book did an ally threaten to use force against its partner in order to restrain that partner.

Even if alliance restraint bears some resemblance to attempts in the regular flow of international affairs to rein in aggressive states, I think it is worth maintaining the distinction and the distinctive terminology. The term *deterrence* may be reserved for relations between non-allies whereas *restraint* may be used for pressure not to act in a certain way within an existing alliance.

Second, the institutional mechanisms created by the alliance facilitate restraint. They may create dependence due to arms transfers, joint planning, or military burden sharing. The case studies demonstrate that alliances facilitate the flow of information between the allies. That information flow is not perfect, however, and allies can still cut it off, as British policy in October 1956 and Israeli policy in the early 1960s demonstrated. But on average the quantity and quality of that information will be more accurate and timelier than information that flows between adversaries. Consultation is an important element in alliance restraint not because it determines the outcome of restraint (success/failure) but rather because it gives the potential restrainer information that might lead to a restraint attempt. As noted in chapter 1, the exchange of information and resultant monitoring and supervision are exactly the kind of functions that some liberals and realists have been ascribing to institutions for the past several decades.

The difference is that these informational functions set the stage for the exercise of power rather than constrain the exercise of power. The alliance institution is neither epiphenomenal nor determinative. It is somewhere in between, consequential yet still subject to the existing power dynamics between allies great and small. So the normative explanation of policy coordination falls short, but the alliance's institutional mechanisms can nonetheless serve a role that distinguishes alliance restraint from run-of-the-mill influence attempts in the international arena.

The Anglo-American and American-Israeli case studies also shed light on the difference between stopping a proposed policy and reversing one already undertaken. For example, is it easier to deter a state from invading its neighbor or to compel it to withdraw after the invasion has taken place? Though the results in terms of alliance restraint are only tentative, it is noteworthy that cases in which restrainees were asked to undo a policy already in motion were always successful. The United States forced Britain out of Suez, pressed Israel to remove its armored personnel carriers from southern Lebanon in 1977, and reversed signed Israeli arms deals with China.[3] The restrainer in these cases—the United States—used material instruments because of the high stakes or overall national security agenda as well as other factors. One may also speculate that because

U.S. officials were seeking to reverse a policy already in place, they recognized the need to go beyond mere alliance restraint rhetoric.

The Richness of the Historical Record: The 1973 War

This book presents almost twenty cases of alliance restraint, but many more exist. Unless alliance restraint is regarded as a distinct category, many of these episodes are not seen as part of a broader phenomenon. One of the cases in this book, the 1973 Arab-Israeli War, nicely illustrates the extent to which intra-alliance interactions are a crucial part of the international historical record. That all these interactions are linked has been overlooked, an omission that could be rectified only by careful attention to multiple cases and relationships.

In chapter 4, the section on the 1973 war dealt with the successful U.S. effort to block an Israeli preemptive strike, but this restraint attempt was just one of the alliance dynamics surrounding the war. For example, Egypt and the Soviet Union, which had been allies since the mid-1950s, signed a Treaty of Friendship and Cooperation on May 27, 1971.[4] Egypt modified its alliance with the Soviet Union in July 1972 by calling for the expulsion of Soviet military advisers. Approximately 15,000–20,000 Soviet military advisers and air and anti-aircraft forces from Egypt left the country.[5] Egyptian president Anwar Sadat publicly announced the expulsion on July 18, 1972.[6]

Egypt expelled the Soviet advisers because it wanted to go to war against Israel but the Soviet Union, as of mid-1972, did not support such a war. Egypt feared restraint by its ally. Karen Dawisha, citing Sadat, claims Leonid Brezhnev warned Sadat in April 1972 and three other times before the war "not to attack Israel within her pre-1967 boundaries."[7] In order to avoid further Soviet restraint attempts, Egypt partially broke with Moscow: "as Sadat said many times, this ability to act independently of Moscow's wishes was the very purpose of the decision to expel the Russians in July 1972."[8] Cairo did not cut all links with Moscow, and Soviet arms transfers to Egypt were an important element leading up to the war. Without the advisers, Egypt could more easily decide to go to war against Israel and worry less about being restrained by its Soviet ally. Yet other states misinterpreted the move, providing support for the idea that outsiders are not always aware of the actual motivation for the formation, management, and collapse of alliances. For example, Kissinger "interpreted Sadat's expulsion of the Soviet presence as a calming of the situation."[9]

At the start of the war, Soviet and American officials both expected the other to rein in its ally. Kissinger called Soviet officials and told them to restrain their Egyptian allies in order to prevent the outbreak of war.[10] At the end of the war, the Soviet Union expected that the United States would be willing and able to rein in its Israeli partner when Israel continued fighting after the passage of the first cease-fire resolution.[11] At the times when the junior allies did not fall into line, the other side was left to wonder if it was the junior ally acting on its own and defying its senior ally or if the other superpower was not actually making an effort to restrain its partner.

The American airlift of arms to Israel exposed a schism in a different alliance, NATO. Though Portugal allowed the United States to use the Lajes air force base in the Azores for refueling and shipment of arms to Israel during the 1973 war and West Germany secretly allowed the United States to draw arms from weapons stored there, many other NATO allies declined on both counts. Britain, France, Greece, Italy, and Turkey were all concerned that if they helped with the American airlift to Israel, they would be the targets of the Arab oil weapon.[12] Over 70 percent of Western Europe's oil came from Arab suppliers; Portugal was less vulnerable because it received a substantial amount of its oil from Angola.[13]

Exactly why Portugal worked with the United States on the airlift is unclear. Some sources suggested that Portugal asked for and received U.S. diplomatic support in debates over Portugal's African colonies. As a result, the "United States subsequently voted against the United Nations resolution welcoming the 'independence' of the Republic of Guinea Bissau and condemning Portugal for its illegal 'occupation' of the Republic."[14] Walter Boyne claims the United States pledged to remove an anti-Portugal amendment from congressional foreign aid legislation.[15] Other sources suggest that the United States pressured Portugal. The Azores deal was concluded "only after a strong personal message from Nixon to Prime Minister Marcelo Caetano, in which Nixon may have threatened that the United States would cease to give Portugal crucial military aid if it did not cooperate."[16]

The war also demonstrated that states simultaneously pursue deterrence and alliance restraint. After the Soviet's threatening message near the end of the war, the U.S. response, Kissinger's "customary diplomatic jujitsu," combined a public response to deter the Soviets, raising the American alert status, and private pressure on Israel to accept the cease-fire on the Egyptian front. Kissinger used a similar combination with the Christmas bombing in North Vietnam in 1972.[17]

Finally, the American airlift affected Israeli fears about a closer alliance with the United States. Some Israelis feared not only being restrained by Washington but also being perceived by their adversaries as militarily weak because they were dependent on the United States. As noted in chapter 4, Sharon was one prominent Israeli strategic thinker who held such a view. At the same time, other Israelis welcomed the U.S. support and saw close ties with the United States as a potentially major deterrent to future Arab attacks. In their eyes, the airlift of American arms was a positive development that demonstrated to all onlookers just how much a superpower, the United States, cared for Israel's survival.

In sum, these examples of intra-alliance interactions related to the 1973 Arab-Israeli War highlight the presence of alliance restraint in international affairs. The universe of cases could be greatly expanded in future research.

Studying the 1973 war and the other cases in the book suggests that in future research one could disaggregate several of the key factors that have been treated similarly here. The type of alliances may vary. Restrainers will target different types of policies; less vital policies will likely be easier to renounce in a restraint dispute. Although the categorization here tended toward lumping together evidence, future scholars might add further nuance on alliance restraint by splitting apart some of the very same categories.

A Unipolar World

Almost all the cases studied in this book took place in a bipolar international system. Two of the alliance formation cases took place in a multipolar world. Yet because the United States is the only remaining great power, today the international system is a unipolar one. Polarity is relevant to the study of alliance restraint, but it is not the central factor explaining the frequency of restraint. We might expect fewer attempts to restrain the superpower, but other allies may still try to restrain each other. Unipolarity might have its greatest effect on the ability of other states to restrain the superpower. With no other great powers, the costs of a go-it-alone approach might seem lower.

Since the start of the unipolar period in 1991, there have been enough differences in interests and enough wars and military interventions to serve as cause for restraint attempts within alliances. Although many of the cases in this book involve the United States, alliance restraint may occur across many types of alliances and with many different types of countries (at least in terms of power). Perhaps if a unipolar world meant fewer alliances overall, the amount of alliance restraint might decrease, but the world has not seen a dwindling number of alliances since the end of the Cold War.

A related possibility is that even if the superpower in a unipolar world has less need for alliances, the 190-plus lesser states still bicker and feud and need partners. Thus it might be that in a unipolar world, in theory, the alliance restraint problem moves "below" the superpower level of international politics.

In terms of the success or failure of restraint, the cases in this book suggest ways that even the most powerful state could fail to restrain or could successfully be restrained by its partners, however small in terms of power those partners may be. If the sole great power in the system is unwilling to mobilize its power resources and either coerce a restrainee or disregard a restrainer and thereby go it alone, weaker states can avoid being restrained by the superpower or they can restrain the mighty state.

But the lone superpower, especially when it is the restrainee, is going to have a clear advantage given the importance of power mobilization for restraint success or failure. A pole will almost always have enough resources to go forward on its own without restraint. By definition, it does not have to worry about being checked by another superpower; there is no other great power.

The George W. Bush administration's coalition of the willing was an example of this phenomenon. If other states wanted to play by American rules, they could be allies in a particular war. But if they did not like something about the U.S. approach, they were free to stand aside. Washington acted with or without them; it had the capabilities to do so. With the invasion of Iraq in 2003, the United States acted without the support of many of the world's middle powers, some of which were close U.S. allies. In 2001 in Afghanistan, the United States wanted to avoid the kinds of military problems created by NATO involvement in the 1999 Kosovo War. As one top senior U.S. official said anonymously, "The fewer people you have to rely on, the fewer permissions you have to get."[18]

A pole could still run into a problem even with its massive capabilities because some issues are much more amenable to multilateral, not unilateral, solutions. The natural environment is a classic example of such an issue, but so too are intelligence gathering, counterterrorism, and nation building. So the Bush administration *could* go to war against Iraq without the approval of many allies, but it ended up paying a very high price for doing so. Capabilities and issue type shape whether the ability to disregard allies and go it alone is a workable option that is likely to lead to policy success.

One puzzle, then, is why U.S. allies even bothered to try to restrain the United States in 2002–2003. In a rational world, one might expect other allies to realize the United States could move without them and therefore not even try to restrain. Perhaps they saw some symbolic or domestic political value in opposing the United States despite the odds. Perhaps they realized they would not stop Washington but hoped for some modifications in the U.S. approach. Alternatively, maybe some recalcitrant allies recognized that at least some aspects of the Iraq situation would ultimately require multilateral cooperation, and so they tried to make that happen up front.

The rational assumption is also questionable. Weak allies usually will not know exactly where the powerful ally draws the line between acceptable policy disagreement and a restraint-worthy military policy. A weaker ally may test the powerful ally, perhaps assuming it knows what it is likely to get away with as a potential restrainee or what it might be able to obstruct as a potential restrainer. When the weaker ally guesses wrong, the result may be a crisis like the tension among Western nations in 1956 as a result of the Suez war.

Future Cases and the 2003 Iraq War

The Iraq case sheds light not only on polarity but also on the alliance relations between strong and weak allies. In this book, only two of the eleven alliance management cases involve a weak state trying to restrain a strong one. In one case, Anglo-American differences over the Taiwan Straits in 1954–1955, the stronger ally, the United States, prevailed. In the other case, the question of military intervention in Indochina in 1954, Britain was able to restrain the United States only because of differences over U.S. policy between members of Congress and the Eisenhower administration.

Future research that looks for more cases of weak states trying to restrain strong ones would help test the strength of the power mobilization explanation and especially verify whether the ways in which weak states prevail in restraint disputes are consistent with the explanation. Is it correct that weak states restrain stronger ones when strong states stumble by failing to mobilize power resources or by disagreeing at the elite level? How important is the national security framework of the stronger ally?

The presence of only two cases of this type also raises a larger question of selection bias. Much as deterrence studies explained in the past, certain types of alliance restraint cases might be less likely because they select out at an earlier stage in the alliance interactions, prior to an actual recorded attempt at restraint.[19] Perhaps weak allies that consider restraint often reject even making the attempt because of their weaker position. Perhaps the idea is not even considered—it is subrationally unthinkable—because of the power disparity. This last possibility would be especially difficult to address because the historical record would not show signs of nonconsideration of alliance restraint. At best, researchers might be able to point to circumstances in which a restraint attempt would have been a logical policy given a weaker ally's interests and note that it was not even considered, let alone attempted.

In 2002–2003, the debate over attacking Saddam Hussein's Iraq pitted the most powerful country in the world, the United States, against several of its lesser allies. The weak states were the restrainers and the strong state was the restrainee. Both the overall decision to attack Iraq and one prominent aspect of the way in which the United States went to war, seeking UN support and then abandoning the UN route, provide further support for the power mobilization explanation.

The United States was willing to carry the military burden in the face of heated opposition from France, Germany, Saudi Arabia, and Turkey. France and Germany led much of the international opposition at the United Nations; Saudi Arabia and Turkey denied the United States the ability to attack Iraq from their territory. Still, the United States did not go it alone because it had support from Britain, Australia, Jordan, Kuwait, and some smaller countries. But if one thinks of a go-it-alone approach versus a multilateral one as a continuum rather than a dichotomous choice, the United States clearly leaned toward the go-it-alone approach. Many called the U.S. approach unilateral, though it was more accurate to call it less multilateral and more ad hoc (a coalition of the willing) than had often been the case in the past. This was quite different from the war the United States fought just before Iraq, the war in late 2001 to topple the Taliban regime in Afghanistan, when the United States had widespread support and military contributions from France and other countries that later opposed the Iraqi debacle.

Thus the Iraq war overall offered several examples of weaker allies failing to restrain a stronger one because the powerful restrainee, the United States, was willing to expend significant blood and treasure and possessed the power-projection capabilities to overcome the objections of some of Iraq's neighbors, Saudi Arabia and Turkey. The U.S. war effort was also effective because the United States was not totally alone; Britain contributed thousands of troops, and Kuwait and several other Gulf States accepted a major U.S. military presence. The behavior of the Gulf States, however, ties back into U.S. power, for they welcomed the security, funds, and technology an alliance with the powerful United States can provide. In other words, the mobilization of America's power made some of these alliances, and the war effort as a whole, possible.

A second policy from the Iraq war debate, the issue of seeking UN support for invading Iraq, illustrates one of the ways in which weaker parties can play a role in modifying the policy of more powerful allies. Half a year prior to the outbreak of war, in August–September 2002, the United States agreed to seek United Nations Security Council (UNSC) support for attacking Iraq. Although one UNSC resolution passed, the UNSC was unable to agree on a second resolution in early 2003, and the United States abandoned the effort.

U.S. decision makers were split about seeking UN approval; Secretary of State Colin Powell and other State Department officials pushed hard for a turn to the United Nations. Britain, led by Prime Minister Tony Blair, also urged the Bush administration to seek UN support. Much as in the Indochina question in 1954, the division of opinion on the American side gave the British opinion greater significance. When officials in the powerful state are not united on the correct course of military action, a weaker ally has greater leverage to restrain, in this example by seeking to modify the way in which the anti-Iraq alliance went to war—with or without covering UN resolutions.

Alliance Restraint and International Stability

This study of alliance restraint begs a larger question about international affairs: What is the overall impact of alliance relations on the stability or instability of the international system? To date, alliances have been credited as both a stabilizing and a destabilizing force. Different schools of thought have emerged.

One prominent argument is that the international system is stable when a balance of power exists. In that case, alliances help restore and maintain that balance. When states need to meet a challenge by balancing, they may build up their own arms (internal balancing) or forge alliances with other states (external balancing). A classic example of external balancing is the Anglo-American-Soviet alliance against Nazi Germany in World War II.

A second claim is that hegemons maintain the stability of the system. If alliances are used to topple a hegemon, then they become a tool for instability. During the hegemonic phase, alliances are a non-issue because the hegemon is, by definition, not dependent on alliances for the maintenance of its superior position in the international system.

A third option is based on the assumption that alliances lead states down the pathway to confrontation and war.[20] George Washington, the first president of the United States, famously warned his fellow Americans to avoid entangling alliances. One popular explanation for World War I is that alliances forced one lemming-like state after another to go over the cliff to war.[21]

Alliance restraint further complicates this picture. Stopping an ally from going to war or forming an alliance could be stabilizing. In 1954, the British helped stop U.S. intervention in Vietnam on behalf of the French. American military intervention ultimately occurred anyway, but perhaps the British move precluded further West European intervention after the French pullout. Yet alliance restraint could also hasten conflict if successful restraint prevents the formation of an alliance or a threat to use force that would have deterred a war. After the United States stopped British intervention in Iran in 1951, one could argue that Washington prevented a potential East-West military clash in Iran, given the fear that the Soviet Union would respond to British intervention with forces of its own. Yet two years later, the United States sponsored a coup to topple the Iranian leader, a coup that reverberates more than fifty years later as American-Iranian hostility lives on.

The lingering question is whether one could disentangle the empirical events and these schools of thought and consider counterfactual events in a convincing enough manner to make some judgment about the overall impact of alliances and alliance restraint on international stability. In the current unipolar international system, this book suggests that the United States could use its material advantage to shape the military policies of its allies. If American leaders are discerning enough to recognize when U.S. allies are pursuing a dangerous, aggressive, or destabilizing military policy, alliance restraint could be a powerful tool for tamping down violence and confrontation. Absent such discernment—and the U.S. track record in the first years of the twenty-first century is not encouraging—the question of whether it should do so in the name of stability remains uncertain.

Notes

1. Alliance Restraint

1. The existing literature on alliance restraint is limited but includes Paul W. Schroeder, "Alliances, 1815–1945: Weapons of Power and Tools of Management," in *Historical Dimensions of National Security Problems,* ed. Klaus Knorr (Lawrence: University Press of Kansas, 1975), pp. 227–263; Glenn Snyder, *Alliance Politics* (Ithaca: Cornell University Press, 1997); and Patricia A. Weitsman, *Dangerous Alliances* (Palo Alto, Calif.: Stanford University Press, 2004). See also Galia Press-Barnathan, "Managing the Hegemon: NATO under Unipolarity," *Security Studies* 15 (April–June 2006): 271–309. For brief references to alliance restraint, see George Liska, *Alliances and the Third World* (Baltimore: Johns Hopkins University Press, 1968), pp. 24–25; Robert E. Osgood, *Alliances and American Foreign Policy* (Baltimore: Johns Hopkins University Press, 1968), pp. 18 and 22; Stephen Van Evera, "Primed for Peace: Europe after the Cold War," *International Security* 15 (winter 1990–1991): 193–243 at 225; Steve Weber, "Shaping the Postwar Balance of Power: Multilateralism in NATO," *International Organization* 46 (summer 1992): 633–680 at 675; and James D. Morrow, "Alliances: Why Write Them Down?" *Annual Review of Political Science* 3 (2000): 63–83 at 65.

2. Thucydides, trans. Rex Warner, *History of the Peloponnesian War* (New York: Penguin Books, 1954/1972), p. 402.

3. See Kenneth Waltz, *Theory of International Politics* (Reading, Mass.: Addison-Wesley, 1979). Benjamin Miller emphasizes that the superpowers have the upper hand in bipolar but not multipolar systems. Miller, *When Opponents Cooperate* (Ann Arbor: University of Michigan Press, 1995), pp. 69–69, 70–71, 74–75, 167–168.

4. See Stanley Hoffmann, *Gulliver's Troubles, or the Setting of American Foreign Policy* (New York: McGraw-Hill, 1968); G. John Ikenberry, *After Victory: Institutions, Strategic Restraint, and the Rebuilding of Order after Major Wars* (Princeton, N.J.: Princeton University Press, 2001); Lisa L. Martin, "Self-Binding," *Harvard Magazine,* September–October, 2004, pp. 33–34, http://www.harvardmagazine.com/on-line/090429.html; Robert A. Pape, "Soft Balancing against the United States," *International Security* 30 (summer 2005): 7–45; Thomas Risse-Kappen, *Cooperation among Democracies* (Princeton, N.J.: Princeton University Press, 1995); and Stephen M. Walt, *Taming American Power* (New York: W. W. Norton, 2005). On how

multidimensional notions of power suggest avenues by which seemingly weaker allies might overcome their larger allies, see Joseph S. Nye, *The Paradox of American Power: Why the World's Only Superpower Can't Go It Alone* (New York: Oxford University Press, 2002), and *Soft Power: The Means to Success in World Politics* (New York: Public Affairs, 2004).

5. Randall L. Schweller, *Unanswered Threats: Political Constraints on the Balance of Power* (Princeton, N.J.: Princeton University Press, 2006). See also Schweller, *Deadly Imbalances: Tripolarity and Hitler's Strategy of World Conquest* (New York: Columbia University Press, 1998); Thomas J. Christensen, *Useful Adversaries: Grand Strategy, Domestic Mobilization, and Sino-American Conflict, 1947–1958* (Princeton, N.J.: Princeton University Press, 1996); Steven R. David, *Choosing Sides: Alignment and Realignment in the Third World* (Baltimore: Johns Hopkins University Press, 1991); Gideon Rose, "Neoclassical Realism and Theories of Foreign Policy," *World Politics* 51 (October 1998): 144–172; Jeffrey W. Taliaferro, "Security Seeking under Anarchy: Defensive Realism Reconsidered," *International Security* 25 (winter 2000–2001): 128–161; and Fareed Zakaria, *From Wealth to Power: The Unusual Origins of America's World Role* (Princeton, N.J.: Princeton University Press, 1998). Stephen Biddle rejects explanations for victory in war based solely on "gross resource advantages" and instead argues that how those capabilities are used—the doctrines and tactics states employ—determines the outcomes of wars. See Biddle, *Military Power: Explaining Victory and Defeat in Modern Battle* (Princeton, N.J.: Princeton University Press, 2004), esp. pp. 2–4, 14–15.

6. See Press-Barnathan, "Managing the Hegemon," p. 283. This section also draws on ideas highlighted by Robert O. Keohane, *After Hegemony* (Princeton, N.J.: Princeton University Press, 1984); Kenneth A. Oye, "Explaining Cooperation under Anarchy: Hypotheses and Strategies," in *Cooperation under Anarchy*, ed. Oye (Princeton, N.J.: Princeton University Press, 1986), pp. 1–24 at 11, 20; Robert Axelrod and Robert O. Keohane, "Achieving Cooperation under Anarchy: Strategies and Institutions," in *Cooperation under Anarchy*, ed. Oye, pp. 226–254 at 239, 250–251; Robert O. Keohane and Joseph S. Nye, *Power and Interdependence*, 2nd ed. (Boston: Scott, Foresman, 1989), pp. 271–272; Lisa L. Martin, *Coercive Cooperation* (Princeton, N.J.: Princeton University Press, 1992); Lisa Martin and Beth A. Simmons, "Theories and Empirical Studies of International Institutions," *International Organization* 52 (autumn 1998): 729–757 at 745. See also David A. Baldwin, ed., *Neorealism and Neoliberalism: The Contemporary Debate* (New York: Columbia University Press, 1993); and Morrow, "Alliances."

7. The quotation was originally used by Tony Evans and Peter Wilson to describe a traditional "realist" view of institutions. I am not going as far as John J. Mearsheimer in his suggestion that the "most powerful states in the system create and shape institutions." I contend that when powerful allies wish, they use the institutions as part of the mobilization of their resources. In my view, institutions may have many of the functions described by neoliberal institutionalists even if the most powerful state is the one that tends to utilize those functions. See Evans and Wilson, "Regime Theory and the English School of International Relations: A Comparison," *Millennium* 21, no. 3 (1992): 329–351 at 330; and Mearsheimer, "The False Promise of International Institutions," *International Security* 19 (winter 1994–1995): 5–49 at 13–14.

8. Clayton L. Thyne, "Cheap Signals with Costly Consequences: The Effect of Interstate Relations on Civil War," *Journal of Conflict Resolution* 50 (December 2006): 937–961 at 947; and Brett Ashley Leeds, "Do Alliances Deter Aggression? The Influence of Military Alliances on the Initiation of Militarized Interstate Disputes," *American Journal of Political Science* 47 (July 2003): 427–439 at 428. See also James Fearon, "Signaling Foreign Policy Interests: Tying Hands versus Sinking Costs," *Journal of Conflict Resolution* 41 (February 1997): 68–90 at 70.

9. Weitsman, in defining the alliance paradox, notes that tethering alliances—one type of alliance restraint—may increase the insecurity of adversaries that do not know the alliance is meant to dampen rivalry. *Dangerous Alliances*, pp. 7 and 171. On the spiral and

deterrence models, see Robert Jervis, *Perception and Misperception in International Politics* (Princeton, N.J.: Princeton University Press, 1976), pp. 58–113.

10. George W. Downs, David M. Rocke, and Randolph M. Siverson, "Arms Races and Cooperation," in *Cooperation under Anarchy*, ed. Oye, pp. 118–146 at 138.

11. Timothy W. Crawford, *Pivotal Deterrence: Third-Party Statecraft and the Pursuit of Peace* (Ithaca: Cornell University Press, 2003), pp. 16, 9, 8, 17–18, and 15. The relationship between alliance restraint and pivotal deterrence is illustrated well in Crawford's case study of German-Austrian-Russian relations in the 1870s. Crawford highlights German efforts to prevent war while avoiding taking sides (p. 47). Yet I use this same case as an example of alliance restraint when Germany and Austria-Hungary signed a pact in 1879 and one of Germany's motives was restraining Austria. In other words, Germany's ultimate goal of war avoidance was the same, but it pursued multiple strategies to achieve that aim.

12. Cuba is the thirty-fifth member of the OAS, but it has been suspended since 1962.

13. Rajan Menon, *The End of Alliances* (London: Oxford University Press, 2007); and Dana H. Allin, "American Power and Allied Restraint: Lessons of Iraq," *Survival* 49 (spring 2007): 123–140.

14. I draw on two previous definitions. The first is from Stephen M. Walt, *The Origins of Alliances* (Ithaca: Cornell University Press, 1987), p. 1: "I define *alliance* as a formal or informal relationship of security cooperation between two or more sovereign states. This definition assumes some level of commitment and an exchange of benefits for both parties; severing the relationship or failing to honor the agreement would presumably cost something, even if it were compensated in other ways." The second definition is from Morrow, "Alliances," p. 64: "Alignments are not written down by states because the common interest is obvious to all. Some alignments, such as the United States and Israel, support close relations over a long period of time, whereas others, such as the United States and Syria during the Gulf War, pass with the immediate issue. The key difference is that an alignment does not carry the expectation of a continuing relationship; the shared interest carries the entire relationship, and therefore that relationship need not be negotiated formally. An alliance entails a formal commitment between the parties wherein certain specific obligations are written out. Alliances require specification because the allies need to clarify their degree of shared interests, both to each other and to others outside the alliance." As I explain in chapter 4, I reject Morrow's characterization of the U.S.-Israeli alliance. On a theoretical level, states may have faith in the continuing nature of the relationship even in the absence of a signed piece of paper attesting to that fact.

15. Liska supports the idea of "an extensive conception of 'alliance,' going beyond the hard core of an explicit, contractual pledge of military assistance." See his *Alliances and the Third World*, p. 3. Consistent with an overemphasis on written alliance agreements, Evans and Wilson note more generally that "the literature on international regimes overwhelmingly focuses on formally negotiated international agreements and tends to ignore the social and political processes that underpin them." They suggest that "the social and political processes" are often the focus of English School theorists. An example is Martin Wight in a chapter on alliances as institutions: "There are associations between powers that seem to be deeper than formal alliances, to be based on affinity and tradition as much as interest, to be not so much utilitarian as *natural*." My discussion in chapter 4 of the American-Israeli alliance considers both the formal aspects and the underlying processes as seen in the rhetorical and documentary record. See Evans and Wilson, "Regime Theory," p. 341; and Martin Wight, *Power Politics*, ed. Hedley Bull and Carsten Holbraad (New York: Holmes and Meier, 1978), p. 123.

16. For more on judging policy success, see David A. Baldwin, "Success and Failure in Foreign Policy," *Annual Review of Political Science* 3 (2000): 167–182. Scholars frequently try to explain the success or failure of a variety of policy categories. The most popular has probably been deterrence. For the most intense deterrence debate and many additional

deterrence citations, see Paul Huth and Bruce Russett, "What Makes Deterrence Work? Cases from 1900 to 1980," *World Politics* 36 (July 1984): 496–526; Richard Ned Lebow and Janice Gross Stein, "Rational Deterrence Theory: I Think, Therefore I Deter," *World Politics* 41 (January 1989): 208–224; Lebow and Stein, "Deterrence: The Elusive Dependent Variable," *World Politics* 42 (April 1990): 336–369; and Huth and Russett, "Testing Deterrence Theory: Rigor Makes a Difference," *World Politics* 42 (July 1990): 466–501. On coercive diplomacy, see Alexander L. George and William E. Simons, *The Limits of Coercive Diplomacy,* 2nd ed. (Boulder, Colo.: Westview Press, 1994); and Robert J. Art and Patrick M. Cronin, eds., *The United States and Coercive Diplomacy* (Washington, D.C.: United States Institute of Peace Press, 2003). On engineered migration, see Kelly Greenhill, "People Pressure: Strategic Engineered Migration as an Instrument of Statecraft and the Rise of the Human Rights Regime" (Ph.D. dissertation, Massachusetts Institute of Technology, 2004).

17. Walt, *Origins of Alliances.* I discuss this issue in greater depth in chapter 2.

18. Schroeder, "Alliances, 1815–1945." See also Paul W. Schroeder, *The Transformation of European Politics, 1763–1848* (New York: Oxford University Press, 1994).

19. Schroeder, "Alliances, 1815–1945," pp. 241, 249–255.

20. For instance, Schroeder notes that Austria thought about using its alliance with Tuscany to replace the Tuscan ruler, Leopold II ("Alliances, 1815–1945," p. 237). Bismarck "wanted to manage, not only Austria's foreign policy, but even Austria's internal policy and constitution" (p. 242).

21. Schroeder, "Alliances, 1815–1945," p. 256.

22. See especially table 6-2 in Snyder, *Alliance Politics,* p. 194. See also Glenn H. Snyder, "The Security Dilemma in Alliance Politics," *World Politics* 36 (July 1984): 461–496.

23. Snyder, *Alliance Politics,* pp. 320–321, 322–323, 325.

24. Ibid., p. 320.

25. Weitsman, *Dangerous Alliances.* See also her earlier article, "Intimate Enemies: The Politics of Peacetime Alliances," *Security Studies* 7 (autumn 1997): 156–192.

26. Walt, *Origins of Alliances,* p. 21. See also Alexander Wendt, "Collective Identity Formation and the International State," *APSR* 88 (June 1994): 384–396 at 386; James D. Morrow, "Alliances and Asymmetry: An Alternative to the Capability Aggregation Model of Alliances," *American Journal of Political Science* 35 (November 1991): 904–933; and Kenneth Waltz, "Structural Realism after the Cold War," in *America Unrivaled: The Future of the Balance of Power,* ed. G. John Ikenberry (Ithaca: Cornell University Press, 2002), pp. 29–67 at 49–50. Other works that challenge Walt but also rely on threats and thus protection rather than control include David, *Choosing Sides;* Steven R. David, "Explaining Third World Alignment," *World Politics* (January 1991): 233–256; and Marc J. O'Reilly, "Omanibalancing: Oman Confronts an Uncertain Future," *Middle East Journal* 52 (winter 1998): 70–84. See also F. Gregory Gause III, "Balancing What? Threat Perception and Alliance Choice in the Gulf," *Security Studies* 13 (winter 2003–2004): 273–305.

27. Michael N. Barnett, "Identity and Alliances in the Middle East," in *The Culture of National Security: Norms and Identity in World Politics,* ed. Peter J. Katzenstein (New York: Columbia University Press, 1996), pp. 400–447 at 400–401 (and n. 1).

28. Christopher Gelpi, "Alliances as Instruments of Intra-Allied Control," in *Imperfect Unions: Security Institutions over Time and Space,* ed. Helga Haftendorn, Robert O. Keohane, and Celeste A. Wallander (New York: Oxford University Press, 1999), pp. 107–139. Wallander agrees: "Although ostensibly motivated by common defense against external threats, alliances have often been motivated at least as much by security management among members as by collective defense concerns." Celeste A. Wallander, "Institutional Assets and Adaptability: NATO after the Cold War," *International Organization* 54 (autumn 2000): 705–735 at 711.

29. Weitsman, *Dangerous Alliances* and Schroeder, "Alliances, 1815–1945," p. 228.

30. In sharp contrast, state A may *want* states B and C to fight, which Mearsheimer characterizes as a "bait and bleed" strategy. John J. Mearsheimer, *The Tragedy of Great Power Politics* (New York: W. W. Norton, 2001), pp. 153–154.

31. Downs et al., "Arms Races and Cooperation," pp. 119–120.

32. Keohane, *After Hegemony,* p. 54.

33. Waltz, *Theory of International Politics,* p. 170. For similar but less categorical statements, see Raymond Aron, *Peace and War: A Theory of International Relations* (Garden City, N.Y.: Doubleday, 1966), p. 69; and Michael Handel, *Weak States in the International System* (London: Frank Cass, 1981), pp. 51, 131.

34. Waltz, *Theory of International Politics,* p. 169.

35. Psychologist Jerome Bruner's comment was mentioned by Karl W. Deutsch, *The Analysis of International Relations* (Englewood Cliffs, N.J.: Prentice-Hall, 1968), p. 184.

36. Sidney Tarrow, *The New Transnational Activism* (New York: Cambridge University Press, 2005), p. 26.

37. Deutsch concludes that in "the pursuit of Western unity, there may be no long-run substitute for consensus politics." Karl W. Deutsch, *Arms Control and the Atlantic Alliance* (New York: John Wiley, 1967), p. 77.

38. Inis L. Claude Jr., *Swords into Plowshares: The Problems and Progress of International Organization,* 3rd ed. (New York: Random House, 1964), pp. 244–245.

39. Risse-Kappen, *Cooperation among Democracies.* He emphasized other factors as well that are less relevant to my study. See also Deutsch et al.'s discussion of community and "mutual responsiveness." Karl W. Deutsch et al., *Political Community and the North Atlantic Area* (1957; repr., New York: Greenwood Press, 1969), pp. 129–133, 164–167. More generally, constructivist authors have highlighted the role of norms in shaping outcomes in international affairs. See Katzenstein, *Culture of National Security.* Steve Weber's discussion of President Dwight D. Eisenhower's multilateral and multipolar vision for NATO is consistent with Risse-Kappen's work. In Weber's view, Eisenhower wanted to use NATO, via the sharing of nuclear weapons, to equalize Western Europe's status with that of the United States, making Western Europe a third pole along with the United States and the Soviet Union. He wanted a relationship with America's European allies built on trust and a "shared sense of purpose among peers" rather than American coercion and dominance. Eisenhower's vision was rejected, Weber argued, in part because the Kennedy administration favored centralized control of Western nuclear forces. Steve Weber, "Shaping the Postwar Balance of Power: Multilateralism in NATO," *International Organization* 46 (summer 1992): 633–680. See also Lisa L. Martin, "Interests, Power, and Multilateralism," *International Organization* 46 (autumn 1992): 765–792; and John Gerard Ruggie, "Multilateralism: The Anatomy of an Institution," *International Organization* 46 (summer 1992): 561–598.

40. Moshe Efrat and Jacob Bercovitch, *Superpowers and Client States in the Middle East* (London: Routledge, 1991).

41. Ikenberry, *After Victory,* pp. 40–41. See also pp. 63–64. Ikenberry cites Schroeder, "Alliances, 1815–1945"; Joseph M. Grieco, "State Interests and Institutional Rule Trajectories: A Neorealist Interpretation of the Maastricht Treaty and European Economic and Monetary Union," *Security Studies* 5 (spring 1996): 288; and Daniel Deudney, "The Philadelphian System: Sovereignty, Arms Control, and Balance of Power in the American States-Union, circa 1781–1861," *International Organization* 49 (spring 1995): 191–228.

42. Ikenberry, *After Victory,* p. 207.

43. Martin, "Self-Binding," pp. 33–34.

44. Thomas Risse, "U.S. Power in a Liberal Security Community," in *America Unrivaled,* ed. Ikenberry, pp. 260–283 at 274. His work is part of a broader discussion of international cooperation. Oye defines cooperation as "conscious policy coordination." *Cooperation under Anarchy,* p. 5. Keohane writes that "cooperation occurs when actors adjust their behavior to

the actual or anticipated preferences of others, through a process of policy coordination."
After Hegemony, p. 51.

45. Daniel Deudney and G. John Ikenberry, "Realism, Liberalism, and the Western Order," in *Unipolar Politics: Realism and State Strategies after the Cold War*, ed. Ethan B. Kapstein and Michael Mastanduno (New York: Columbia University Press, 1999), pp. 103–137 at 110–111.

46. On using case studies, see Alexander L. George and Timothy McKeown, "Case Studies and Theories of Organizational Decision Making," in *Advances in Information Processing in Organizations* (Greenwich, Conn.: JAI Press, 1985), pp. 21–58; and Stephen Van Evera, *Guide to Methods for Students of Political Science* (Ithaca: Cornell University Press, 1997).

47. The same distinction is made between general and specific (immediate) cases in the deterrence literature. See, for instance, Yair Evron, *War and Intervention in Lebanon: The Israeli-Syrian Deterrence Dialogue* (London: Croom Helm, 1987), p. 177.

48. One area in which I do not have variation is prior to the question of success and failure. I did not study in-depth a case in which restraint was considered but not attempted; in all my case studies, restraint was attempted. This type of variation would help address the question of why states choose restraint over other policy options such as abandonment or acquiescence. For some helpful ideas, see Press-Barnathan, "Managing the Hegemon."

49. This finding sets the stage for future research on the conditions under which restraint is likely to lead to the formation of an alliance.

50. I am not proposing an exact formula for the relationship between lesser security objectives and overarching ones. In terms of great powers, relations with other great powers will probably trump other national security issues. For all states, questions of imminent survival—the enemy is massing at the border—will have a different weight than other military decisions. Richard E. Neustadt referred to "different orders of priority." See his *Alliance Politics* (New York: Columbia University Press, 1970), p. 59.

51. In their study of coercive diplomacy, George and Simons note that a weaker state may challenge a more powerful state if the former cares more about what is at stake. See George and Simons, *Limits of Coercive Diplomacy*, p. 9. Other authors who highlight the possible importance of state interests in explaining political outcomes are T. V. Paul, *Asymmetric Conflicts: War Initiation by Weaker Powers* (New York: Cambridge University Press, 1994), p. 16–17; and Risse-Kappen, *Cooperation among Democracies*, p. 21. After noting the difficulty of operationalizing this variable in a nontautological manner, Risse-Kappen tried to control for this factor by including cases in which the survival of the smaller ally was not at stake. For a balance-of-interest explanation for the victory of less powerful states in wars, see Andrew J. R. Mack, "Why Big Nations Lose Small Wars: The Politics of Asymmetric Conflict," *World Politics* 27 (January 1975): 175–200. This explanation is challenged by Ivan Arreguín-Toft, "How the Weak Win Wars: A Theory of Asymmetric Conflict," *International Security* 26 (summer 2001): 93–128. See also Robert A. Pape, *Bombing to Win: Air Power and Coercion in War* (Ithaca: Cornell University Press, 1996), p. 4 n. 9; and Judith Kelley, "Strategic Noncooperation as Soft Balancing: Why Iraq Was Not Just about Iraq," *International Politics* 42 (2005): 153–173 at 159.

2. Allying to Restrain

1. On treaty language, see Gregory D. Miller, "Hypotheses on Reputation: Alliance Choices and the Shadow of the Past," *Security Studies* 12 (spring 2003): 40–78.

2. For a seminal example of categorizing alliances, see J. David Singer and Melvin Small, "Formal Alliances, 1815–1939: A Quantitative Description," *Journal of Peace Research* 3 (January 1966): 1–32.

3. For related points, see Glenn H. Snyder, "The Security Dilemma in Alliance Politics," *World Politics* 36 (July 1984): 461–496.

4. On regime type, see Michael W. Simon and Erik Gartzke, "Political System Similarity and the Choice of Allies: Do Democracies Flock Together, or Do Opposites Attract?" *Journal of Conflict Resolution* 40 (December 1996): 617–635; Brian Lai and Dan Reiter, "Democracy, Political Similarity, and International Alliances, 1816–1992," *Journal of Conflict Resolution* 44 (April 2000): 203–227; and Douglas M. Gibler and Scott Wolford, "Alliances, Then Democracy: An Examination of the Relationship between Regime Type and Alliance Formation," *Journal of Conflict Resolution* 50 (February 2006): 129–153. On reputation, see Miller, "Hypotheses on Reputation." On ideology, see Mark L. Haas, *The Ideological Origins of Great Power Politics, 1789–1989* (Ithaca: Cornell University Press, 2005).

5. My discussion of the Austro-German alliance was greatly informed by Glenn Snyder, *Alliance Politics* (Ithaca: Cornell University Press, 1997), pp. 84–101, 133–135.

6. Nicholas Mansergh, *The Coming of the First World War: A Study in the European Balance, 1878–1914* (London: Longmans, Green, 1949), p. 26.

7. William L. Langer, *European Alliances and Alignments, 1871–1890*, 2nd ed. (New York: Alfred A. Knopf, 1950), p. 196.

8. A. J. P. Taylor, *The Struggle for Mastery in Europe, 1848–1918* (London: Oxford University Press, 1954), p. 264.

9. Snyder, *Alliance Politics*, pp. 87–88, 90.

10. Taylor, *Struggle for Mastery*, p. 263.

11. Langer, *European Alliances*, pp. 178–179, 180. See also Taylor, *Struggle for Mastery*, p. 267; and Raymond James Sontag, *European Diplomatic History, 1871–1932* (New York: Appleton-Century-Crofts, 1933), p. 19.

12. Snyder, *Alliance Politics*, pp. 88, 90, 91.

13. Ibid., p. 89. See also Taylor, *Struggle for Mastery*, p. 265. The Russian threat cannot be wholly dismissed, however. See Langer, *European Alliances*, pp. 180 and 184.

14. Langer, *European Alliances*, p. 176. Taylor downplays the possibility of other alliances against Germany: Franco-Russian (made more likely by an Austro-German alliance), Russo-Austrian (not "remotely probable"), and Franco-Austrian ("hardly worth making an alliance in order to avoid this"). Taylor, *Struggle for Mastery*, p. 261. See also Sontag, *European Diplomatic History*, pp. 20–21.

15. Taylor, *Struggle for Mastery*, pp. 259–260.

16. Ibid., p. 266.

17. Snyder, *Alliance Politics*, p. 91. According to Langer, Bismarck "argued that Austria, as the weaker of the allied powers, could be led by Germany." *European Alliances*, p. 196.

18. Sontag, *European Diplomatic History*, p. 19.

19. Taylor, *Struggle for Mastery*, p. 259.

20. Langer, *European Alliances*, p. 196.

21. Sontag, *European Diplomatic History*, p. 20.

22. This is an example of moral hazard: insurance against risk may result in riskier behavior.

23. Snyder, *Alliance Politics*, p. 91. See also Taylor, *Struggle for Mastery*, p. 263.

24. Taylor, *Struggle for Mastery*, p. 263.

25. John J. Mearsheimer, *The Tragedy of Great Power Politics* (New York: W. W. Norton, 2001), pp. 71 and 187.

26. But some claim Britain would have intervened if Russia was crushing Japan in a war, even if France stood aside. Snyder, *Alliance Politics*, p. 355.

27. The date is variously given as March 16, 17, or 19. See Amos S. Hershey, *The International Law and Diplomacy of the Russo-Japanese War* (London: Macmillan, 1906), pp. 28–29; Alfred L. P. Dennis, *The Anglo-Japanese Alliance* (Berkeley: University of California Publications, 1923), p. 8; and Snyder, *Alliance Politics*, p. 270.

28. On British concern about Russian advances in China, see Zara S. Steiner, "Great Britain and the Creation of the Anglo-Japanese Alliance," *Journal of Modern History* 31

(March 1959): 27–36 at 36. On the Russo-French naval threat, see Ian H. Nish, *The Anglo-Japanese Alliance: The Diplomacy of Two Island Empires, 1894–1907* (London: Athlone Press, 1966), pp. 174–175 and 183–184; David Steeds, "Anglo-Japanese Relations, 1902–23: A Marriage of Convenience," in *The History of Anglo-Japanese Relations, Volume 1: The Political-Diplomatic Dimension, 1600–1930*, ed. Ian Nish and Yoichi Kibata with assistance from Tadashi Kuramatsu (New York: St. Martin's Press, 2000), p. 201; and Steiner, "Anglo-Japanese Alliance," pp. 29–30. On the British desire to prevent a Russo-Japanese understanding, see Snyder, *Alliance Politics*, pp. 139 and 270; Dennis, *Anglo-Japanese Alliance*, p. 5; and Steeds, "Anglo-Japanese Relations," p. 202.

29. Snyder, *Alliance Politics*, p. 149; Steeds, "Anglo-Japanese Relations," pp. 199, 203. Hershey gives details of the failed Russo-Japanese negotiations over a settlement in the Far East. See Hershey, *International Law and Diplomacy*, pp. 55–61.

30. See Snyder, *Alliance Politics*, pp. 270 and 272; Steeds, "Anglo-Japanese Relations," p. 201; Dennis, *Anglo-Japanese Alliance*, p. 17; Steiner, "Anglo-Japanese Alliance"; Nish, *Anglo-Japanese Alliance*, pp. 181, 205, 207, 232; J. A. S. Grenville, "Lansdowne's Abortive Project of 12 March 1901 for a Secret Agreement with Germany," *Bulletin of the Institute of Historical Research* (November 1954): 201–213; and Miller, "Hypotheses on Reputation," pp. 69–72.

31. Nish, *Anglo-Japanese Alliance*, p. 205.

32. The dispatch is reproduced in K. Asakawa, *The Russo-Japanese Conflict: Its Causes and Issues* (Boston: Houghton Mifflin, 1904), pp. 206–207.

33. The letter appears in Nish, *Anglo-Japanese Alliance*, p. 240.

34. The text of the treaty appears in Nish, *Anglo-Japanese Alliance*, pp. 216–217.

35. Britain helped Japan but only at the margin; British forces were never directly engaged in the fighting. On Britain's tilt toward Japan during the war, see Miller, "Hypotheses on Reputation," pp. 74–75.

36. *Public Papers of the Presidents of the United States: Harry Truman, 1948* (Washington, D.C.: U.S. Government Printing Office, 1964), pp. 182–186.

37. Timothy P. Ireland, *Creating the Entangling Alliance: The Origins of the North Atlantic Treaty Organization* (Westport, Conn.: Greenwood Press, 1981) p. 100. See also Robert E. Osgood, *NATO: The Entangling Alliance* (Chicago: University of Chicago Press, 1962), pp. 85–86 and 91–98.

38. Ireland, *Creating the Entangling Alliance*, pp. 109, 186.

39. Ibid., p. 63.

40. Ibid., pp. 64–65 n. 64. See also p. 68 and p. 75. The United States favored the idea that any attack activated the treaty. See p. 67.

41. Sir Nicholas Henderson, *The Birth of NATO* (Boulder, Colo.: Westview Press, 1983), p. 49.

42. Ireland, *Creating the Entangling Alliance*, pp. 158–159.

43. Ibid., p. 196.

44. Celeste A. Wallander, "Institutional Assets and Adaptability: NATO after the Cold War," *International Organization* 54 (autumn 2000): 705–735 at 716 and 732.

45. James Chace, "New World Disorder," *New York Review of Books*, December 17, 1998.

46. The United States and the ROK were already multilateral allies under the United Nations Command (UNC), but the bilateral security pact proposed a stronger alliance bond. For instance, the bilateral pact would be an open-ended commitment rather than linked to a particular conflict.

47. A further twist is that South Korea then pushed the United States for a broad treaty that would allow for a wide range of military steps in the face of communist aggression. In early August 1953, Dulles successfully opposed these pressures and blocked Rhee's efforts for a tighter U.S. commitment in the wording of the treaty. Thus a treaty signed in order to restrain an ally (ROK) had to be worded in such a way to avoid giving that more aggressive ally the freedom to pursue additional provocative and aggressive military policies. On

Rhee's efforts and Dulles's resistance, see Yong-Pyo Hong, *State Security and Regime Security* (New York: St. Martin's Press, 2000), p. 55. Also, as noted below, the U.S. Congress added an understanding to the treaty on the limitations of U.S. support for South Korea.

48. Hong, *State Security*, pp. 42, 45.

49. Ibid., pp. 52–53.

50. The U.S. position was sent from Washington to U.S. officials in Korea on May 22, 1953; they presented it, including U.S. reluctance to sign a bilateral security pact, to Rhee on May 25. The Korean president promptly rejected it. See *Foreign Relations of the United States [FRUS], 1952–1954: Korea*, vol. 15, part 1, ed. Edward C. Keefer (Washington, D.C.: U.S. Government Printing Office, 1984), pp. 1086–1090 and 1097–1098.

51. See "Letter from U.S. President Eisenhower to Korean President Rhee on Proposed Armistice, June 9, 1953," in *Documents on Korean-American Relations, 1943–1976*, ed. Se-Jin Kim (Seoul: Research Center for Peace and Unification, 1976), pp. 151–153; and Hong, *State Security*, pp. 46–47.

52. The statement is from July 31, 1953, as quoted in Hong, *State Security*, p. 40. The ellipses appear in Hong's version of Dulles's comment. See also Fred Greene, *U.S. Policy and the Security of Asia* (New York: McGraw-Hill for the Council on Foreign Relations, 1968), pp. 77–78.

53. Hong, *State Security*, pp. 43–44, 46, 47, 52, 57. The South Korean public supported Rhee's policy of opposing an armistice and getting a U.S. security commitment (p. 58).

54. James F. Schnabel and Robert J. Watson, *The History of the Joint Chiefs of Staff: The Joint Chiefs of Staff and National Policy, Volume 3: The Korean War*, part 2 (Wilmington, Del.: Michael Glazier, 1979), pp. 983–984. See also Hong, *State Security*, p. 43; and Richard C. Allen, *Korea's Syngman Rhee: An Unauthorized Portrait* (Rutland, Vt.: Charles E. Tuttle, 1960), p. 157.

55. *FRUS, 1952–1954*, vol. 15, pp. 1112–1114 and 1116. Robertson took Korean threats seriously, especially after the prisoner release in mid-June. Hong, *State Security*, p. 53. The United States warned Rhee not to undertake unilateral steps. See Sydney D. Bailey, *The Korean Armistice* (London: Macmillan, 1992), p. 139.

56. Allen, *Korea's Syngman Rhee*, p. 160.

57. Hong, *State Security*, p. 50.

58. May 30, 1953, *FRUS, 1952–1954*, vol. 15, pp. 1123. For another example of the linkage between ROK cooperation on the armistice and the signing of the security pact, see details of a June 5 meeting between U.S. and ROK officials in Schnabel and Watson, *Joint Chiefs of Staff*, part 2, p. 1000. See also Peter Lowe, "The Significance of the Korean War in Anglo-American Relations, 1950–1953," in *British Foreign Policy, 1945–56*, ed. Michael Dockrill and John W. Young (London: Macmillan, 1989), pp. 126–148.

59. May 29, 1953, *FRUS, 1952–1954*, vol. 15, p. 1118.

60. The north-south political conference was part of the armistice deal and was expected to be held within three months of the conclusion of the armistice (by October 27, 1953). The United States agreed to withdraw from the conference after 90 days if it was "fruitless." See "Joint Statement Issued at Seoul by Korean President Syngman Rhee and U.S. Secretary of State John Foster Dulles Regarding Post-Armistice R.O.K.-U.S. Policy, August 7, 1953," in *Documents on Korean-American Relations*, ed. Kim, pp. 183–185.

61. Other than the mutual security pact, the ROK received an aid package from the United States. In addition, Chinese forces attacked ROK units, perhaps in an effort to force the ROK to accept the terms of armistice. See Donald W. Boose Jr., "The Korean War Truce Talks: A Study in Conflict Termination," *Parameters* (U.S. Army War College Quarterly) (spring 2000): 102–116; and Hong, *State Security*, p. 54.

62. The text of the treaty and the additional understanding may be found at http://www.yale.edu/lawweb/avalon/diplomacy/korea/kor001.htm or in *Documents on Korean-American Relations*, ed. Kim, pp. 185–186. The treaty, as well as the Dulles-Rhee statement of August 7, highlighted the need to combat the "common danger" from the north

(Dulles-Rhee statement). But we should expect states to highlight threat-based reasons in public rather than restraint-based motivations. Public disclosure of restraint issues would reveal fissures that adversaries might try to exploit.

63. Robert A. Divine, *Eisenhower and the Cold War* (New York: Oxford University Press, 1981), p. 57.

64. The text of the treaty may be found at http://www.yale.edu/lawweb/avalon/diplomacy/china/chin001.htm.

65. The text of the letter may be found at http://www.yale.edu/lawweb/avalon/diplomacy/china/chin002.htm. See also William T. Tow, *Encountering the Dominant Player: U.S. Extended Deterrence Strategy in the Asia-Pacific* (New York: Columbia University Press, 1991), pp. 80–81.

66. Greene uses the term *releash* in *U.S. Policy,* p. 80.

67. John W. Garver, *The Sino-American Alliance* (Armonk, N.Y.: M. E. Sharpe, 1997), pp. 84–85.

68. *Foreign Relations of the United States [FRUS], 1952–1954: China and Japan,* vol. 14, part 1, ed. David W. Mabon and Harriet D. Schwar (Washington, D.C.: U.S. Government Printing Office, 1985), pp. 833–835, as cited in Garver, *Sino-American Alliance,* p. 126.

69. Garver, *Sino-American Alliance,* p. 133.

70. Robert Accinelli, *Crisis and Commitment: United States Policy toward Taiwan, 1950–1955* (Chapel Hill: University of North Carolina Press, 1996), pp. xi–xii, 108–109; and Gordon Chang and He Di, "The Absence of War in the US-Chinese Confrontation over Quemoy and Matsu in 1954–55: Contingency, Luck, Deterrence," *American Historical Review* 98 (December 1993): 1500–1524 at 1508.

71. Divine, *Eisenhower and the Cold War,* p. 58.

72. Ralph N. Clough, *Island China* (Cambridge, Mass.: Harvard University Press, 1978), p. 12. At a deeper level, the U.S.-ROC treaty also probably staved off a Taiwanese nuclear weapons program. See ibid., pp. 30, 117, 119.

73. Nancy Bernkopf Tucker, "Cold War Contacts: America and China, 1952–1956," in *Sino-American Relations, 1945–1955,* ed. Harry Harding and Yuan Ming (Wilmington, Del.: Scholarly Resources, 1989), pp. 238–266 at 251. See also Harry Harding, "The Legacy of the Decade for Later Years: An American Perspective," in *Sino-American Relations,* ed. Harding and Ming, pp. 311–329 at 321.

74. Tow, *Encountering the Dominant Player,* p. 81.

75. Accinelli, *Crisis and Commitment,* p. 109.

76. Garver, *Sino-American Alliance,* p. 57. See also p. 130.

77. *FRUS, 1952–1954,* vol. 14, as cited in Garver, *Sino-American Alliance,* p. 114.

78. Wang Jisi, "The Origins of America's 'Two China' Policy," in *Sino-American Relations,* ed. Harding and Ming, p. 205; see also Garver, *Sino-American Alliance,* p. 114.

79. On the support side, see Clough, *Island China,* pp. 17–18; and Document 133, "Telegram from the Embassy in the Republic of China [Drumright] to the Department of State," September 27, 1958, in *Foreign Relations of the United States [FRUS], 1958–1960: China,* vol. 19, ed. Harriet Dashiell Schwar (Washington, D.C.: U.S. Government Printing Office, 1996), pp. 284–285. On restraint, see Clough, *Island China,* p. 18; J. H. Kalicki, *The Pattern of Sino-American Crises: Political-Military Interactions in the 1950s* (London: Cambridge University Press, 1975), pp. 196–197 and 206; and Document 65, "Memorandum from the Commander, U.S. Taiwan Defense Command (Smoot) to the Chief of General Staff, Republic of China (Wang)," September 4, 1958, *FRUS, 1958–1960,* vol. 19, pp. 128–129. See also point 6 in Document 127, "Telegram from the Department of State [Dulles] to the Embassy in the United Kingdom," September 25, 1958, ibid., pp. 272–273. Dulles told the prime minister of New Zealand that "we have been restraining the GRC [Government of the Republic of China]." See Document 144, "Memorandum of Conversation," September 30, 1958, ibid., p. 303. See also Documents 161–162, ibid., pp. 337–339.

80. Clough, *Island China*, p. 18; see also He Di, "The Evolution of the People's Republic of China's Policy toward the Offshore Islands," in *The Great Powers in East Asia, 1953-1960*, ed. Warren I. Cohen and Akira Iriye (New York: Columbia University Press, 1990), p. 235; Garver, *Sino-American Alliance*, pp. 138, 139; and Thomas J. Christensen, *Useful Adversaries: Grand Strategy, Domestic Mobilization, and Sino-American Conflict, 1947-1958* (Princeton, N.J.: Princeton University Press, 1996), pp. 196, 228.

81. Document 60, "Memorandum of Telephone Conversation between President Eisenhower and Secretary of State Dulles," September 1, 1958, *FRUS, 1958-1960*, vol. 19, p. 113.

82. Document 159, "Memorandum from Acting Secretary of State Herter to Secretary of State Dulles," October 6, 1958, *FRUS, 1958-1960*, vol. 19, p. 335.

83. Dwight D. Eisenhower, *Waging Peace, 1956-1961* (Garden City, N.Y.: Doubleday, 1965), p. 301. On September 11, 1958, McElroy met with Eisenhower and "commented that Chiang's only hope is to provoke a big fight." See Document 78, "Editorial Note," *FRUS, 1958-1960*, vol. 19, p. 161. For similar thoughts expressed by Dulles in an October 22, 1958, memorandum, see Kalicki, *Sino-American Crises*, 200. On September 29, 1958, General Nathan F. Twining, chairman of the JCS, told Eisenhower that "there has been concern that Chiang might do something rash, but General [Laurence S.] Kuter [commander, Pacific Air Forces], who has just visited him, feels that this is not likely." Document 140, "Memorandum of Conference with President Eisenhower," September 29, 1958, *FRUS, 1958-1960*, vol. 19, p. 296.

84. Document 106, "Memorandum by the Regional Planning Adviser in the Bureau of Far Eastern Affairs ([Marshall] Green)," September 18, 1958, *FRUS, 1958-1960*, vol. 19, pp. 222-223. See also p. 224. In a September 19, 1958, telegram to State, the U.S. ambassador to the ROC, Everett F. Drumright, disagreed: "I have yet to find evidence that GRC leadership has sought in this crisis to involve US deliberately in war with Communists." The United States should "release restraints on [the] GRC." See Document 108, "Telegram from the Embassy in the Republic of China to the Department of State," *FRUS, 1958-1960*, vol. 19, pp. 227-228. However, on September 27, Drumright cabled that "President Chiang... will try to involve us more directly... but it is my belief that he understands necessity of keeping in step with us and will do so." See Document 133, "Telegram from the Embassy in the Republic of China [Drumright] to the Department of State," September 27, 1958, *FRUS, 1958-1960*, vol. 19, p. 285.

85. Document 113, "Memorandum of Conversation," September 20, 1958, *FRUS, 1958-1960*, vol. 19, p. 244.

86. Document 124, "Editorial Note," September 25, 1958, *FRUS, 1958-1960*, vol. 19, pp. 269-270.

87. Nancy Bernkopf Tucker, "Taiwan Expendable? Nixon and Kissinger Go to China," *Journal of American History* 92 (June 2005): 109-135 at 115. See also p. 113.

88. Walt calls Egypt's summit effort "an attempt to balance against the Syrians." I believe the term *restraint* is more appropriate because the effort was made within the confines of a multilateral military alliance that included both Egypt and Syria. Stephen M. Walt, *The Origins of Alliances* (Ithaca: Cornell University Press, 1987), p. 87. Walt notes three motives for the summits, including "Balance Israel." Ibid., table 10, p. 159. As I explain in the text, I think the Israeli threat was less of a factor for Egypt than the desire to restrain Syria out of fear that Syria would provoke Israel. Shlomo Ben-Ami argues that Israel wanted a war with Syria to stop Syrian support of Palestinian guerrillas. Even so, the Egyptian support for the alliance was directly aimed at changing Syrian behavior more than Israeli action. I say "directly" because the indirect implication of changing Syrian behavior would be to change Israeli policy. See Ben-Ami, *Scars of War, Wounds of Peace* (New York: Oxford University Press, 2006), pp. 100-101.

89. Fred J. Khouri, "The Jordan River Controversy," *Review of Politics* 27 (January 1965): 44.

90. Fred J. Khouri, *The Arab-Israeli Dilemma*, 3rd ed. (Syracuse, N.Y.: Syracuse University Press, 1985), p. 227.

91. Yair Evron, *The Middle East: Nations, Superpowers, and Wars* (New York: Praeger, 1973), p. 54. Nasser later claimed that the Syrian delegate stated that Syria could not divert the Jordan tributaries for fear of an Israeli attack. Nasser thus implied that the meeting revealed Syrian weakness. "President Nasser's Speech at the Airforce Academy's Graduation," July 1, 1964, pp. 251–254 at 253, in *Arab Political Documents, 1964*, ed. Walid Khalid and Yusuf Ibish (Beirut: Political Studies and Public Administration Department of American University of Beirut, n.d.).

92. Howard M. Sachar, *A History of Israel from the Rise of Zionism to Our Time*, 2nd ed. (New York: Alfred A. Knopf, 1996), p. 617.

93. Khouri, *Arab-Israeli Dilemma*, p. 227. See also Khouri, "Jordan River Controversy," p. 44.

94. Evron, *Middle East*, pp. 54–55. Patrick Seale agrees that Nasser was seeking to restrain Syria; see Seale with Maureen McConville, *Asad: The Struggle for the Middle East* (Berkeley: University of California Press, 1988), pp. 121–123, 126–132. Interestingly, Seale claims Syria itself was trying to restrain Yasser Arafat and slow the Palestinian raids against Israel. Whereas the Palestinians wanted a people's war to spark a conventional Arab-Israeli war, Syria saw a people's war as a "substitute" for a conventional one (p. 125).

95. See Malcolm Kerr, *The Arab Cold War: Gamal 'Abd al-Nasir and His Rivals, 1958–1970*, 3rd ed. (London: Oxford University Press, 1971), p. 98.

96. Ibid., p. 100.

97. Khouri, "Jordan River Controversy," p. 46.

98. Evron, *Middle East*, p. 56. At some point, a Board for Exploitation of the Jordan Waters was established. *Arab Report and Record*, 15–28 February 1966, no. 4, p. 48.

99. *Arab Report and Record*, 1–15 March 1966, no. 5, p. 52.

100. Khouri, "Jordan River Controversy," p. 32.

101. Ibid., p. 45.

102. Kerr, *Arab Cold War*, p. 100.

103. Khouri, "Jordan River Controversy," p. 49.

104. Ibid., p. 50. Avi Shlaim calls the first summit "the first time that the Arab states collectively declared in an official document that their ultimate aim was the destruction of the State of Israel." Israel "took a very grave view" of the second summit as well. The Israeli prime minister saw it as a sign of careful Arab preparation for war with Israel. Still, Shlaim notes that at the third summit, "Nasser injected a characteristic note of caution by warning against resuming the [water] diversion work before the Arabs had improved their land and air defense capabilities. He hinted that if Syria acted unilaterally, it would not be able to count on his assistance." Avi Shlaim, *The Iron Wall: Israel and the Arab World* (New York: W. W. Norton, 2001), pp. 230–232. Nadav Safran says that in the period of the summits, "the Arab states were openly preparing to go to war with Israel over the Jordan waters." Safran, *Israel: The Embattled Ally* (Cambridge, Mass.: Harvard University Press, 1978, 1981), p. 385.

105. "Joint Communiqué of the Second Arab Summit Conference," September 3, 1964, in *Arab Political Documents*, ed. Khalid and Ibish, pp. 389–391.

106. "President Nasser's Speech at a Rally Held to Commemorate Victory Day," December 23, 1964, in *Arab Political Documents*, ed. Khalid and Ibish, pp. 543–554 at 549.

107. Khouri, "Jordan River Controversy," p. 54.

108. David Kimche and Dan Bawley, *The Sandstorm: The Arab-Israeli War of June, 1967* (New York: Stein and Day, 1968), p. 33.

109. *Arab Report and Record*, 1–15 August 1966, no. 15, p. 180.

110. Khouri, *Arab-Israeli Dilemma*, p. 232. Mark Tessler cites Khouri in *A History of the Israeli-Palestinian Conflict* (Bloomington: Indiana University Press, 1994), p. 378. See also *Arab Report and Record*, 1–15 August 1966, no. 15, p. 177, and 16–31 August 1966, no. 16, pp. 188–189.

111. *The USSR and Arab Belligerency* (Jerusalem: Information Division, Ministry of Foreign Affairs, 1967), p. 24.

112. *Arab Report and Record*, 16–31 August 1966, no. 16, p. 189.

113. On Nasser's calls for delaying the next military confrontation with Israel, see Kerr, *Arab Cold War*, pp. 98–99; and Khouri, "Jordan River Controversy," pp. 44–45.

114. *Arab Report and Record*, 1–15 November 1966, no. 21, p. 249.

115. Kerr, *Arab Cold War*, p. 122. Seale concurs that Egypt was using the defense pact to try to regain control of Syrian policy. Seale, *Asad*, p. 126.

116. *Arab Report and Record*, 1–15 November 1966, no. 21, p. 250.

117. Anthony Nutting, *Nasser* (New York: E. P. Dutton, 1972), pp. 389, 391–392.

118. Evron, *Middle East*, p. 72.

119. James Feron, "Israel Sees Arabs' Defense Pact and U.N. Vote as Curbing Syria," *New York Times*, November 7, 1966, p. 9. Tessler writes: "Israel was deeply concerned about the Syrian-Egyptian rapprochement, and especially about the mutual defense treaty concluded by the two countries.... As seen from the Israeli capital, the November defense pact had allied the Jewish state's two most dangerous enemies and, equally important, it had given the more aggressive and irresponsible of the two an ability to determine the behavior of the other, militarily stronger partner." Tessler, *Israeli-Palestinian Conflict*, p. 368.

120. Sachar, *History of Israel*, p. 620.

3. Anglo-American Relations and Alliance Restraint

1. The data are from Jan Faber, "Annual Data on Nine Economic and Military Characteristics of 78 Nations (SIRE NATDAT)," 1948–1983 [computer file]. Amsterdam: Europa Instituut [producer], 1989; Ann Arbor, Mich.: Inter-university Consortium for Political and Social Research, and Amsterdam: Steinmetz Archive [distributors], 1990.

2. Natural Resources Defense Council, "Table of Global Nuclear Weapons Stockpile, 1945–2002," http://www.nrdc.org/nuclear/nudb/datab19.asp, accessed September 22, 2005.

3. One scholar argues that there was a brief split just after 1945 as the two sides competed for dominance in the Middle East. See Amikam Nachmani, *Great Power Discord in Palestine* (London: Frank Cass, 1987).

4. Richard E. Neustadt, *Alliance Politics* (New York: Columbia University Press, 1970), pp. 3–4. See also Louise Richardson, *When Allies Differ: Anglo-American Relations during the Suez and Falklands Crises* (New York: St. Martin's Press, 1996).

5. Secretary of State to Embassy in Iran, telegram #2088, May 11, 1951, *Foreign Relations of the United States [FRUS], 1952–1954: Iran, 1951–1954*, vol. 10, ed. Carl N. Raether and Charles S. Sampson (Washington, D.C.: U.S. Government Printing Office, 1989), p. 52. Ambassador Franks called on Secretary of State Dean Acheson, H. Freeman Matthews (deputy undersecretary of state), and George C. McGhee, assistant secretary of state for Near Eastern–South Asian–African affairs, to discuss the new British note to Iran. See also *FRUS, 1952–1954*, vol. 10, pp. 35–36, and the British National Archives (BNA) version, FO 371/91471, EP 1023/49, April 19, 1951 (which includes text excised from *FRUS*).

6. Mentioned in *FRUS, 1952–1954*, vol. 10, p. 56 n. 4.

7. Oliver S. Crosby, *Account of the Iranian Oil Controversy*, vol. 1 of 3, 888.2553/7–1452, RG 59, National Archives and Records Administration (NARA), p. 69 (hereinafter the Crosby report), which cites State to London, telegram #5310, May 18, 1951.

8. *FRUS, 1952–1954*, vol. 10, p. 74. NSC 107 (approved March 24, 1951) called for an update by July 1, 1951.

9. *FRUS, 1952–1954*, vol. 10, pp. 39–40.

10. For additional sources, see Franks to Foreign Office, No. 3097, FO 371/91472, September 25 [received in London on the 26th], 1951, BNA. See also Acheson-Lovett

Memorandum of Conversation, September 26, 1951, Digital National Security Archive, http://nsarchive.chadwyck.com/home.do. For Frank's characterization of the Elliot-Lovett meeting, see Washington to Foreign Office, No. 3117, FO 371/91591, September 26 [received early in the morning on the 27th], 1951, BNA.

11. A British document says September 11 (No. 929, FO 371/91472, September 11, 1951, BNA), but the U.S. version contains the minutes of U.S.-British meetings on both days. According to the minutes in *FRUS*, the two parties discussed the Middle East on the 10th and the Far East on the 11th. See *Foreign Relations of the United States [FRUS], 1951: European Security and the German Question*, vol. 3, ed. John A. Bernbaum, Charles S. Sampson, Lisle A. Rose, William Z. Slany, and David H. Stauffer (Washington, D.C.: U.S. Government Printing Office, 1981), pp. 1128–1249.

12. No. 929, FO 371/91472, September 11, 1951, BNA. See also Dennis Merrill, ed., *Documentary History of the Truman Presidency*, vol. 29, *Oil Crisis in Iran* (Bethesda, Md.: University Publications of America, 2000), pp. 126–127.

13. "Meeting of the U.S.-U.K. Foreign Ministers—Minutes of the First Meetings," U.S.-U.K. MIN-1, September 10, 1951, RG 43, Lot No. M-88, Box 63, NARA. In the position paper prepared for the bilateral talks on September 10, Washington ruled out providing support for British intervention: "The United States could not support the introduction of British troops into Iran in connection with the oil controversy for any purpose other than the evacuation of British nationals whose lives were in immediate danger from mob violence." This was point number 3 under "Position to Be Presented." See "Washington Foreign Ministers Meetings, British Talks: Iran," WFM-B-2/2c, September 6, 1951, NARA.

14. Washington to Foreign Office, No. 3115, FO 371/91591, September 26 [received early in the morning on the 27th], 1951, BNA. *FRUS* refers to but does not print Truman's reply to Attlee. See *FRUS, 1952–1954*, vol. 10, p. 169.

15. Entry for August 8, 1951, in *The Diary of Hugh Gaitskell, 1945–1960*, ed. Philip Williams (London: Jonathan Cape, 1983).

16. CAB 128/20, CM 60 (51) 6, September 27, 1951, BNA.

17. On the United Nations and the issue of international approval, see "Record of Conversation between the Secretary of State and the South African Minister of Labour on the 24th July, 1951," FO 800/649, July 24, 1951, BNA; CAB 128/19, CM 35 (51) 7, May 10, 1951, BNA; CAB 128/19, CM 45 (51) 4, June 21, 1951, BNA; CAB 130/67, GEN 363, 22nd meeting, September 25, 1951, BNA; and CAB 128/20, CM 60 (51) 6, September 27, 1951, BNA. The evidence on the Soviet issue is less explicit. See Letter from the Foreign Office (G. W. Furlonge) to the Chiefs of Staff Committee, March 20, 1951, as copied in DEFE 5/29, COS (51) 156, March 21, 1951, BNA; "Implications of Military Action in Persia," DEFE 5/29, COS (51) 173, March 27, 1951, BNA. The Chiefs of Staff amended and approved this report at DEFE 4/41, COS 53rd meeting (51), item 1, March 27, 1951, BNA. On March 27, 1951, the Chiefs of Staff agreed to forward the report to the Foreign Office for presentation to ministers; *FRUS, 1952–1954*, vol. 10, pp. 54–56; DEFE 4/42, COS 79 (51) 2, May 8, 1951, BNA; and CAB 130/67, GEN 363/3rd, May 9, 1951, BNA.

18. Central Intelligence Agency (CIA), "Special Estimate: Current Developments in Iran," SE-6, May 22, 1951, http://www.foia.cia.gov, accessed May 20, 2005. See also section 5 of CIA, "Iran's Position in the East-West Conflict," NIE-6, April 5, 1951; and section 3 of CIA, "Special Estimate: The Current Crisis in Iran," SE-3, March 16, 1951.

19. CIA, "Key Problems Affecting US Efforts to Strengthen the Near East," NIE-26, April 25, 1951, http://www.foia.cia.gov, accessed June 7, 2006.

20. Rapp (British Middle East Office in Cairo) to Bowker, FO 141/1442, 107/3/5, July 6, 1951 (and appended minutes), BNA; and FO 141/1442, 1077/24/51G, July 31, 1951, BNA.

21. Excerpt in report "Military Action in Persia," June 19, 1951, DEFE 4/44, JP (51) 109, which was considered at DEFE 4/44, COS 101 (51) 5, June 22, 1951, BNA.

22. See FO 371/91459, No. 2415, June 8, 1951, BNA. See also "Conversation between the [British] Secretary of State and the United States Ambassador," FO 800/653, EP 1531/484, June 1, 1951, BNA.

23. See Foreign Office to Washington, No. 4638, FO 371/91592, September 28, 1951, BNA.

24. *FRUS, 1952–1954,* vol. 10, September 26, 1951, p. 173.

25. June 22, 1951, *FRUS, 1952–1954,* vol. 10, p. 67. For comments on the British belief that the United States might be motivated to act contrary to British interests in order to help American companies, see *FRUS, 1952–1954,* vol. 10, p. 53.

26. *FRUS, 1952–1954,* vol. 10, p. 178.

27. October 8, 1951, *FRUS, 1952–1954,* vol. 10, pp. 208–210. See also Morrison's comments in ibid., p. 69.

28. *FRUS, 1952–1954,* vol. 10, pp. 82–83.

29. Study Paper, Appendix to WFM B-2/2b, "The Position of the United States in Iran," September 6, 1951, p. 7, as cited in Crosby report, p. 124. WFM-B were U.S. papers prepared for the Washington Foreign Ministers' talks between Britain, France, and the United States. The *B* refers to the bilateral Anglo-American element of the talks. See *FRUS, 1951,* vol. 3, p. 1196.

30. *FRUS, 1952–1954,* vol. 10, pp. 188–190 at 189. See also pp. 205–208.

31. July 7, 1951, *FRUS, 1952–1954,* vol. 10, p. 83. In this instance, Morrison relented and accepted Truman's idea of sending Harriman to try to restart talks between Iran and Britain. Mohammad Mossadegh was prime minister of Iran.

32. Crosby report, p. 35.

33. "Washington Foreign Ministers Meetings, British Talks: Iran," WFM-B-2/2c, September 6, 1951, NARA.

34. "Oral History Interview with George C. McGhee," conducted by Richard D. McKinzie, Washington, D.C., June 11, 1975, Truman Library, http://www.trumanlibrary.org/oralhist/mcgheeg.htm.

35. *FRUS, 1952–1954,* vol. 10, p. 54.

36. Acheson-Lovett Memorandum of Conversation, September 26, 1951, Digital National Security Archive. For Frank's characterization of the Elliot-Lovett meeting, see Washington to Foreign Office, No. 3117, FO 371/91591, September 26 [received early in the morning on the 27th], 1951, BNA.

37. *FRUS, 1952–1954,* vol. 10, pp. 60–61. The document is also at the BNA. See also McGhee's comments to Franks, *FRUS,* pp. 37–38.

38. *FRUS, 1952–1954,* vol. 10, pp. 149–150.

39. Ibid., pp. 21–23. Some sections of the document have been removed. See also the editorial note, pp. 23–24.

40. *FRUS, 1952–1954,* vol. 10, pp. 71–76. Some sections of the document have been removed. See also the Crosby report, pp. 1–3.

41. The telegram was written by Loy Henderson, U.S. ambassador-designate to Iran. *FRUS, 1952–1954,* vol. 10, September 28, 1951, p. 178.

42. FO 800/653, PM/51/29, May 1, 1951, BNA. For an example of Anglo-American differences on Iran and communism, see *FRUS, 1952–1954,* vol. 10, October 8, 1951, p. 209.

43. This definition of United Action is distinct from either unilateral (U.S.) military intervention or a security organization for Southeast Asia along the lines of NATO.

44. Townsend Hoopes, *The Devil and John Foster Dulles* (Boston: Little, Brown, 1973), p. 211.

45. The meeting included five senators: William F. Knowland (R-Calif.), the majority leader; Eugene D. Millikin (R-Colo.); Lyndon B. Johnson (D-Tex.), the minority leader; Earle C. Clements (D-Ky.); and Richard Russell (D-Ga.). The meeting included three representatives: Joseph W. Martin Jr. (R-Mass.), the Speaker of the House; John McCormack, (D-Mass.), the minority whip; and James Percy Priest (D-Tenn.).

46. George C. Herring and Richard H. Immerman, "Eisenhower, Dulles, and Dienbienphu: 'The Day We Didn't Go to War' Revisited," *Journal of American History* 71 (September 1984): 343–363 at 353.

47. George C. Herring, *America's Longest War: The United States and Vietnam, 1950–1975,* 2nd ed. (New York: Alfred A. Knopf, 1986), p. 33.

48. "U.S.-U.K. Statement," dated April 13, 1954, *Department of State Bulletin* 30 (April 26, 1954): 622.

49. Lloyd C. Gardner blames Dulles for the misunderstanding. See Gardner, *Approaching Vietnam: From World War II through Dienbienphu* (New York: W. W. Norton, 1988), pp. 224–228. Waldo Heinrichs writes that "Eden later reneged" on what they had agreed on in London. Heinrichs, "Eisenhower and Sino-American Confrontation," in *The Great Powers in East Asia, 1953–1960,* ed. Warren I. Cohen and Akira Iriye (New York: Columbia University Press, 1990), pp. 86–103 at 96. Cable also says "Dulles...was probably right." James Cable, *The Geneva Conference of 1954 on Indochina* (New York: St. Martin's Press, 1986), p. 59. Anthony Short suggests it could be understood either way. Short, "British Policy in Southeast Asia: The Eisenhower Era," in *Great Powers in East Asia,* ed. Cohen and Iriye, pp. 246–271 at 253. Geoffrey Warner writes that Eden went back on his word but the United States went public without British permission about the proposed defense organization. Warner, "Britain and the Crisis over Dien Bien Phu, April 1954: The Failure of United Action," in *DIEN BIEN PHU and the Crisis of Franco-American Relations 1954–1955,* ed. Lawrence S. Kaplan, Denise Artaud, and Mark R. Rubin (Wilmington, Del.: Scholarly Resources, 1990), pp. 55–77. Hoopes seems to accept Eden's version. Hoopes, *Devil and John Foster Dulles,* p. 215.

50. Gardner, *Approaching Vietnam,* pp. 237–240. Makins reported that U.S. officials were constantly asking him about Britain's likely reaction to a larger U.S. role in Indochina. See ibid., pp. 172, 203–204.

51. "It is clear that the ministerial meetings of [April] 25th marked the end of any prospect of United Action in Indochina, at any rate before the Geneva Conference." Warner, "Crisis over Dien Bien Phu," p. 73. Melanie Billings-Yun agrees that the need for British support was the key obstacle to United Action. See Billings-Yun, *Decision against War: Eisenhower and Dien Bien Phu, 1954* (New York: Columbia University Press, 1988), p. 96. See also Cable, *Geneva Conference,* p. 69. Short agrees: "In the climatic year of 1954 it would seem, therefore, that the object of British policy in Southeast Asia was as much to restrain the United States as it was to contain communism." Short, "British Policy in Southeast Asia," p. 256. Gary R. Hess concurs: "That [U.S.] urgency, however, was not shared by the British....In the end the United States had to accept delaying movement on collective defense." Hess uses the term *collective defense* in the context of United Action. Hess, "The American Search for Stability in Southeast Asia: The SEATO Structure of Containment," in *Great Powers in East Asia,* ed. Cohen and Iriye, pp. 272–295 at 277. According to Herring, in late April, Dulles "made frantic efforts to convert Eden, urgently warning that without support from its allies France might give up the fight. The British would have none of it, however, and the administration was forced to back off." Herring, *America's Longest War,* p. 37. See also Hoopes, *Devil and John Foster Dulles,* p. 218.

52. Dwight D. Eisenhower, *The White House Years: Mandate for Change, 1953–1956* (Garden City, N.Y.: Doubleday, 1963), p. 351.

53. Eden telegram #1696, April 19, 1954, FO 371/112053, Public Record Office (PRO; now BNA), as cited in Warner, "Crisis over Dien Bien Phu," p. 70. Warner also mentions Evelyn Shuckburgh, *Descent to Suez: Diaries, 1951–1956* (London: Weidenfeld and Nicolson, 1986), p. 21.

54. Short, "British Policy in Southeast Asia," p. 256 (citing Eden and Churchill in CAB 129/68, PRO). See also Warner, "Crisis over Dien Bien Phu," p. 73, also citing CAB documents: "The foreign secretary [Eden] made it clear that he believed that the proposal for

a strike at Dien Bien Phu was a red herring and that the real objective would turn out to be China."

55. Gardner, *Approaching Vietnam*, pp. 273–274, 277–278.

56. Ibid., pp. 260–261.

57. Ibid., pp. 286–289.

58. Short, "British Policy in Southeast Asia," p. 247.

59. Gardner, *Approaching Vietnam*, p. 274.

60. Ibid., pp. 256–257.

61. Ibid. On the details of Dulles's comments to Molotov, Gardner cites Louis L. Gerson, *John Foster Dulles* (New York: Cooper Square, 1967), and April 27, 1954, *Foreign Relations of the United States [FRUS], 1952–1954: The Geneva Conference*, vol. 16, ed. Allen H. Kitchens and Neal H. Petersen (Washington, D.C.: U.S. Government Printing Office, 1981), pp. 570–580.

62. Gardner, *Approaching Vietnam*, p. 277.

63. A second question is why members of Congress demanded British participation. I have not found much evidence on this question. I attempted to trace some of the participants in the April 3, 1954, meeting. Sen. Richard Russell has notes on the meeting, but it is not possible to distinguish between what were his thoughts and what were his notes on what others were saying. The papers of Rep. Joseph Martin (Stonehill College), Rep. James Percy Priest (Tennessee State Library and Archives), Sen. Eugene Millikin (U. of Colorado-Boulder), and Sen. Earle C. Clements (U. of Kentucky) do not contain any useful material. Other possible avenues include checking Johnson's papers at his presidential library and visiting NARA to see the papers of another attendee, the assistant secretary for congressional relations, Thruston B. Morton. One may speculate that the fear of getting dragged into another ground war in Asia, so close on the heels of the Korean War, was not appealing.

64. *Foreign Relations of the United States [FRUS], 1952–1954: Indochina*, vol. 13, part 1, ed. Neal H. Petersen (Washington, D.C.: U.S. Government Printing Office, 1982), p. 1323.

65. Warner, "Crisis over Dien Bien Phu," p. 67.

66. Billings-Yun, *Decision against War*, p. 10.

67. Gardner, *Approaching Vietnam*, pp. 173, 244.

68. Ibid., p. 218. See also p. 252.

69. *FRUS, 1952–1954*, vol. 13, p. 1323.

70. Ibid., pp. 1232–1233, 1311–1313, 1316.

71. Short, "British Policy in Southeast Asia," p. 255.

72. Gardner, *Approaching Vietnam*, p. 241. See also p. 244. See also Short, "British Policy in Southeast Asia," p. 258; and Billings-Yun, *Decision against War*, p. 89.

73. CAB 128/27, CC 26 (54) 4, April 7, 1954, microfilm, Lamont Library, Harvard University. See also Warner, "Crisis over Dien Bien Phu," pp. 65–66 and 73.

74. Gardner, *Approaching Vietnam*, pp. 151, 184–185.

75. Robert A. Divine, *Eisenhower and the Cold War* (New York: Oxford University Press, 1981), p. 51. See also Richard Betts, *Nuclear Blackmail and Nuclear Balance* (Washington, D.C.: Brookings Institution, 1987), pp. 48–54.

76. Warner, "Crisis over Dien Bien Phu," p. 74.

77. Cable, *Geneva Conference*, p. 65.

78. April 7, 1954, *FRUS, 1952–1954*, vol. 13, pp. 1270–1272. See also Gardner, *Approaching Vietnam*, pp. 159–160, 162, 186, 213, 215, 222, and 380 n. 10.

79. Shuckburgh, *Descent to Suez*, p. 172, as cited in Warner, "Crisis over Dien Bien Phu," p. 72. See also Gardner, *Approaching Vietnam*, pp. 244 and 253.

80. Shuckburgh, *Descent to Suez*, p. 175, as cited in Warner, "Crisis over Dien Bien Phu," p. 74.

81. *FRUS, 1952–1954*, vol. 13, p. 1320.

82. Michael Dockrill, "Britain and the First Chinese Off-Shore Islands Crisis, 1954–55," in *British Foreign Policy, 1945–1956,* ed. Dockrill and John W. Young (London: Macmillan, 1989), pp. 173–196 at 179–180. See also Eisenhower, *White House Years,* p. 464.

83. Foreign Office to Washington, telegram #5795, November 24, 1954, FO 371/110233; and Makins, telegram #2556, November 28, 1954, FO 371/110239, as cited in Dockrill, "Chinese Off-Shore Islands Crisis," pp. 181–182.

84. Eisenhower, *White House Years,* pp. 467–469.

85. Peter G. Boyle, ed., *The Churchill-Eisenhower Correspondence, 1953–1955* (Chapel Hill: University of North Carolina Press, 1990), pp. 193–195.

86. Eisenhower, *White House Years,* p. 475. See also p. 483.

87. Boyle, *Churchill-Eisenhower Correspondence,* p. 210. Dockrill, "Chinese Off-Shore Islands Crisis," concurs on p. 190.

88. Letter to Churchill on February 18, 1955, in Boyle, *Churchill-Eisenhower Correspondence,* p. 198.

89. *Public Papers of the Presidents of the United States: Dwight D. Eisenhower, 1956* (Washington, D.C.: U.S. Government Printing Office, 1958), pp. 1060–1066 at 1064.

90. This is an excerpt of Robert D. Murphy's draft statement for the first tripartite meeting to discuss the Suez situation. Murphy, U.S. deputy undersecretary of state for political affairs, met with Selwyn Lloyd (British foreign secretary) and Christian Pineau (French foreign minister) on July 29. See *Foreign Relations of the United States [FRUS], 1955–1957: Suez Crisis, July 26–December 31, 1956,* vol. 16, ed. Nona J. Noring (Washington, D.C.: U.S. Government Printing Office, 1990), p. 36. See also W. Scott Lucas, *Divided We Stand: Britain, the US and the Suez Crisis* (London: Hodder and Stoughton, 1991), pp. 148–149.

91. "Letter from President Eisenhower to Prime Minister Eden," July 31, 1956, *FRUS, 1955–1957,* vol. 16, pp. 69–71. See also Lucas, *Divided We Stand,* pp. 151–152. Eden responded on August 5: *FRUS, 1955–1957,* vol. 16, pp. 146–148.

92. Eisenhower sent the note on September 2; Eden received it on September 3. *FRUS, 1955–1957,* vol. 16, pp. 355–358. On September 2, Hoover told U.S. embassies that the "U.S. is committed to endeavoring find peaceful solution." *FRUS, 1955–1957,* vol. 16, p. 350. See also p. 692.

93. *Public Papers of the Presidents,* p. 737.

94. *FRUS, 1955–1957,* vol. 16, pp. 435–438. See also PREM 11/1177, Eisenhower to Eden, September 8, 1956, PRO (BNA), as cited in Lucas, *Divided We Stand,* p. 184. Eden's letter to Eisenhower, sent on September 6, appears in *FRUS, 1955–1957,* vol. 16, pp. 400–403.

95. Dulles's idea was an organization of canal users that would protect the rights of users as outlined in the 1888 treaty signed at Constantinople. Dulles conceived of the Suez Canal Users' Association (SCUA) as a provisional way of avoiding the need for Egyptian cooperation while delaying Anglo-French pressures for using force. At the Second London Conference (September 19–21), the eighteen members agreed to form the SCUA. But it soon began to compete with British and French efforts at the United Nations; the two U.S. allies referred the Suez dispute to the UN Security Council (UNSC) on September 23, having informed the UNSC of the matter on September 12. The next meeting on the SCUA took place on October 1, just before the start of the discussions of the UNSC on October 5. The SCUA had several different names; *SCUA* was adopted on September 21, according to *FRUS, 1955–1957,* vol. 16, p. 552, and I use it throughout for the sake of clarity.

96. Diane B. Kunz, *The Economic Diplomacy of the Suez Crisis* (Chapel Hill: University of North Carolina Press, 1991), p. 110. For notes on this meeting, see *FRUS, 1955–1957,* vol. 16, pp. 639–645. This came just after a National Security Council meeting at which Eisenhower said, and Dulles agreed, that "the United States would be dead wrong to join in any resort to force." *FRUS, 1955–1957,* vol. 16, p. 633 (October 4).

97. *FRUS, 1955–1957*, vol. 16, p. 766; cited in Kunz, *Economic Diplomacy*, p. 114. Dillon's response is in *FRUS, 1955–1957*, vol. 16, pp. 766–767.

98. Kunz, *Economic Diplomacy*, pp. 84, 97.

99. *FRUS, 1955–1957*, vol. 16, p. 68.

100. Ibid., pp. 226, 195.

101. Ibid., pp. 392, 396.

102. Ibid., p. 703.

103. Kunz, *Economic Diplomacy*, p. 98 (especially n. 13); and Lucas, *Divided We Stand*, p. 199.

104. *FRUS, 1955–1957*, vol. 16, p. 435. See also the points Dulles made to Eisenhower on August 29, 1956, p. 315.

105. *FRUS, 1955–1957*, vol. 16, p. 586 (September 26, 1956).

106. Ibid., p. 767 (October 23, 1956). This echoes a Special National Intelligence Estimate, September 19, 1956, paragraph 9, *FRUS, 1955–1957*, vol. 16, p. 527.

107. Eisenhower himself also brainstormed about possible diplomatic options. See his letter to Hoover in *FRUS, 1955–1957*, vol. 16, p. 662–663 (October 8).

108. The first international effort to avert a military confrontation was the London Conference, August 16–23, 1956. The conference of twenty-two states resulted in the eighteen-power plan, which would have created a new international authority to manage and control the canal. A subgroup of the eighteen countries supporting the plan, the five-member Suez Committee led by Australian premier Robert Menzies, presented the plan to Egypt on September 3–9. Egypt rejected it.

109. The major exceptions include Eden's understanding of Dulles's use of the word *disgorge* and Macmillan's report of his trip to the United States.

110. CAB 128/30, CM 56 (56), August 1, 1956, microfilm, Lamont Library, Harvard University.

111. There is a slight discrepancy about dates. In his entry for September 5, Clark refers to "last night's telegram" from Eisenhower. But according to *FRUS*, the British received the message on September 3. See William Clark, *From Three Worlds* (London: Sidgwick and Jackson, 1986), p. 183.

112. CAB 128/30, CM 63 (56), September 6, 1956, microfilm, Lamont Library, Harvard University.

113. Washington to Foreign Office, telegram #1849, FO 800/740, September 9, 1956, PRO (BNA); cited in Kunz, *Economic Diplomacy*, p. 94.

114. CAB 128/30, CM 64 (56) 4, September 11, 1956, microfilm, Lamont Library, Harvard University.

115. Anthony Eden, *Full Circle* (Boston: Houghton Mifflin, 1960), p. 561.

116. CAB 128/30, CM 74 (56) 1, October 25, 1956, microfilm, Lamont Library, Harvard University.

117. CAB 128/30, CM 75 (56) 1, October 30, 1956, microfilm, Lamont Library, Harvard University.

118. Lucas, *Divided We Stand*, pp. 171–172; and *FRUS, 1955–1957*, vol. 16, p. 226. On August 9, Dulles told the NSC that he "felt the United States must make it clear that we would be in the hostilities if the Soviets came in." He called for studying the implications of such a statement (*FRUS, 1955–1957*, vol. 16, p. 174).

119. Kunz, *Economic Diplomacy*, p. 92. See also *FRUS, 1955–1957*, vol. 16, pp. 176–177, 177–178, and 185–187. Yet during the crisis, the U.S. military also interfered with the operation of the British navy. Clark, *From Three Worlds*, p. 205.

120. Lucas, *Divided We Stand*, pp. 260–261.

121. Ibid., pp. 269–270, 307.

122. This quotation is from document 352, an editorial note that quotes from a transcript of the conversation. *FRUS 1955–1957*, vol. 16, p. 745.

123. Document 384, *FRUS, 1955–1957,* vol. 16, p. 790.

124. Document 403, *FRUS, 1955–1957,* vol. 16, p. 815.

125. Dwight D. Eisenhower, *Waging Peace, 1956–1961* (Garden City, N.Y.: Doubleday, 1965), p. 77. The ellipse and emphasis appear in *Waging Peace.* See also Douglas Stuart and William Tow, *The Limits of Alliance: NATO Out-of-Area Problems since 1949* (Baltimore: Johns Hopkins University Press, 1990), pp. 63–65.

126. *FRUS, 1955–1957,* vol. 16, p. 974. See also Eisenhower's comment on p. 988 (November 5, 10:20 a.m.). The United States recognized that Western Europe's oil supply "may soon be endangered" (987).

127. *FRUS, 1955–1957,* vol. 16, pp. 1070–1086 at 1076–1078.

128. Ibid., pp. 1127–1132.

129. Ibid., p. 1194.

130. Ibid., p. 1195.

131. Ibid., p. 1201.

132. Lucas, *Divided We Stand,* p. 317.

133. On oil, see also Eisenhower, *Waging Peace,* p. 98.

134. In his memoirs, Eisenhower did not explicitly mention U.S. currency pressure on Britain, but he noted the "great drain in British gold and dollar reserves." Eisenhower, *Waging Peace,* p. 92.

135. Harold Macmillan, *Riding the Storm, 1956–1959* (London: Macmillan, 1971), p. 164.

136. Selwyn Lloyd, *Suez, 1956: A Personal Account* (New York: Mayflower Books, 1978), pp. 209–211.

137. Ibid., pp. 210–211; Alistair Horne, *Harold Macmillan: Volume 1, 1894–1956* (New York: Viking, 1988), pp. 440–445; Kunz, *Economic Diplomacy,* pp. 131–133; Betts, *Nuclear Blackmail,* pp. 62–65.

138. R. A. Butler, *The Art of the Possible: The Memoirs of Lord Butler* (London: Hamish Hamilton, 1971), p. 195.

139. Walter Monckton, unpublished memoirs, http://www.spartacus.schoolnet.co.uk/PRmonckton.htm, accessed July 21, 2005.

140. Divine, *Eisenhower and the Cold War,* p. 90.

141. *Foreign Relations of the United States, 1955–1957: Western European Security and Integration,* vol. 4, ed. Nancy E. Johnson (Washington, D.C.: U.S. Government Printing Office, 1986), pp. 137–145 at 140–142. December 13, 1956, "Telegram from the United States Delegation at the North Atlantic Council Ministerial Meeting to the Department of State," document 47. "The NAC at its May 5, [1956] Ministerial meeting appointed a Committee of Three Foreign Ministers to advise the Council on ways and means to improve and extend NATO cooperation in nonmilitary fields and to develop greater unity within the Atlantic Community" (137). The authors of the report took into account the alliance crisis caused by the Suez war. The full report is printed in *Department of State Bulletin,* January 7, 1957, pp. 18–28.

142. *FRUS, 1955–1957,* vol. 16, p. 65 July 31, 1956.

143. Ibid., p. 745.

144. Ibid., p. 816 (October 29, 1956, 11:17 a.m.).

145. Dillon characterizes the French argument in *FRUS, 1955–1957,* vol. 16, p. 655. Dulles agreed (657).

146. *FRUS, 1955–1957,* vol. 16, p. 643.

147. Ibid., p. 651.

148. CAB 128/30, CM 68 (56) 11, October 3, 1956, microfilm, Lamont Library, Harvard University.

149. The report highlighted Britain and France on one side and West Germany and the smaller NATO countries on the other side. See *FRUS, 1955–1957,* vol. 16, p. 387.

150. Lucas, *Divided We Stand*, p. 37 n. 73. For a minor example, see *FRUS, 1955–1957*, vol. 16, p. 590.

151. *FRUS, 1955–1957*, vol. 16, p. 133.

152. Ibid., p. 149.

153. Ibid., pp. 156–160, 226.

154. Ibid., p. 649 (October 5).

155. The opposite question is also of interest in the case of the U.S. invasion of Iraq in 2003: does the restrainee become responsible for the outcome if restraint fails?

156. In *FRUS, 1955–1957*, vol. 16, the French blamed the United States, pp. 551 (#2) and 655. The scapegoat question appears on pp. 397, 551 (#4), 625, 632ff., and 679. Evidence that the United States tried to mollify France is on p. 552.

157. *FRUS, 1955–1957*, vol. 16, p. 591.

158. Ibid., p. 404 (September 7, 1956).

159. Ibid., p. 579 (September 25, 1956).

160. Ibid., pp. 641 and 642.

161. Ibid., pp. 679, 680, 770.

162. Ibid., p. 67 (July 31, 1956).

163. Ibid., p. 63.

164. Ibid., p. 640 (October 5) and p. 816 (October 29).

165. Ibid., pp. 106–107. Byroade was ambassador to Egypt until September 10, 1956.

166. *FRUS, 1955–1957*, vol. 16, p. 334. Eisenhower's letter to Eden on September 2 used this same language (357). See also pp. 95–96, 99, 430.

167. SNIE, September 5, 1956, *FRUS, 1955–1957*, vol. 16, pp. 384–385, 388.

168. *FRUS, 1955–1957*, vol. 16, p. 194.

169. Ibid., p. 334. See also p. 640 and p. 816 (October 29).

170. SNIE, September 5, 1956, in *FRUS, 1955–1957*, vol. 16, p. 386.

171. *FRUS, 1955–1957*, vol. 16, p. 390. See also pp. 95–96, 189, 313, 440.

172. November 3, 1956, *FRUS, 1955–1957*, vol. 16, pp. 968–972.

173. *FRUS, 1955–1957*, vol. 16, pp. 1018–1019. See p. 1030 (#1) and n. 2 on the U.S. decision not to share this estimate with Britain or Canada. Lucas writes that after U.S. intelligence concluded that the Soviets would not attack, Britain's Joint Intelligence Committee was told this on November 6 as the cabinet was meeting. Lucas, *Divided We Stand*, p. 294.

174. For expressions of U.S. concern, see *FRUS, 1955–1957*, vol. 16, pp. 990, 1000, 1001, 1014, 1016–1017 (contrasted with p. 995), 1041, 1048.

175. For instance, see Hoover's comments to the French ambassador, November 6, 1956, *FRUS, 1955–1957*, vol. 16, p. 1024.

176. *FRUS, 1955–1957*, vol. 16, p. 1028.

177. Ibid., p. 987.

178. Ibid., p. 1014. On Syria, see also pp. 966–967, 973, 977.

179. Kunz, *Economic Diplomacy*, p. 131.

180. Herman Finer, *Dulles over Suez* (Chicago: Quadrangle Books, 1964), p. 411ff.

181. For a list of the steps taken, see *FRUS, 1955–1957*, vol. 16, pp. 1035–1037. During this meeting, Eisenhower called Eden (1025–1027). On military steps, see also p. 1002. On the issue of meeting notes, see p. 1035 n. 1.

182. *FRUS, 1955–1957*, vol. 16, p. 1051. In his memoirs, Eisenhower wrote almost nothing about U.S. economic pressure on Britain in November. See Eisenhower, *Waging Peace*, especially pp. 91–92 and 98.

183. "Memorandum of Discussion at the 302nd Meeting of the National Security Council, Washington, November 1, 1956, 9 a.m.," *FRUS, 1955–1957*, vol. 16, pp. 902–916 at 914 and 911. Dulles was out of the room when the president stated that fighting with these two allies was unthinkable (914).

184. *FRUS, 1955–1957*, vol. 16, p. 167.
185. Compare ibid., pp. 432 and 436. Eisenhower mentioned this same point to Dulles on September 7, 1956 (430).
186. *FRUS, 1955–1957*, vol. 16, p. 642. See also p. 189 (August 12, 1956).
187. Ibid., p. 835 (October 29, 1956).
188. Ibid., pp. 833–839 (October 29, 1956). Just minutes later, Eisenhower repeated his stance to Coulson (U.K.). *FRUS, 1955–1957*, vol. 16, pp. 839–840.
189. See also *FRUS, 1955–1957*, vol. 16, pp. 98, 436.
190. *FRUS, 1955–1957*, vol. 16, pp. 48, 63, 167, 356.
191. Ibid., p. 356 (September 2, 1956).
192. Ibid., pp. 63 and 65 (July 31, 1956).
193. Ibid., p. 65.
194. Ibid., p. 313 (August 28, 1956).
195. Ibid., p. 440 (September 8, 1956).
196. Ibid., p. 330.
197. Ibid., p. 546.
198. Ibid., p. 581. For more examples, see pp. 140–143, 334–335, 357, 436–437, 440.
199. Ibid., p. 626.
200. For instance, see *FRUS, 1955–1957*, vol. 16, pp. 639–645 (October 5).
201. *FRUS, 1955–1957*, vol. 16, p. 143 n. 3.
202. For the November 3 date, see Neustadt, *Alliance Politics*, p. 27.
203. Neustadt, *Alliance Politics*, p. 121. Neustadt also posits the possibility that Dulles's failure to threaten England materially was a failure of "imagination" (121).
204. Neustadt, *Alliance Politics*, p. 23.

4. American-Israeli Relations and Alliance Restraint

1. Although a restrainee may have an incentive to withhold information so as to avoid restraint, once it has been restrained it may want to highlight the fact that it held back. This is a useful argument for the restrainee when it asks for side payments for capitulating to the restrainer's demands: I was restrained and now you owe me one. This probably affected Israeli statements in cases of Israeli restraint, including the 1973 war and the 1991 Persian Gulf War. See also Tom Segev, *1967*, trans. Jessica Cohen (New York: Henry Holt, 2005/2007), p. 200.

2. I am suggesting not that these were always the only concerns but rather that they were always central ones.

3. Abraham Ben-Zvi, *The United States and Israel: The Limits of the Special Relationship* (New York: Columbia University Press, 1993).

4. The data are from Jan Faber, "Annual Data on Nine Economic and Military Characteristics of 78 Nations" (SIRE NATDAT), 1948–1983 [computer file]. Amsterdam: Europa Institut [producer], 1989; Ann Arbor, Mich.: Inter-university Consortium for Political and Social Research, and Amsterdam: Steinmetz Archive [distributors], 1990.

5. In 1959, Eisenhower supported $100 million "in technical and financial assistance." The next year the United States sold $10 million of radar equipment. Douglas Little, *American Orientalism* (Chapel Hill: University of North Carolina Press, 2002), p. 94.

6. The Johnson administration had also sold tanks and aircraft to Israel before the 1967 war, but with the hope of avoiding a binding security guarantee at that time. Israelis, however, saw such sales as further steps toward a tighter relationship. See Zach Levey, "The United States' Skyhawk Sale to Israel, 1966: Strategic Exigencies of an Arms Deal," *Diplomatic History* 28 (April 2004): 255–276.

7. The arms figure is from Scott Lasensky, "Dollarizing Peace: Nixon, Kissinger and the Creation of the US-Israeli Alliance," *Israel Affairs* 13 (January 2007): 164–186 at 168.

8. Itamar Rabinovich, *Waging Peace: Israel and the Arabs, 1948–2003*, rev. ed. (Princeton, N.J.: Princeton University Press, 2004), p. 17. See also the cable from K. Keating, U.S. ambassador to Israel, to State, October 31, 1973, http://aad.archives.gov/aad/createpdf? rid=91501&dt=1573&dl=823.

9. William B. Quandt, *Peace Process: American Diplomacy and the Arab-Israeli Conflict since 1967*, rev. ed. (Washington, D.C.: Brookings Institution Press; Berkeley: University of California Press, 2001), pp. 44, 121–124.

10. Avner Yaniv, *Deterrence without the Bomb* (Lexington, Mass.: Lexington Books/D. C. Heath, 1987), pp. 157, 220.

11. For example, see Keating to State, October 31, 1973, http://aad.archives.gov/aad/ createpdf?rid=77596&dt=1573&dl=823. The Soviets did the same. See Drew Middleton, "Middle East War Is Vast Test Range for the Most Advanced Soviet Weapons," *New York Times*, October 24, 1973.

12. Michael Karpin, *The Bomb in the Basement* (New York: Simon and Schuster, 2006), pp. 183–184.

13. The episode started when Syrian tanks moved against Jordan. Jordan requested air and land strikes from the United States against the Syrian forces. The United States asked Israel to fly reconnaissance missions to prepare the groundwork for a possible U.S. strike. Israel and the United States then discussed possible Israeli ground and air strikes instead of American ones; Washington approved both Israeli options in principle. On September 22, Israel was "poised to act," but King Hussein of Jordan, cognizant of American and Israeli support, attacked the Syrian forces with his own air force. Syrian forces were pushed back, thus eliminating the need for Israeli intervention on America's behalf. As a result, "U.S.-Israeli relations were stronger than ever." See Quandt, *Peace Process*, pp. 80–83.

14. Nadav Safran, *Israel: The Embattled Ally* (Cambridge, Mass.: Harvard University Press, Belknap Press, 1981), p. 455.

15. Quandt, *Peace Process*, p. 83. See also Kissinger's view on p. 103.

16. Quandt, *Peace Process*, pp. 103–104. See also Jeremy M. Sharp, *U.S. Foreign Aid to Israel* (Washington, D.C.: Congressional Research Service, 2006).

17. Quandt, *Peace Process*, p. 87.

18. Safran, *Israel*, p. 456; and Quandt, *Peace Process*, p. 87.

19. Safran, *Israel*, p. 466.

20. William B. Quandt, *Peace Process: American Diplomacy and the Arab-Israeli Conflict since 1967* (Washington, D.C.: Brookings Institution Press; Berkeley: University of California Press, 1993), p. 131; Safran, *Israel*, p. 466; and Lasensky, "Dollarizing Peace," p. 166.

21. Bernard Gwertzman, "Congressmen Get Mideast Briefing," *New York Times*, January 22, 1974; Quandt, *Peace Process* (1993), p. 200; Lasensky, "Dollarizing Peace," p. 172.

22. The text of the agreement is at http://www.jewishvirtuallibrary.org/jsource/Peace/ mou1975.html, accessed January 3, 2007. For an earlier example of an Israeli call for a security agreement, see Keating to State, December 3, 1973, http://aad.archives.gov/aad/ createpdf?rid=110014&dt=1573&dl=823.

23. Shai Feldman, *The Future of U.S.-Israel Strategic Cooperation* (Washington, D.C.: Washington Institute for Near East Policy, 1996), p. 10. See also Yaniv, *Deterrence without the Bomb*, pp. 216–217. The text of the agreement is at http://www.mfa.gov.il/MFA/ Peace%20Process/Guide%20to%20the%20Peace%20Process/US-Israel%20Memorandu m%20of%20Agreement, accessed June 19, 2007.

24. Quandt, *Peace Process* (2001), p. 258. For the full text of the 1981 agreement, see Nimrod Novik, *Encounter with Reality: Reagan and the Middle East (The First Term)* (Boulder, Colo.: Westview Press for the Jaffee Center for Strategic Studies, 1985), pp. 86–88, as cited in Quandt, *Peace Process* (2001), p. 442. Reagan lifted the suspension as part of National Security Decision Directive 111, "Next Steps toward Progress in Lebanon and the Middle East," October 28, 1983, http://www.fas.org/irp/offdocs/nsdd/nsdd-111.htm. Most of

the document has not been declassified. On October 31, 1998, the two allies also signed a Memorandum of Agreement that was meant to enhance "Israel's defense and deterrent capabilities" and upgrade "the framework of the U.S.-Israel strategic and military relationship." See http://www.cns.miis.edu/research/wmdme/isrl_moa.htm, accessed January 3, 2007. Yaniv, *Deterrence without the bomb* (p. 220), points out that despite the many contentious Israeli policies in the early 1980s—attacking Iraqi nuclear facilities, extending Israeli law to the occupied Golan Heights, invading Lebanon—the alliance held strong.

25. Bernard Gwertzman, "Reagan Turns to Israel," *New York Times Magazine,* November 27, 1983.

26. The text of the agreement is at http://www.jewishvirtuallibrary.org/jsource/US-Israel/mou0488.html, accessed January 4, 2007.

27. The letter is cited but not reproduced in *Foreign Relations of the United States [FRUS], 1958–1960: Arab-Israeli Dispute; United Arab Republic; North Africa,* vol. 13, ed. Suzanne E. Coffman and Charles S. Sampson (Washington, D.C.: U.S. Government Printing Office, 1992), p. 74. See also Peter L. Hahn, *Caught in the Middle East: U.S. Policy toward the Arab-Israeli Conflict, 1945–1961* (Chapel Hill: University of North Carolina Press, 2004), p. 245. This letter may also be what Shlomo Aronson was referring to when he wrote that Eisenhower secretly promised Israel that the United States "will not permit Israel's destruction." Aronson, *Conflict and Bargaining in the Middle East: An Israeli Perspective* (Baltimore: Johns Hopkins University Press, 1978), p. 40.

28. Document 35, "Memorandum of Conversation," August 3, 1958, *FRUS, 1958–1960,* vol. 13, pp. 82–83.

29. Document 35, "Paper Prepared by the National Security Council Planning Board," July 29, 1958, *Foreign Relations of the United States [FRUS], 1958–1960: Near East Region; Iraq; Iran; Arabian Peninsula,* vol. 12, ed. Edward C. Keefer (Washington, D.C.: U.S. Government Printing Office, 1993), p. 117.

30. The document was NSC 5820/1. Document 51, "National Security Council Report," November 4, 1958, *FRUS, 1958–1960,* vol. 12, pp. 187–199 at 189–190.

31. Document 121, Memorandum of Conversation between Kennedy and Meir, Palm Beach, Florida, December 27, 1962, *Foreign Relations of the United States [FRUS], 1961–1963: Near East, 1962–1963,* vol. 18, ed. Nina J. Noring (Washington, D.C.: U.S. Government Printing Office, 1995), pp. 280–281, or http://www.state.gov/r/pa/ho/frus/kennedyjf/xviii/26200.htm. See also Little, *American Orientalism,* pp. 96–97.

32. Shlomo Aronson with Oded Brosh, *The Politics and Strategy of Nuclear Weapons in the Middle East* (Albany: State University of New York Press, 1992), pp. 72, 83. See also Mordechai Gazit, "The Genesis of the U.S.-Israeli Military-Strategic Relationship and the Dimona Issue," *Journal of Contemporary History* 35 (July 2000): 413–422 at 414–415.

33. George Lenczowski, *American Presidents and the Middle East* (Durham, N.C.: Duke University Press, 1990), p. 71.

34. Lyndon Baines Johnson, *The Vantage Point: Perspectives of the Presidency, 1963–1969* (New York: Holt, Rinehart and Winston, 1971), p. 297. See also Little, *American Orientalism,* p. 97.

35. Merle Miller, *Lyndon* (New York: G. P. Putnam's Sons, 1980), p. 477. See also Karpin, *Bomb in the Basement,* pp. 242–247; Segev, *1967,* p. 109; and Transcript, Arthur B. Krim Oral History Interview III, June 29, 1982, by Michael Gillette, p. 27, LBJ Library. Online: http://www.lbjlib.utexas.edu/johnson/archives.hom/oralhistory.hom/Krim-A/Krim3.pdf, accessed June 15, 2007.

36. Little, *American Orientalism,* p. 106.

37. Lenczowski, *American Presidents,* pp. 139–140.

38. Cable from Keating to State, October 16, 1973, http://aad.archives.gov/aad/creat epdf?rid=86750&dt=1573&dl=823.

39. Given the material power imbalance between the two sides, it is not surprising that the United States gave more than it got. Ben-Zvi compares the relationship to that between

a patron and a client. In my view, the patron-client dynamic is one type of alliance. See Ben-Zvi, *United States and Israel*.

40. The meeting included the U.S. ambassador to Cairo and a few State Department officials. Document 117, Memorandum of Conversation, December 21, 1962, *FRUS, 1961–1963*, vol. 18, p. 271.

41. The strong sense in Ben-Zvi's work is that the United States already considered Israel a strategic asset during Eisenhower's second term and under Kennedy. See Abraham Ben-Zvi, *Decade of Transition* (New York: Columbia University Press, 1998).

42. Uri Bialer, *Between East and West: Israel's Foreign Policy, 1948–1956* (Cambridge: Cambridge University Press, 1990), pp. 261–262, 264, 279. See also Zach Levey, *Israel and the Western Powers* (Chapel Hill: University of North Carolina Press, 1997), especially chap. 1; and Yaniv, *Deterrence without the Bomb*, pp. 53–54 and 153–157. See also Karpin, *Bomb in the Basement*, pp. 9, 20, 23.

43. Ariel Sharon with David Chanoff, *Warrior* (New York: Simon and Schuster, 1989), p. 345. On Dayan, see Yaniv, *Deterrence without the Bomb*, p. 215. Sharon had changed his tune by the time he was prime minister in the 2000s. He fostered a very close relationship with the United States. Yaniv (p. 218) contends Sharon changed his view by the 1980s. See also Jonathan Rynhold, "The View from Jerusalem: Israeli-American Relations and the Peace Process," *Middle East Review of International Affairs* 4 (June 2000). On Dayan in the Begin years, see Scott B. Lasensky, "Buying Peace and Security? US Positive Economic Inducement Strategies for Reducing Regional Conflicts and Retarding Weapons of Mass Destruction Proliferation" (Ph.D. dissertation, Brandeis University, 2001), p. 57.

44. Dean Rusk as told to Richard Rusk, *As I Saw It* (New York: W. W. Norton, 1990), p. 381.

45. Avner Cohen, *Israel and the Bomb* (New York: Columbia University Press, 1998), p. 103.

46. Ibid., p. 109.

47. Ibid., p. 112. See also pp. 118–119, 121.

48. Ibid., p. 128.

49. Ben-Zvi, *Decade of Transition*, p. 122; and Warren Bass, *Support Any Friend: Kennedy's Middle East and the Making of the U.S.-Israel Alliance* (New York: Oxford University Press, 2003), p. 189.

50. One could argue that the two are not separate. By inspecting Dimona, perhaps the United States hoped to block Israel from producing the fissile material that is the sine qua non of any nuclear weapons program.

51. Cohen, *Israel and the Bomb*, p. 154; Bass, *Support Any Friend*, p. 216; and Karpin, *Bomb in the Basement*, pp. 232–233.

52. Cohen, *Israel and the Bomb*, p. 101; Bass, *Support Any Friend*, p. 193.

53. Cohen, *Israel and the Bomb*, pp. 108–109. See also Avner Cohen, "The Nuclear Ambiguity Route," *Ha'aretz*, February 12, 2007.

54. Cohen, *Israel and the Bomb*, p. 113.

55. Bass, *Support Any Friend*, p. 207.

56. Cohen, *Israel and the Bomb*, p. 119.

57. Looking back, Evron thinks it was an "open question." Yair Evron, *Israel's Nuclear Dilemma* (Ithaca: Cornell University Press, 1994), p. 150.

58. Cohen, *Israel and the Bomb*, p. 43; on U.S.-Israeli negotiations, see Michael Bar-Zohar, *Ben-Gurion: A Biography*, trans. Peretz Kidron (New York: Delacorte Press, 1977), p. 223.

59. Cohen, *Israel and the Bomb*, p. 55.

60. Ibid., p. 48.

61. Ben-Zvi, *Decade of Transition*, pp. 126–129.

62. Bass, *Support Any Friend*, pp. 213–214, 223, 231. For Kennedy's rejection on July 23, 1963, see pp. 230, 236. For the suggestion that over time Ben-Gurion lost faith in the idea

of a military pact and came to depend on the nuclear option, see Cohen, *Israel and the Bomb*, pp. 13, 48, 65; and Aronson, *Conflict and Bargaining*, p. 43. Karpin argues that Israel in the 1950s would have readily traded away its nuclear aspirations for a security guarantee, especially a NATO-like deal. By 1962–1963, however, he thinks Israel was no longer willing. He also cites Peres, Ben-Gurion's point man on nuclear relations with France, on this issue. Karpin, *Bomb in the Basement*, pp. 94, 144, 195, 222, 235, 238. If Karpin is correct, the American ability to restrain Israel would have been limited.

63. Document 300, "Memorandum from Robert W. Komer of the National Security Council Staff to President Kennedy," July 23, 1963, *FRUS, 1961–1963*, vol. 18, p. 651, or http://www.state.gov/r/pa/ho/frus/kennedyjf/xviii/26215.htm.

64. Document 298, "Memorandum from Robert W. Komer of the National Security Council Staff to President Kennedy," July 19, 1963, *FRUS, 1961–1963*, vol. 18, p. 648, or http://www.state.gov/r/pa/ho/frus/kennedyjf/xviii/26215.htm.

65. Little, *American Orientalism*, p. 96.

66. Aronson, *Politics and Strategy*, p. 80.

67. Document 327, "Memorandum from the Department of State Executive Secretary (Read) to the President's Special Assistant for National Security Affairs (Bundy)," September 20, 1963, pp. 705–708, or http://www.state.gov/r/pa/ho/frus/kennedyjf/xviii/26376.htm. On State, see also document 317: "We continue to favor disassociation of the Dimona problem and Israel's quest for special security relations" (p. 687). See document 308 for the JCS: "In summary, the Joint Chiefs of Staff recommend that: a. No US security assurance to Israel be given beyond that enunciated by the President on 8 May 1963." "Memorandum from the Joint Chiefs of Staff to Secretary of Defense McNamara," JCSM-611–63, August 7, 1963, p. 669, or http://www.state.gov/r/pa/ho/frus/kennedyjf/xviii/26215.htm. See also document 316, "Letter from the Deputy Assistant Secretary of Defense for International Security Affairs (Sloan) to the Deputy Assistant Secretary of State for Near Eastern and South Asian Affairs (Grant)," August 22, 1963, pp. 684–685, or http://www.state.gov/r/pa/ho/frus/kennedyjf/xviii/26376.htm. All the documents in this note are in *FRUS, 1961–1963*, vol. 18.

68. Document 303, "Memorandum of Conversation," July 23, 1963, *FRUS, 1961–1963*, vol. 18, p. 660, or http://www.state.gov/r/pa/ho/frus/kennedyjf/xviii/26215.htm. The meeting included President Kennedy, Acting Secretary of State George Ball, John J. Mc-Cloy, Assistant Secretary of State Phillips Talbot, Ambassador John Badeau (American ambassador to the United Arab Republic [Egypt]), CIA director John McCone, Assistant Secretary of Defense Paul Nitze, National Security Advisor McGeorge Bundy, NSC staffer Robert Komer, and Hermann F. Eilts from State.

69. Document 332, "Telegram from the Department of State to the Embassy in Israel," October 2, 1963, *FRUS, 1961–1963*, vol. 18, pp. 720–722, or http://www.state.gov/r/pa/ho/frus/kennedyjf/xviii/26376.htm.

70. See Karpin, *Bomb in the Basement*, pp. 181, 184, 185, 194.

71. Document 301, "Memorandum from Secretary of State Rusk to President Kennedy," July 23, 1963, *FRUS, 1961–1963*, vol. 18, p. 655.

72. Bass, *Support Any Friend*, p. 188.

73. Roland Popp, "Stumbling Decidedly into the Six-Day War," *Middle East Journal* 60 (Spring 2006): 281–309 at 287. Popp's work is in sharp contrast to a recent book on the Soviet role, Isabella Ginor and Gideon Remez, *Foxbats over Dimona: The Soviets' Nuclear Gamble in the Six-Day War* (New Haven, Conn.: Yale University Press, 2007).

74. Norman G. Finkelstein disputes this claim in *Image and Reality of the Israel-Palestine Conflict*, 2nd ed. (New York: Verso, 2003). See also the comments by Gen. Earle G. Wheeler, chairman of the Joint Chiefs of Staff: "Israel could maintain the present level of mobilization for two months without causing serious economic trouble." Popp, "Stumbling Decidedly," p. 302.

75. Document 3, and also documents 16 and 36, *Foreign Relations of the United States [FRUS], 1964–1968: Arab-Israeli Crisis and War, 1967*, vol. 19, Harriet Dashiell Schwar (Washington, D.C.: U.S. Government Printing Office, 2004), p. 3. This *FRUS* volume is available online at http://www.state.gov/r/pa/ho/frus/johnsonlb/xix/.

76. Document 8, *FRUS, 1964–1968*, vol. 19, pp. 10–11.

77. Document 18, ibid., p. 27.

78. Document 25, ibid., pp. 34–35.

79. Document 58, ibid., p. 97.

80. Richard B. Parker, ed., *The Six-Day War: A Retrospective* (Gainesville: University Press of Florida, 1996), p. 220.

81. Richard B. Parker, *The Politics of Miscalculation in the Middle East* (Bloomington: Indiana University Press, 1993), pp. 114–115. For other general comments that the United States was restraining Israel, see Wheeler's remark in Steven L. Spiegel, *The Other Arab-Israeli Conflict: Making America's Middle East Policy from Truman to Reagan* (Chicago: University of Chicago Press, 1985), p. 150; Saunders's quotation in Quandt, *Peace Process* (2001), p. 399 n. 9; and Quandt, *Peace Process* (2001), p. 28.

82. Parker, *Six-Day War*, pp. 129, 138.

83. Rusk, *As I Saw It*, p. 387. Johnson himself later wrote that he was "working as hard as I could to forestall [war]," and "I used all the energy and experience I could muster to prevent war." Johnson, *Vantage Point*, pp. 287 and 294.

84. Documents 50, 57, and 72, *FRUS, 1964–1968*, vol. 19, pp. 81–82, 94–95, 127–136; Spiegel, *Other Arab-Israeli Conflict*, p. 137; Michael Oren, *Six Days of War* (New York: Oxford University Press, 2002), p. 90; Michael Brecher, *Decisions in Israel's Foreign Policy* (New Haven, Conn.: Yale University Press, 1975), pp. 319, 322, 332, 380.

85. Document 71, *FRUS, 1964–1968*, vol. 19, p. 123.

86. Document 69, ibid., pp. 118–119.

87. Document 72, ibid., p. 136. See also Johnson's displeasure with Eshkol's public phrasing of Johnson's words to Eban, document 109, *FRUS, 1964–1968*, vol. 19, pp. 201–202; and Spiegel, *Other Arab-Israeli Conflict*, p. 146. Oren, *Six Days of War*, p. 139, writes that in this Johnson-Eshkol dispute, Johnson went back on his word; this is a correct assessment, based on documents 77 and 102 (and documents 114 and 130). According to Evron, the linguistic spat signaled to Israel that it would have to act on its own. Parker, *Six-Day War*, p. 152. Yitzhak Rabin, chief of staff: "There was no way of misinterpreting the cable [from Evron in Washington informing Israel on June 1 of Johnson's clarification]: we could not expect any action on the part of the United States for it was not possible to assemble an international flotilla to break the Egyptian blockade.... That cable from Washington had the look and feel of the proverbial last straw." Yitzhak Rabin, *The Rabin Memoirs*, expanded ed. (Berkeley: University of California Press, 1996), p. 95.

88. Document 139, *FRUS, 1964–1968*, vol. 19, p. 264.

89. Quandt, *Peace Process* (2001), pp. 29, 49.

90. Document 72, *FRUS, 1964–1968*, vol. 19, p. 132.

91. Document 64, ibid., p. 111.

92. Ibid., p. 110, and also documents 69, 71, and 80.

93. Document 71, *FRUS, 1964–1968*, vol. 19, p. 123. Segev later argued that Eban overstated Johnson's promise when Eban reported back to the Israeli cabinet. Segev, *1967*, pp. 289, 292.

94. Document 77, *FRUS, 1964–1968*, vol. 19, p. 143.

95. Ibid., p. 145.

96. Quandt, *Peace Process* (2001), pp. 36, 42.

97. Lyndon B. Johnson daily diary, May 26, 1967, Johnson Presidential Library, p. 11.

98. For instance, see documents 68, 71, 77, 80, *FRUS, 1964–1968*, vol. 19, pp. 116–117, 123–126, 140–146, 151–153.

99. U.S. officials told their Israeli counterparts that they had to go through the motions of appealing for UN action in order to secure domestic and international support for the multilateral regatta idea. *FRUS, 1964–1968,* vol. 19; Spiegel, *Other Arab-Israeli Conflict,* p. 139. Later in the crisis, Spiegel contends, rival groups of U.S. officials favored the regatta and ad hoc diplomacy (pp. 143–144). See also Oren, *Six Days of War,* p. 122.

100. Documents 85, 86, 88, 108, 141, and 148, *FRUS, 1964–1968,* vol. 19, pp. 160–164, 167–168, 198–200, 266–268, 283–286.

101. Rabin, *Memoirs,* p. 91.

102. Document 89, *FRUS, 1964–1968,* vol. 19, p. 168 n. 3.

103. Document 97 and also documents 98 and 102, *FRUS, 1964–1968,* vol. 19, p. 179 and also pp. 180–181 and 187–189; Spiegel, *Other Arab-Israeli Conflict,* p. 143; Oren, *Six Days of War,* pp. 123–124; Quandt, *Peace Process* (2001), p. 36; Brecher, *Israel's Foreign Policy,* pp. 400–401. See also Segev, *1967,* pp. 245, 276, 310.

104. Document 98, *FRUS, 1964–1968,* vol. 19, p. 181. Spiegel, *Other Arab-Israeli Conflict,* p. 143: "The Israeli Cabinet concluded that if the Western community would establish the international status of the waterway through action, Israel could avoid force." Ibid., p. 147: "If the naval force had appeared more effective, with plans progressing and international support growing, it is improbable that the Israelis would have dared attack." See also Quandt, *Peace Process* (2001), pp. 29–30; and Parker, *Politics of Miscalculation,* pp. 117–118.

105. Documents 77, 80, 101, 130, and 139, *FRUS, 1964–1968,* vol. 19, pp. 140–146, 151–153, 186–187, 237–244, 262–264; Quandt, *Peace Process* (2001), p. 35. On Vietnam, see Komer in Parker, *Six-Day War,* pp. 229–230; and Moshe Gat, "Let Someone Else Do the Job: American Policy on the Eve of the Six Day War," *Diplomacy and Statecraft* 14, no. 1 (2003): 131–158 at 139 and 142.

106. Spiegel, *Other Arab-Israeli Conflict,* pp. 144, 146; Oren, *Six Days of War,* p. 140; Quandt, *Peace Process* (2001), pp. 30–31. For other Vietnam references by Johnson, see Quandt, *Peace Process* (2001), pp. 28–29, 35. Members of Congress also expressed concern; for example, Sen. John Stennis (D-Mississippi) did not support U.S. unilateral steps given Vietnam. See Hedrick Smith, "Johnson Is Told of Mideast Clash," *New York Times,* June 5, 1967, p. 6.

107. Documents 38, 57, 130, 131, 144, and 148, *FRUS, 1964–1968,* vol. 19, pp. 65, 94–95, 237–246, 272–277, 283–286.

108. Document 101, ibid., p. 186.

109. Richard Helms with William Hood, *A Look over My Shoulder* (New York: Random House, 2003), pp. 299–300. In Johnson's memoir, the president created the impression that U.S. officials thought they had more time. Johnson, *Vantage Point,* pp. 293–294.

110. Documents 108 (May 31) and 109, *FRUS, 1964–1968,* vol. 19, pp. 198–202. See also Brecher, *Israel's Foreign Policy,* pp. 412, 416–417; and Parker, *Six-Day War,* pp. 218–219.

111. Document 124, *FRUS, 1964–1968,* vol. 19, p. 223–225; Oren, *Six Days of War,* p. 147; Gat, "Let Someone Else," p. 148.

112. Amit in Parker, *Six-Day War,* pp. 139, 141; Spiegel, *Other Arab-Israeli Conflict,* p. 146; Oren, *Six Days of War,* pp. 146–147; and Quandt, *Peace Process* (2001), p. 38.

113. M. Amit, *Head On...* (Or Yehuda, Israel: Hed Arzi, 1999), p. 239, as cited in Gat, "Let Someone Else."

114. Document 132, *FRUS, 1964–1968,* vol. 19, pp. 247–251.

115. Segev, *1967,* pp. 333–334.

116. Oren, *Six Days of War,* p. 153; Quandt, *Peace Process* (2001), p. 40; and Segev, *1967,* p. 335. Evron later cautioned against overemphasizing Fortas's role. Parker, *Six-Day War,* pp. 225–226.

117. Quandt, *Peace Process* (2001), pp. 38–39.

118. Spiegel, *Other Arab-Israeli Conflict,* pp. 146–148; Oren, *Six Days of War,* p. 147; Finkelstein, *Image and Reality,* pp. 190–191; Parker, *Politics of Miscalculation,* p. 118.

119. Document 139, *FRUS, 1964–1968,* vol. 19, p. 263.

120. Moshe Dayan, *Moshe Dayan: Story of My Life* (New York: William Morrow, 1976), pp. 342–346.

121. There is one possible exception. On May 31, Israelis heard a report that Rusk said, "I don't think it is our business to restrain anyone." Michael Bar-Zohar, *Embassies in Crisis: Diplomats and Demagogues behind the Six-Day War* (Englewood Cliffs, N.J.: Prentice-Hall, 1970), p. 157, as cited in Quandt, *Peace Process* (2001), p. 38; also in Abba Eban, *An Autobiography* (Jerusalem: Steimatsky's, 1977), pp. 384–386, as cited by Parker, *Politics of Miscalculation*, p. 119. Quandt says Rusk opposed Israeli action until the end. Parker, *Six-Day War*, pp. 207, 210–211.

122. Document 128, *FRUS, 1964–1968*, vol. 19, p. 231–232. See also documents 103, 114 (Saunders), 122, 137, and 146–147, pp. 190–194, 208–211, 220–221, 259–262, 279–283; Oren, *Six Days of War*, pp. 106, 140–141. Many members of Congress expressed opposition to the regatta. Oren, *Six Days of War*, p. 140.

123. Amit thought Israel also needed to address the Egyptian military buildup in Sinai. Parker, *Six-Day War*, pp. 145, 151.

124. Oren, *Six Days of War*, pp. 146–148; see also Rusk's cable to U.S. ambassadors in Arab capitals, document 141, *FRUS, 1964–1968*, vol. 19, pp. 266–268. Recognition that Israel would go to war came even earlier according to some versions of what Johnson said after his May 26 meeting with Eban (that restraint would fail). See Oren, *Six Days of War*, p. 115; Quandt, *Peace Process* (2001), p. 35.

125. Quandt, *Peace Process* (2001), p. 40; Dayan, *Moshe Dayan*, pp. 341–342; Parker, *Politics of Miscalculation*, p. 120; Brecher, *Israel's Foreign Policy*, p. 420; Amit in Parker, *Six-Day War*, p. 141.

126. Brecher, *Israel's Foreign Policy*, p. 420.

127. Ibid., p. 421.

128. Dayan, *Moshe Dayan*, pp. 345–347; and Amit in Parker, *Six-Day War*, p. 141.

129. Quandt, *Peace Process* (2001), pp. 34, 41–42, 51; Oren, *Six Days of War*, p. 153.

130. Parker, *Politics of Miscalculation*, pp. 120–121. My argument is consistent with Gat, "Let Someone Else."

131. Documents 54, 69, 76, 130, and 142, *FRUS, 1964–1968*, vol. 19, pp. 87–91, 118–122, 138–139, 237–244, 268–269; Quandt, *Peace Process* (2001), p. 26; Finkelstein, *Image and Reality*, pp. 192–193; Eugene Rostow in Parker, *Six-Day War*, p. 202; and Popp, "Stumbling Decidedly," pp. 299, 305.

132. Document 77, *FRUS, 1964–1968*, vol. 19, pp. 142–143. In his memoir, Johnson wrote that he said if Egypt attacks, "you will whip [the] hell out of them." Johnson, *Vantage Point*, p. 293.

133. Rusk, *As I Saw It*, p. 386; and Helms, *Look over My Shoulder*, p. 299.

134. Parker, *Politics of Miscalculation*, p. 114.

135. Brecher, *Israel's Foreign Policy*, pp. 333–335, 348–349.

136. Helms, *Look over My Shoulder*, pp. 298–299. See also Popp, "Stumbling Decidedly," p. 298; and Segev, *1967*, pp. 187, 189.

137. Rabin, *Memoirs*, pp. 77, 81. Rabin's argument is a clear example of Robert Jervis's deterrence model. Jervis, *Perception and Misperception in International Politics* (Princeton: Princeton University Press, 1976), pp. 58–113.

138. Merle Miller, *Lyndon: An Oral Biography* (New York: G. P. Putnam's Sons, 1980), p. 478. See also Segev, *1967*, pp. 113, 259, 265, 304.

139. John P. Roche, an adviser to the president and author of the May 23 televised statement, made this claim in Miller, *Lyndon*, p. 479. I did not find evidence of calls to Johnson himself in Johnson's daily diary, which, among other things, served as a log of his phone calls. The diary was maintained by his secretaries.

140. "Statement by the President on Rising Tensions in the Near East," May 23, 1967, *Public Papers of the Presidents of the United States* (Washington, D.C.: U.S. Government Printing Office), or http://www.presidency.ucsb.edu/ws/index.php?pid=28265&st=&st1=.

141. Segev, *1967*, p. 265.

142. Douglas Little, a historian, comes to a broader conclusion: "Clearly, Lyndon Johnson's handling of the crisis was influenced in part by pressure from friends of Israel in Congress, on the White House staff, and among the American Jewish community." By not differentiating among these groups, however, Little limits the value of his statement for assessing the role of domestic actors outside government. Little, *American Orientalism*, p. 101.

143. Richard Witkin, "Johnson, in City, Vows to Maintain Peace in Mideast," *New York Times*, June 4, 1967, p. 1.

144. Netanel Lorch, "The Arab-Israeli Wars," September 2, 2003, http://www.mfa.gov.il/MFA/History/Modern+History/Centenary+of+Zionism/The+Arab-Israeli+Wars.htm, accessed January 24, 2007.

145. William B. Quandt, *Decade of Decisions: American Policy toward the Arab-Israeli Conflict, 1967–1976* (Berkeley: University of California Press, 1977), pp. 169–170. See also Marvin Kalb and Bernard Kalb, *Kissinger* (Boston: Little, Brown, 1974), p. 459.

146. Edward R. F. Sheehan, *The Arabs, Israelis, and Kissinger* (New York: Reader's Digest Press, 1976), p. 31.

147. Kalb and Kalb, *Kissinger*, p. 456.

148. National Security Archive (NSA) document no. 63, October 23, 1973, http://www.gwu.edu/~nsarchiv/NSAEBB/NSAEBB98/octwar-63.pdf. The same document appears in Richard Parker, ed., *The October War: A Retrospective* (Gainesville: University Press of Florida, 2001), pp. 339–351.

149. Kalb and Kalb, *Kissinger*, p. 460.

150. NSA document no. 18, October 7, 1973, on a meeting in Kissinger's office with Dinitz and Shalev, http://www.gwu.edu/~nsarchiv/NSAEBB/NSAEBB98/octwar-18.pdf.

151. Golda Meir, *My Life* (New York: G. P. Putnam's Sons, 1975), p. 426.

152. Quoted by Mordechai Gazit in Parker, *October War*, p. 229.

153. Dayan, *Moshe Dayan*, p. 461.

154. Ibid.

155. Insight Team of the London *Sunday Times*, *The Yom Kippur War* (Garden City, N.Y.: Doubleday, 1974), p. 125. Meir made the same point in an interview on December 21, 1973, in *Yediot Ahronot* (Israeli newspaper). See the cable Keating to State, December 22, 1973, http://aad.archives.gov/aad/createpdf?rid=107471&dt=1573&dl=823. Dayan made the same point to a meeting of Labor party leaders. See the cable Keating to State, October 26, 1973, http://aad.archives.gov/aad/createpdf?rid=76871&dt=1573&dl=823.

156. Matti Golan, *The Secret Conversations of Henry Kissinger: Step-by-Step Diplomacy in the Middle East*, trans. Ruth Geyra Stern and Sol Stern (New York: Quadrangle, 1976), p. 45.

157. NSA document, October 5, 1973, Meir via Shalev to Kissinger via Scowcroft, http://www.gwu.edu/~nsarchiv/NSAEBB/NSAEBB98/octwar-07.pdf. According to Kalb and Kalb, *Kissinger*, p. 458, Kissinger got this document at 8 p.m. on Friday, October 5.

158. Kalb and Kalb, *Kissinger*, p. 458. Elazar's request to strike first was also confirmed by Dinitz in a conversation with Kissinger on October 7, 1973. According to Dinitz, Meir responded: "No, I don't want to have a preemptive strike and then have to spend the rest of my life explaining why we struck first." NSA document no. 18, October 7, 1973, on a meeting in Kissinger's office with Dinitz and Shalev.

159. Kalb and Kalb, *Kissinger*, p. 457.

160. Insight Team, *Yom Kippur War*, p. 119.

161. Kalb and Kalb, *Kissinger*, p. 459.

162. Henry Kissinger, *Crisis* (New York: Simon and Schuster, 2003), p. 18. See also Kalb and Kalb, *Kissinger*, p. 460; and Golan, *Secret Conversations*, p. 41.

163. NSA document no. 10, October 6, 1973, Kissinger to Nixon, http://www.gwu.edu/~nsarchiv/NSAEBB/NSAEBB98/octwar-10.pdf.

164. Golan, *Secret Conversations*, p. 43.

165. Meir, *My Life,* p. 426.
166. Golan, *Secret Conversations,* p. 44.
167. Insight Team, *Yom Kippur War,* p. 122.
168. Ibid., pp. 122–123; and Harold Saunders in Parker, *October War,* pp. 138–139. According to Sheehan, Israel did not preempt "because of Kissinger's warning and above all because they were confident they could swiftly repel the Arabs on both fronts." Sheehan, *Arabs, Israelis, and Kissinger,* p. 31.
169. NSA document, October 6, 1973, Keating to Kissinger. The document also appears at http://aad.archives.gov/aad/createpdf?rid=77417&dt=1573&dl=823. See also Kissinger, *Crisis,* p. 25, 27, 36; and NSA document no. 18, October 7, 1973, on a meeting in Kissinger's office with Dinitz and Shalev.
170. Meir, *My Life,* p. 427. See also Walter Laqueur, *Confrontation* (New York: Quadrangle, 1974), p. 89; Henry Kissinger, *Years of Upheaval* (Boston: Little, Brown, 1982), p. 451; and Kalb and Kalb, *Kissinger,* p. 459.
171. Golan, *Secret Conversations,* p. 44. Keating himself believed U.S. warnings led Israel to stay its hand: "[The] failure of Israel to launch pre-emptive strikes [was] due primarily, I believe, to recognition of our concerns." See Keating to State, October 7, 1973, http://aad. archives.gov/aad/createpdf?rid=77383&dt=1573&dl=823.
172. Kalb and Kalb, *Kissinger,* p. 460; the same version is repeated by Insight Team, *Yom Kippur War,* pp. 124–125.
173. Kalb and Kalb, *Kissinger,* pp. 460–461.
174. NSA document no. 18, October 7, 1973, on a meeting in Kissinger's office with Dinitz and Shalev. See also Tad Szulc, *The Illusion of Peace: Foreign Policy in the Nixon Years* (New York: Viking Press, 1978), p. 729.
175. Kissinger, *Years of Upheaval,* p. 296.
176. The United States wanted neither an Israeli loss nor an "outright" win. William Bundy, *A Tangled Web: The Making of Foreign Policy in the Nixon Presidency* (New York: Hill and Wang, 1998), p. 442.
177. Alan Dowty, *Middle East Crisis* (Berkeley: University of California Press, 1984), pp. 204–205.
178. Kissinger, *Years of Upheaval,* pp. 297–299; and Nixon, *RN: The Memoirs of Richard Nixon* (New York: Grosset and Dunlap, 1978), pp. 884–886. See also Raymond L. Garthoff, *Détente and Confrontation* (Washington, D.C.: Brookings Institution, 1985). A more definitive evaluation of U.S. opposition to an Israeli attack must await further document declassification. I do not have direct evidence that the strategic thinking I describe here led to the warnings against preemptive attack.
179. Nixon, *RN,* p. 885.
180. Kissinger, *Years of Upheaval,* p. 299. See also Garthoff, *Détente and Confrontation,* pp. 382, 594. I am indebted to Garthoff's book for spurring my thinking about possible explanations for the U.S. desire to restrain Israel in 1973. The explanation I suggest here is also consistent with U.S. pressure on Israel at the end of the 1973 war to adhere to the cease-fire. In a different way, continued Israeli action at the end of the war could have hurt U.S. chances of negotiating a peace and thereby marginalizing Moscow.
181. Walter LaFeber, *America, Russia, and the Cold War, 1945–1984* (New York: Alfred A. Knopf, 1985), p. 277. See also Walter J. Boyne, *The Two O'Clock War* (New York: Thomas Dunne Books/St. Martin's Press, 2002), p. 29. Bundy treated protecting détente and reducing Soviet influence as equally important goals of the Nixon administration. See Bundy, *Tangled Web,* p. 442.
182. I draw heavily on William B. Quandt, *Camp David: Peacemaking and Politics* (Washington, D.C.: Brookings Institution, 1986), pp. 103–104; and a phone interview with William B. Quandt, January 16, 2007. The case is also mentioned in Jimmy Carter, *Palestine: Peace Not Apartheid* (New York: Simon and Schuster, 2006), pp. 44–45. Carter mistakenly dates the incident in 1978.

183. Quandt, *Camp David*, p. 79. Carter wrote only that the two "discussed" Lebanon. See Jimmy Carter, *Keeping Faith: Memoirs of a President* (New York: Bantam Books, 1982), p. 291.

184. Quandt, *Camp David*, p. 103.

185. Ibid.

186. Phone interview with William B. Quandt, January 16, 2007.

187. For instance, see Alexander M. Haig Jr., *Caveat: Realism, Reagan, and Foreign Policy* (New York: Macmillan, 1984), p. 333.

188. Samuel W. Lewis, "The United States and Israel: Constancy and Change," in *The Middle East: Ten Years after Camp David*, ed. William B. Quandt (Washington, D.C.: Brookings Institution, 1988), pp. 217–257 at 231.

189. Ben-Zvi, *United States and Israel*, p. 129.

190. Ibid., p. 124; Haig, *Caveat*, pp. 328–329.

191. Lewis, "United States and Israel," p. 238. See also Little, *American Orientalism*, p. 111.

192. Haig, *Caveat*, p. 332.

193. Ibid., p. 334.

194. Ibid., pp. 326–327; George W. Ball, *Error and Betrayal in Lebanon* (Washington, D.C.: Foundation for Middle East Peace, 1984), p. 34.

195. Ze'ev Schiff and Ehud Ya'ari, *Israel's Lebanon War* (New York: Simon and Schuster, 1984), pp. 67–68, 73–74. During the May meeting, Haig said he had a "strenuous argument with Sharon in the presence of my staff." Haig, *Caveat*, p. 335.

196. William B. Quandt, "U.S. Policy toward the Arab-Israeli Conflict," in *Middle East*, ed. Quandt, pp. 357–386 at 364.

197. Haig, *Caveat*, p. 327.

198. Ibid., p. 317; see also pp. 342–344.

199. Schiff and Ya'ari, *Israel's Lebanon War*, pp. 77–76; Benny Morris, *Righteous Victims: A History of the Zionist-Arab Conflict, 1881–1999* (New York: Alfred A. Knopf, 1999), p. 514; Spiegel, *Other Arab-Israeli Conflict*, p. 414; Haig, *Caveat*, p. 330.

200. Schiff and Ya'ari, *Israel's Lebanon War*, p. 74.

201. For instance, see Morris, *Righteous Victims*, p. 514; and Ben-Zvi, *United States and Israel*, p. 140.

202. Ball, *Error and Betrayal*, p. 35 (see also 39 and 40); and Spiegel, *Other Arab-Israeli Conflict*, p. 414.

203. Schiff and Ya'ari, *Israel's Lebanon War*, p. 75.

204. Haig, *Caveat*, p. 330.

205. Howard Teicher and Gayle Radley Teicher, *Twin Pillars to Desert Storm: America's Flawed Vision in the Middle East from Nixon to Bush* (New York: Morrow, 1993), p. 204, as cited in Kathleen Christison, *Perceptions of Palestine: Their Influence on U.S. Middle East Policy* (Berkeley: University of California Press, 1999), p. 323 n. 33. For other examples, see Ben-Zvi, *United States and Israel*, pp. 271–272 n. 5; Haig, *Caveat*, pp. 338–339, 341, 345.

206. Ben-Zvi, *United States and Israel*, pp. 146–147.

207. Quandt, *Peace Process* (2001), p. 252.

208. Morris, *Righteous Victims*, pp. 529–530.

209. Moshe Arens, *Broken Covenant* (New York: Simon and Schuster, 1995), pp. 159–160.

210. Yitzhak Shamir, *Summing Up: An Autobiography* (Boston: Little, Brown, 1994), p. 221.

211. Laura Zittrain Eisenberg, *Restraint or Retaliation? Israel's Response to Iraqi Missile Attacks during the 1991 Gulf War*, Case 361 (Washington, D.C.: Institute for the Study of Diplomacy, 1994), pp. 1–16.

212. Arens, *Broken Covenant*, pp. 171–174.

213. National Security Directive 54, January 15, 1991, http://bushlibrary.tamu.edu/research/nsd/NSD/NSD%2054/0001.pdf.

214. Lawrence Freedman and Efraim Karsh, *The Gulf Conflict, 1990–1991* (Princeton, N.J.: Princeton University Press, 1993), p. 334.

215. Bob Woodward, *The Commanders* (New York: Simon and Schuster, 1991), p. 363.

216. James A. Baker III with Thomas M. DeFrank, *The Politics of Diplomacy: Revolution, War, and Peace, 1989–1992* (New York: G. P. Putnam's Sons, 1995), p. 383.

217. George Bush and Brent Scowcroft, *A World Transformed* (New York: Alfred A. Knopf, 1998), p. 454; and Arens, *Broken Covenant*, pp. 183–184.

218. Bush and Scowcroft, *World Transformed*, p. 456; Freedman and Karsh, *Gulf Conflict*, p. 337.

219. Freedman and Karsh, *Gulf Conflict*, pp. 334–335. See also Baker, *Politics of Diplomacy*, pp. 386–387; Eisenberg, *Restraint or Retaliation?* p. 5.

220. Freedman and Karsh, *Gulf Conflict*, p. 337.

221. Baker, *Politics of Diplomacy*, p. 389.

222. Freedman and Karsh, *Gulf Conflict*, pp. 334–338. Arens's detailed account of the period presents Shamir as an important element in Israel's restraint.

223. Arens, *Broken Covenant*, pp. 181–182, 191, 197.

224. Freedman and Karsh, *Gulf Conflict*, p. 336; Woodward, *Commanders*, pp. 363–364; and Arens, *Broken Covenant*, pp. 169, 179, 185.

225. Scott B. Lasensky, "Friendly Restraint: U.S.-Israel Relations during the Gulf Crisis of 1990–1991," *MERIA* 3 (June 1999); and Shai Feldman, "Israeli Deterrence and the Gulf War," in *War in the Gulf: Implications for Israel*, ed. Joseph Alpher (Boulder, Colo.: Westview Press, 1993), pp. 184–208. On IFF and "deconfliction," see Bush and Scowcroft, *World Transformed*, p. 453.

226. Baker, *Politics of Diplomacy*, p. 390.

227. Eisenberg, *Restraint or Retaliation?* p. 5. Eisenberg lists many of the same positive and negative sanctions.

228. Arens, *Broken Covenant*, p. 171.

229. Lasensky, "Friendly Restraint."

230. Ibid.; Freedman and Karsh, *Gulf Conflict*, p. 338; and Feldman, "Israeli Deterrence," p. 195.

231. Some have suggested that Iraq was not deterred but rather lacked the technical capacity to use WMD warheads. See Kenneth Pollack, *The Threatening Storm* (New York: Random House, 2002), p. 263. Iraqi general Wafic al-Samarrai, then head of Iraqi military intelligence, told PBS's *Frontline*, "Part of these missiles, the scud missiles, were loaded with chemical warheads but they were not used and they were kept till after the war. We told him [Saddam] very clearly that should he use chemical weapons they will use their nuclear weapons." The episode, titled "The Gulf War," was first broadcast January 9, 1996. See http://www.pbs.org/wgbh/pages/frontline/gulf/oral/samarrai/7.html. Iraq could have armed the warheads but was deterred by the threat of American or Israeli nuclear attack, according to Timothy V. McCarthy and Jonathan B. Tucker, "Saddam's Toxic Arsenal: Chemical and Biological Weapons in the Gulf Wars," in *Planning the Unthinkable*, ed. Peter R. Lavoy, Scott D. Sagan, and James J. Wirtz (Ithaca: Cornell University Press, 2000), pp. 47–78 at 69 and 71–72; Feldman, "Israeli Deterrence," pp. 199–204; Saad al-Bazzaz, former editor of the Iraqi newspaper *Al-Jumhuriya*, in an interview in "Saad al-Bazzaz: An Insider's View of Iraq," *Middle East Quarterly* (December 1995): 67–75 at 68–69; Gerald M. Steinberg, "Parameters of Stable Deterrence in a Proliferated Middle East: Lessons from the 1991 Gulf War," *Nonproliferation Review* (fall–winter 2000): 43–60 at 57; and Arens, *Broken Covenant*, p. 216.

232. Shamir, *Summing Up*, p. 224.

233. Feldman, "Israeli Deterrence," p. 192.

234. This is not a direct quotation. William A. Orme Jr., "Americans and Israelis Spar over Sale of Radar to China," *New York Times*, June 16, 2000.

235. John Lancaster, "Israel Halts China Arms Deal," *Washington Post*, July 13, 2000.

236. Ibid.

237. Ibid. Some reports state that Barak told Clinton on July 12. See also Jane Perlez, "Israel Drops Plan to Sell Air Radar to China Military," *New York Times*, July 13, 2000.

238. Lancaster, "Israel Halts China Arms Deal."

239. Edward Cody, "China Scolds U.S. for Blocking Israeli Arms Sale," *Washington Post*, June 28, 2005.

240. Bill Gertz, "U.S. to Restart Arms Technology Transfers to Israel," *Washington Times*, August 17, 2005.

241. Cody, "China Scolds U.S."

242. Miles A. Pomper, "U.S., Israel Seek to Cut Deal on China Arms Sales," *Arms Control Today*, July/August 2005, http://www.armscontrol.org/act/2005_07–08/IsraelChina_ArmsSales.asp.

243. Miles A. Pomper, "U.S., Israel Reach China Arms Deal," *Arms Control Today*, September 2005, http://www.armscontrol.org/act/2005_09/USIsraelChinaDeal.asp.

244. Conal Urquhart, "US Acts over Israeli Arms Sales to China," *The Guardian*, June 13, 2005.

245. Pomper (who also cited a *Ha'aretz* report), "U.S., Israel Seek to Cut Deal"; and Gertz, "U.S. to Restart."

246. Marc Perelman, "Israel Miffed over Lingering China Flap," *The Forward* (New York), October 7, 2005; and Ze'ev Schiff, "Selling Arms to China, or Not," *Ha'aretz*, December 22, 2004.

247. Ze'ev Schiff, "Taking on U.S. over China—a Lost Cause," *Ha'aretz*, June 14, 2005.

248. Pomper, "U.S., Israel Seek to Cut Deal."

249. Aluf Benn, "Israel, U.S. Pledging Openness in Arms Deals," *Ha'aretz*, June 27, 2005.

250. Shmuel Rosner and Aluf Benn, "U.S., Israel Sign Deal on Defense Exports," *Ha'aretz*, August 17, 2005. See also Pomper, "U.S., Israel Reach China Arms Deal."

251. Urquhart, "US Acts over Israeli Arms Sales."

252. Benn, "Israel, U.S. Pledging Openness."

253. "Israel Sorry over China Arms Sale," June 19, 2005, http://www.aljazeera.com/me.asp?service_ID=9009.

254. Joseph Alpher, "Sharon Warned Bush," *The Forward*, January 12, 2007, http://www.forward.com/articles/sharon-warned-bush/.

255. In a 2002 interview, then Israeli prime minister Ariel Sharon did not express any concerns about the impending U.S. invasion of Iraq. See Stephen Farrell, Robert Thomson, and Danielle Haas, "Attack Iran the Day Iraq War Ends, Demands Israel," *Times of London*, November 5, 2002. For the argument that Israel pushed the United States toward war with Iraq, see John Mearsheimer and Stephen Walt, "The Israel Lobby," *London Review of Books*, March 23, 2006, http://www.lrb.co.uk/v28/n06/mear01_.html.

5. Expanding the Restraint Story

1. As noted in chapter 4, some later accounts claim that Israeli leaders knew they would win quickly while other reports said they feared for Israel's survival.

2. This explanation accounts only for why the United States did not offer a security guarantee. It does not explain why the United States did not mobilize power in other ways to stop the Israeli nuclear weapons program.

3. The case of Israeli nuclear proliferation might fit here too, and sit as a contrasting example of failure, but one would need to know more about the standing of Israel's nuclear weapons program in 1961–1963. That information is not publicly available at this time.

4. For the text of the treaty, see Yaacov Ro'i, *From Encroachment to Involvement: A Documentary Study of Soviet Policy in the Middle East, 1945–1973* (New York: John Wiley, 1974), pp. 550–552.

5. Benny Morris, *Righteous Victims: A History of the Zionist-Arab Conflict, 1881–1999* (New York: Alfred A. Knopf, 1999), p. 391; and Galia Golan, *Yom Kippur and After: The Soviet Union and the Middle East Crisis* (Cambridge: Cambridge University Press, 1977), p. 21. Egypt did not abrogate the treaty itself.

6. For the Radio Cairo announcement, see Ro'i, *From Encroachment to Involvement*, pp. 572–575.

7. Sadat's ASU speech, *SWB IV*, ME/4050/A/1–17, July 26, 1972; and Sadat's interviews in *al-Hawadith*, March 19, 1975, and *al-Anwar*, June 27, 1975, as cited in Karen Dawisha, *Soviet Foreign Policy towards Egypt* (New York: St. Martin's Press, 1979), p. 63.

8. Golan, *Yom Kippur and After*, p. 73.

9. William Bundy, *A Tangled Web: The Making of Foreign Policy in the Nixon Presidency* (New York: Hill and Wang, 1998), p. 433.

10. Henry Kissinger, *Crisis* (New York: Simon and Schuster, 2003), pp. 16, 18, 25.

11. Raymond L. Garthoff, *Détente and Confrontation* (Washington, D.C.: Brookings Institution, 1985), p. 383.

12. Leslie H. Gelb, "U.S. Jets for Israel Took Route around Some Allies," *New York Times*, October 25, 1973. What is not clear is whether these U.S. allies hoped to stop the airlift or whether they were just passing the buck, knowing that some U.S. ally would capitulate.

13. Insight Team of the London *Sunday Times, The Yom Kippur War* (Garden City, N.Y.: Doubleday, 1974), p. 284; and Ibrahim Sus, "Western Europe and the October War," *Journal of Palestine Studies* 3 (winter 1974): 65–83 at 74.

14. Sus, "Western Europe," p. 74.

15. Walter J. Boyne, *The Two O'Clock War: The 1973 Yom Kippur Conflict and the Airlift That Saved Israel* (New York: Thomas Dunne Books/St. Martin's Press, 2002), p. 120.

16. Bundy, *Tangled Web*, p. 437. According to then secretary of defense James Schlesinger, Nixon sent a "strong cable" to Portugal's prime minister, Marcelo Caetano, on Saturday, October 13, 1973, and "we finally received Portuguese acquiescence early Saturday afternoon." Richard Parker, ed., *The October War: A Retrospective* (Gainesville: University Press of Florida, 2001), p. 157.

17. See Garthoff, *Détente and Confrontation*, p. 384.

18. Elaine Sciolino and Steven Lee Myers, "Bush Says 'Time Is Running Out,' as U.S. Forces Move into Place," *New York Times*, October 7, 2001.

19. For instance, see James D. Fearon, "Signaling versus the Balance of Power and Interests: An Empirical Test of a Crisis Bargaining Model," *Journal of Conflict Resolution* 38 (June 1994): 236–269; and Eugene Gholz and Daryl G. Press, "Overcoming Selection Effects in Studies of Coercion," unpublished manuscript, 2005.

20. Kenneth Waltz, *Theory of International Politics* (Reading, Mass.: Addison-Wesley, 1979), p. 167. For work on chainganging and buckpassing, see Barry R. Posen, *The Sources of Military Doctrine: France, Britain, and Germany between the World Wars* (Ithaca: Cornell University Press, 1984), p. 63; and Thomas J. Christensen and Jack Snyder, "Chain Gangs and Passed Bucks: Predicting Alliance Patterns in Multipolarity," *International Organization* 44 (spring 1990): 137–168. Snyder uses the terms *entrapment* and *abandonment*. Glenn H. Snyder, "The Security Dilemma in Alliance Politics," *World Politics* 36 (July 1984): 461–496. For a quantitative indictment of alliances and war, see John Vasquez, "The Steps to War: Toward a Scientific Explanation of Correlates of War Findings," *World Politics* 40 (October 1987): 108–145 at 121; and Bruce Bueno de Mesquita, *The War Trap* (New Haven, Conn.: Yale University Press, 1981), pp. 159–160.

21. Barbara W. Tuchman, *The Guns of August* (New York: Macmillan, 1962).

Index

Acheson, Dean, 28, 46–47, 49, 50, 149n5
Afghanistan, 130, 132
alignments, 5, 20, 139n14
alliance formation: and balance-of-threat theory, 3, 6, 8–9, 11, 13, 18, 19, 21, 120; and choice of ally, 6, 20–21; external orientation of, 18–19, 41; intra-ally dimension of, 41, 129; offensive/defensive alliances, 4; and restraint explanation, 2, 7, 11–15, 18, 19, 40–41, 120–21; role of alliance restraint in, 6, 7–8, 18, 19, 21, 29, 86
alliance management: and decision-making process, 2, 6, 9, 42; and power mobilization, 3, 8, 11, 12, 131–33; and power variants, 2, 3, 9–12, 14–15, 122, 131–32. *See also* restraint failure; restraint success
alliance restraint: case studies of, 127, 129, 131–32, 142n48; defined, 6; impact on international stability, 120, 133–35; and institutional links, 4, 17, 126; and military policies, 6, 8, 16; and power mobilization, 3, 15–16; restraint attempts among non-allies distinguished from, 16–17, 125–26; role in alliance formation, 6, 7–8, 18, 19, 21, 29, 86; and simultaneous deterrence, 128; and unipolar system, 129–31. *See also* restraint failure; restraint success

alliances: conceptions of, 5, 8, 139nn14, 15; and international stability, 133–35; origins of, 2, 6, 11, 18
American-Israeli relations: evolution of relations, 81–87, 159–60n24, 160n27, 160–61n39; formal and underlying processes of, 139n15; and institutional links, 11; and Israeli arms sales to China, 14, 79, 80, 114–17, 118, 121, 122, 124; and Israeli attack of 1967, 78, 81, 83, 91–99, 121, 123, 124, 125, 164nn99, 104, 109, 165n124, 166n142, 170n1; and Israeli intervention in Lebanon of 1977, 78–79, 81, 105–6, 114, 118, 121, 122, 124, 126; and Israeli invasion of Lebanon of 1982, 78, 79, 106–9, 118, 121–22, 124; Israel in restrainer role, 118–19; and Israeli nuclear proliferation, 78, 79, 81, 86, 87–91, 121, 125, 126, 161n50, 161–62n62, 162n67, 170nn2, 3; and Israeli preemptive strike attempt of 1973, 78–82, 87, 97, 100–105, 121, 123, 124, 127, 128–29, 158n1, 167nn171, 178, 180; and military policies, 5, 78, 81–84, 106, 114, 119; Morrow on, 139n14; possible Israeli retaliatory attacks on Iraq in 1991, 1, 79, 80, 109–14, 121, 123, 124, 158n1; and power mobilization, 3, 78–80, 87–93, 96, 97, 104, 107, 108,